The Geometry of Information Retrieval

Information retrieval, IR, is the science of extracting information from documents. It can be viewed in a number of ways: logical, probabilistic and vector space models are some of the most important. In this book, the author, one of the leading researchers in the area, shows how these three views can be combined in one mathematical framework, the very one used to formulate the general principles of quantum mechanics. Using this framework, van Rijsbergen presents a new theory for the foundations of IR, in particular a new theory of measurement. He shows how a document can be represented as a vector in Hilbert space, and the document's relevance by an Hermitian operator. All the usual quantum-mechanical notions, such as uncertainty, superposition and observable, have their IR-theoretic analogues. But the approach is more than just analogy: the standard theorems can be applied to address problems in IR, such as pseudo-relevance feedback, relevance feedback and ostensive retrieval. The relation with quantum computing is also examined. To help keep the book self-contained, appendices with background material on physics and mathematics are included, and each chapter ends with some suggestions for further reading. This is an important book for all those working in IR, AI and natural language processing.

KEITH VAN RIJSBERGEN'S research has, since 1969, been devoted to information retrieval, working on both theoretical and experimental aspects. His current research is concerned with the design of appropriate logics to model the flow of information and the application of Hilbert space theory to content-based IR. This is his third book on IR: his first is now regarded as the classic text in the area. In addition he has published over 100 research papers and is a regular speaker at major IR conferences. Keith is a Fellow of the IEE, BCS, ACM, and the Royal Society of Edinburgh. In 1993 he was appointed Editor-in-Chief of *The Computer Journal,* an appointment he held until 2000. He is an associate editor of *Information Processing and Management*, on the editorial board of *Information Retrieval*, and on the advisory board of the *Journal of Web Semantics.* He has served as a programme committee member and editorial board member of the major IR conferences and journals. He is a non-executive director of a start-up: Virtual Mirrors Ltd.

The Geometry of Information Retrieval

C. J. VAN RIJSBERGEN

CAMBRIDGE
UNIVERSITY PRESS

CAMBRIDGE
UNIVERSITY PRESS

University Printing House, Cambridge CB2 8BS, United Kingdom

Cambridge University Press is part of the University of Cambridge.

It furthers the University's mission by disseminating knowledge in the pursuit of education, learning and research at the highest international levels of excellence.

www.cambridge.org
Information on this title: www.cambridge.org/9780521838054

First published 2004
Fourth printing 2007

A catalogue record for this publication is available from the British Library

Library of Congress Cataloguing in Publication data
Van Rijsbergen, C. J., 1943–
The geometry of information retrieval / by C. J. van Rijsbergen.
p. cm.
Includes bibliographical references and index.
ISBN 0 521 83805 3 (hb)
1. Computer science – Mathematics. 2. Information storage and retrieval systems – Mathematics. I. Title.
QA76.9.M35.V38 2004 025.04 – dc22 2004045683

ISBN 978-0-521-83805-4 Hardback

To make a start,
Out of particulars
And make them general, rolling
Up the sum, by defective means

Paterson: Book I
William Carlos Williams, 1992

for
Nicola

Contents

Preface

This book begins and ends in information retrieval, but travels through a route constructed in an abstract way. In particular it goes through some of the most interesting and important models for information retrieval, a vector space model, a probabilistic model and a logical model, and shows how these three and possibly others can be described and represented in Hilbert space. The reasoning that occurs within each one of these models is formulated algebraically and can be shown to depend essentially on the geometry of the information space. The geometry can be seen as a 'language' for expressing the different models of information retrieval.

The approach taken is to structure these developments firmly in terms of the mathematics of Hilbert spaces and linear operators. This is of course the approach used in quantum mechanics. It is remarkable that the application of Hilbert space mathematics to information retrieval is very similar to its application to quantum mechanics. A document in IR can be represented as a vector in Hilbert space, and an observable such as 'relevance' or 'aboutness' can be represented by a Hermitian operator. However, this is emphatically not a book about quantum mechanics but about using the same language, the mathematical language of quantum mechanics, for the description of information retrieval. It turns out to be very convenient that quantum mechanics provides a ready-made interpretation of this language. It is as if in physics we have an example semantics for the language, and as such it will be used extensively to motivate a similar but different interpretation for IR. We introduce an appropriate logic and probability theory for information spaces guided by their introduction into quantum mechanics. Gleason's Theorem, which specifies an algorithm for computing probabilities associated with subspaces in Hilbert space, is of critical importance in quantum mechanics and will turn out to be central for the same reasons in information retrieval. Whereas quantum theory is about a theory of measurement for *natural* systems, The Geometry of Information Retrieval is about such a theory for *artificial* systems, and in particular for information retrieval. The important notions in quantum mechanics, state vector, observable, uncertainty, complementarity, superposition and compatibility readily translate into analogous notions in information retrieval, and hence the theorems of quantum theory become available as theorems in IR.

One of the main aims of this book is to present the requisite mathematics to explore in detail the foundation of information retrieval as a parallel to that of quantum mechanics. The material is principally addressed to students and researchers in information retrieval but will also be of interest to those working in such disciplines as AI and quantum computation. An attempt is made to lay a sound mathematical foundation for reasoning about existing models in IR sufficient for their modification and extension. The hope is that the treatment will inspire and enable the invention of new models. All the mathematics is introduced in an elementary fashion, step-by-step, making copious references to matching developments in quantum mechanics. Any reader with a good grasp of high school mathematics, or A-level equivalent, should be able to follow the mathematics from first principles. One exception to this is the material in the Prologue, where some more advanced notions are rapidly introduced, as is often the case in dialogue, but even there a quick consultation of the appropriate appendices would clarify the mathematics.

Although the material is not about quantum computation, it could easily be adopted as an elementary introduction to that subject. The mathematics required to understand most discussions on quantum computation is covered. It will be interesting to see if the approach taken to modelling IR can be mapped onto a quantum computer architecture. In the quantum computation literature the Dirac notation is used as a *lingua franca*, and it is also used here and is explained in some detail as it is needed.

Students and researchers in IR are happy to use mathematics to define and specify algorithms to implement sophisticated search strategies, but they seem to be notoriously resistant to investing energy and effort into acquiring new mathematics. Thus there is a threshold to be overcome in convincing a person to take the time to understand the mathematics that is here. For this reason we begin with a Prologue. In it fundamental concepts are presented and discussed with only a little use of mathematics, to introduce by way of a dialogue the new way of thinking about IR. It is hoped that illustrating the material in this way will overcome some of the reader's resistance to venturing into this new mathematical territory for IR.

A further five chapters followed by three technical appendices and an extensive annotated Bibliography constitute the full extent of the book. The chapters make up a progression. Chapter 1, the Introduction, goes some way to showing the extent to which the material depends on ideas from quantum mechanics whilst at the same time motivating the shift in thinking about IR notions. Chapter 2 gives an account of traditional Boolean algebra based on set theory and shows how non-Boolean structures arise naturally when classes are no longer sets, but are redefined in an appropriate way. An illustration of the breakdown of the law of distribution in logic then gives rise to non-classical logic. Chapter 3 introduces vector and Hilbert spaces from first principles, leading to Chapter 4 which describes linear operators, their representation and properties as vehicles for measurement and observation. Chapter 5 is the first serious IR application for the foregoing theory. It builds on the earlier work of many researchers on logics for IR and it shows how conditionals in logic can be represented as objects in Hilbert space. Chapter 6, by far the longest, takes the elementary theory presented thus far and recasts it, using the Dirac notation, so that it can be applied to a number of specific problems in IR, for example, pseudo-relevance feedback, relevance feedback and ostensive retrieval.

Each chapter concludes with some suggestions for further reading, thus providing guidance for possible extensions. In general the references collected at the end of the book are extensively annotated. One reason for this is that readers, not necessarily acquainted with quantum mechanics or its mathematics, may enjoy further clarification as to why pursuing any further reference may be worthwhile. Scanning the bibliography with its annotations is intended to provide useful information about the context for the ideas in the book. A given reference may refer to a number of others because they relate to the same topic, or provide a commentary on the given one.

There are three detailed appendices. The first one gives a potted introduction to linear algebra for those who wish to refresh their memories on that subject. It also conveniently contains a summary of the Dirac notation which takes some getting used to. The second appendix is a self-contained introduction to quantum mechanics, and it uses the Dirac notation explained in the previous appendix. It also contains a simple proof of the Heisenberg Uncertainty Principle which does not depend on any physics. The final appendix gives the classical axioms for probability theory and shows how they are extended to quantum probability.

There a number of ways of reading this book. The obvious way is to read it from beginning to end, and in fact it has been designed for that. Another way is to read the Prologue, the Introduction and the appendices, skipping the intervening chapters on a first pass; this would give the reader a conceptual grasp of the material without a detailed understanding of the mathematics. A third way is to read the Prologue last, and then the bulk of the book will provide grounding for some of the advanced mathematical ideas that are introduced rapidly in the Prologue. One can also skip all the descriptive and motivational material and start immediately with the mathematics, for that one begins at Chapter 2, and continues to the end. A fifth way is to read only Chapter 6, the geometry of IR, and consult the relevant earlier chapters as needed.

There are many people who have made the writing of this book possible. Above all I would like to thank Juliet and Nicola van Rijsbergen for detailed and constructive comments on earlier drafts of the manuscripts, and for the good humour with which they coped with my frustrations. Mounia Lalmas, Thomas Roelleke and Peter Bruza I thank for technical comments on an early draft. Elliott Sober I thank for help with establishing the origin of some of the quotations as well as helping me clarify some thinking. Dealing with a publisher can sometimes be fraught with difficulties; fortunately David Tranah of CUP ensured that it was in fact wonderfully straightforward and agreeable, for which I express my appreciation; I also thank him for his constant encouragement. The ideas for the monograph were conceived during 2000–1 whilst I was on sabbatical at Cambridge University visiting the Computer Laboratory, Department of Engineering and King's College, all of which institutions deserve thanks for hosting me and making it possible to think and write. Taking on a task such as this inevitably means that less time is available for other things, and here I would like to express my appreciation to the IR group at Glasgow University for their patience. Finally, I would like record my intellectual debt to Bill Maron whose ideas in many ways foreshadowed some of mine, also to the writings of John von Neumann for his insights on geometry, logic and probability without which I could not have begun.

Prologue

Where did that come from?

Strictly Ballroom, film, directed by Baz Luhrmann, Australia: M&A Film Corporation, 1992.

Scene

A sunny office overlooking a cityscape of Victorian roofs and elm trees. K, an academic of some seniority judging by his white beard, and the capaciousness of his bookshelves, is sitting at his desk. The sign outside his door reads 'Please disturb'.

B: (A younger academic) enters without knocking, shortly followed by N (not so young).

B: I hear that you have been re-inventing IR.

K: Well, I am writing a book.

B: Yes, the story is that you have been looking at quantum mechanics, in order to specify a new model. Also (looks at N) that you are looking at quantum computation.

K: I have certainly been looking at quantum mechanics, but *not* because I want to specify a new model; I am looking at quantum mechanics because it gives insight into how one might combine probability, logic and vector spaces into one formalism. The role of quantum computation in all this is not clear yet. It may be that having reformulated IR in this way, using the language of quantum mechanics, that it will be obvious how quantum computation may help at the algorithmic level, but I have not been thinking that far . . .

N: (Interrupting) Well, I listen patiently as ever – but it seems to me that you are – yet again – taking an entirely system-based approach to IR leaving no room for the user. For years now I have been saying that we need to spend more time on improving the interaction of the user with *any* system. Support for the user will make a bigger difference than any marginal improvements to a system. A new . . .

K: (Interrupting in turn) I know you think we should stop developing new theories and models and instead spend the time making existing ones work from a user perspective. Well, in a way that is what all this is about. Currently, we really do not have a way of describing formally, or in theoretical terms, how a user interacts with an IR system. I think . . .

N: – here we go. It has to be 'formal' –

K: we need a new paradigm, and the QM paradigm –

N: (Interrupting for the third time) Why? Why do we need this extra formalism? We have spent years describing how a user interacts with an IR system.

K: (Holds up hand) Hang on. We have had this argument over and over again. My reply has always been that if you do not formally describe or specify something then trying to arrive at a computational form becomes nigh impossible. Or if you do achieve a computational form without formal description then transferring a design from one approach or system to another becomes a nightmare. There is also the scientific imperative, that we cannot hope to make predictions about systems if we cannot reason about their underlying structure, and for this we need some kind of formality, and, dare I say it, –

N: I suppose I can't stop you –

K: a theory. Einstein always claimed that you need a theory to tell you what to measure.

N: Must you drag Einstein into this?

B: Let me get a word in edgewise. One could argue that a computer programme is a description, or a formal theory of a system. Why do we need more than that?

K: (Becomes instantly enthusiastic) Good question. It is certainly true that a computer program can be considered as a formal description of a process or a theory. Unfortunately it is very difficult to reason about such a description, and it is difficult to recover the semantics. What's more, computer programs are strongly influenced by the design of the digital computer which they run, that is, their von Neumann architecture. In developing this new IR paradigm I intend it perhaps to be implemented on a quantum computer.

N: Delusions of grandeur. So, tell us what is the essence or central idea of your new way of looking at things?

K: (Becomes even more enthusiastic) This will take some time, how long have you got?

B, N: We have got all afternoon.

K: (Hesitates) Of course, it would easier for you to understand what I am doing if you knew some elementary quantum mechanics. Let's see: you could start with Hughes' book on 'The Structure and Interpretation of Quantum Mechanics' . . .

N: I said we had this afternoon, not the next five years.

K: . . . I found his account invaluable to understanding some of the basics.

B: Can't you just give us the gist?

K: (Gets up and inspects his bookshelf) Well, the story really begins with von Neumann. As you know, in the thirties he wrote a now famous book on the foundations of quantum mechanics. One could argue that all later developments in quantum logic and probability are footnotes to his book. Of course von Neumann did not *do* QM, like say Feynman and Dirac, he theorised about it. He took the pioneering work of Bohr, Schrödinger, Heisenberg, Born and others, and tried to construct a consistent formal theory for QM It is much in the same spirit as what I am attempting for IR.

N: (Laughs) When I ascribed you delusions of grandeur I underestimated you. Are you now equating QM and IR in importance? Or merely yourself with von Neumann? In IR we deal only with artefacts and the way humans interact with them. Everything is man made. Whereas in QM we attempt to describe a piece of reality and many of the paradoxes arise because we are uncertain how to go about that.

K: (Focusing on the last point) Ah, exactly. You have put your finger on the problem. Both in IR and QM we are uncertain about how to describe things – be they real or artificial. In QM we have the problem of measurement; we don't know how to model the result of an observation which arises from the interaction of an 'observable' with a piece of reality. In IR we face the same problem when we attempt to model the interaction of a 'user' with an artefact.

B: (Gloomily) This is all getting a bit abstract for me. How about you try to make it more concrete?

K: (Cheerfully now) Well imagine the world in IR *before* keywords or index terms. A document, then, was not simply a set of words, it was much more: it was a set of ideas, a set of concepts, a story, etc., in other words a very abstract object. It is an accident of history that a representation of a document is so directly related to the text in it. If IR had started with documents that were images then such a dictionary kind of representation would not have arisen immediately. So let us begin by leaving the representation of a document unspecified. That does not mean that there will be none, it simply means it will not be defined in advance.

B: (Even gloomier) Great. So how do I get a computer to manipulate it – this piece of fiction?

K: Actually that is exactly what it is – a document is a kind of fictive object. Strangely enough Schrödinger . . .

N: (As an aside) Here we go with the name dropping again.

K: (continues, ignoring N) . . . in his conception of the state-vector for QM envisaged it in the same way. He thought of the state-vector as an object encapsulating all the possible results of potential measurements. Let me quote: 'It (ψ-function) is now the means for predicting probability of measurement results. In it is embodied the momentarily attained sum of theoretically based future expectation, somewhat as laid down in a catalogue.'[1] Thus a state-vector representing a document may be viewed the same way – it is an object that encapsulates the answers to all possible queries.

N: (Perks up) Ah, I can relate to this. You mean a document is defined with respect to the queries that a user might ask of it?

K: Yes, in more than one way, as will emerge later. By the way, one could view Maron and Kuhns' original paper on probabilistic indexing in this sort of way. Indeed, Donald Mackay (1969, 1950), who worked with Maron, anticipated the use of QM in theorising about IR.

N: Good, keep going; we seem to be getting somewhere at last.

K: So what have we got? We have a collection of artefacts each of which is represented by a highly abstract object called a 'state-vector'. Of course using the term 'vector' gives the game away a little. These abstract objects are going to live in some kind of space (an information space), and it will come as no surprise to you that it will be a vector space, an infinite-dimensional vector space: a Hilbert space.

B: (With some frustration) Terrific. After all this verbiage we end up with a vector space, which is a traditional IR model. So, apart from being able to add ourselves as footnotes to von Neumann, what is the big deal?

K: The big deal is that we do not say in advance what the vectors in this space look like. All we require is a notion of dimensionality, which can be infinite, and objects that satisfy the axioms of a vector space, for example, vectors can be added and multiplied by scalars. Moreover, the

[1] Schrödinger, p. 158 in Wheeler and Zurek (1983).

space has a geometry given by an inner product which allows one to define a distance on the space. The fact that it is infinite is not immediately important, but there is no reason to restrict the dimensionality.

B: Why do you talk of scalars and not of real numbers?

K: You noticed that did you? Well, scalars here can be complex numbers.

N: Hold it, are you saying that we can attach a meaning to complex or for that matter imaginary numbers in IR?

K: No, I am not saying that. I am implying that we do not need to restrict our representational power to just real numbers. Rest assured that our observation or measurements will always deliver a real number, but it may be that we represent things on the way by complex numbers. There are many examples in mathematics where this is done, in addition to quantum mechanics, for example, Fourier analysis.

B: I don't buy this. Why introduce what appears to be an unnecessary complexity into the representation? What on earth would you want to represent with complex numbers?

K: To be honest I am not sure of this yet. But a simple example would arise in standard text retrieval where both term-frequency and document-frequency counts are used (per term, or per dimension) during a matching process. I imagine that we may wish to represent that combination of features in such a way that algebraic operations on them become easier. Right now when we combine *tf* and *idf* their identities are lost at the moment of combination.

N: So, from a mathematical, or algorithmic, point of view this may make sense. But, tell me, are you expecting the user to formulate their queries using complex numbers? If so, you can forget it.

K: No, of course not. But just as a person may write down a polynomial with real coefficients which has *complex roots*, a user may write down a query which from another point of view may end up being represented by complex numbers. The user is only expected to generate the point of view, and in changing it the query will change.

N: (With some impatience) This sounds great but I do not fully understand it. What do you mean by a 'point of view'?

B: Yes, what do you mean? I am lost now.

K: In conventional index term based retrieval the point of view in the vector space model is given by the axes in the space corresponding to the index terms in the query. Thus, if the query is $(a, b, c, \ldots)$ then a might lie along the x-axis, b the y-axis, c the z-axis, etc. Usually these are assumed to be orthogonal and linearly independent. Notice how convenient it is that the user has specified a set of axes. Now imagine that the query is simply an abstract vector in the space, we would still have to define it with respect to the basis of the space, but it would be up to us, or the user, to refer the objects in the space to different bases depending on their point of view. A change of basis constitutes a change of point of view.

B: Well, I am not sure this buys us anything but I'll hang in there for the moment. I see that you are still talking about queries as vectors. I infer that much of what you have said so far is a dressed up version of the standard vector space model of IR. Am I right?

K: You are right. I am trying to inspire the introduction of some of the new ways of talking by referring to the old way.

N: Get on with it – I am still waiting too.

K: All right. But first here is a small example of how we can go beyond standard vector space ideology. By assuming that the query is a vector in a high (maybe infinite) dimensional space, we are making assumptions about the dimensions that are not mentioned in the query. We could assume that those components are zero, or have some other default value. Why? No good reason, and perhaps the query would be better represented by a *subspace*, the subspace spanned by the basis vectors that are mentioned in the query. So we have grasped the need for talking about subspaces. The problem is how to handle that symbolically. More about this later.

(B and N look bored, so K quickly moves on)

K: Given the space of objects is a Hilbert space which we may fondly call an information space. How do we interact with it?

N: (With a sigh of relief) At last something about interaction.

B: Shut up, N. Let him talk. Although, I am still puzzled about how you will interact with these objects when you do not describe them explicitly in any way.

K: (With a grin) That is right. I forgot to tell you that. Once you have specified the basis (point of view) for the space, you can express the object in terms of the basis. This is done by projecting the object onto the different basis vectors. The effect of this is to give a 'co-ordinate' for the object with respect to each basis vector. It is a bit like defining an object by giving the answers to a set of simple questions, one question for each basis vector. If the object (state-vector) is normalised these projections are given by calculating the inner product between each basis vector and the state-vector. Of course, if we allow complex numbers then we would need to take the modulus (size) of the inner product to get a real number. In the case where we have a real Hilbert space, the state-vector is simply expanded as a real linear combination of the basis vectors. The expansion would differ from basis to basis.

N: You are getting too technical again; let's get back to the issue of interaction.

B: Yes, let's.

K: The basic idea is that an observable, such as a query or a single term, is to be represented by a linear operator which is self-adjoint in the Hilbert space. This means that in the finite case it corresponds to a matrix which can have complex numbers as entries but is such that the conjugate transpose is equal to itself. Let me illustrate. If A represents an observable, then A is self-adjoint if A = A*.

(K writes some symbols on the white board)

$$\mathrm{A} = \begin{pmatrix} a & b \\ c & d \end{pmatrix}$$

$$\mathrm{A}^* = \overline{\mathrm{A}'} = \begin{pmatrix} \overline{a} & \overline{c} \\ \overline{b} & \overline{d} \end{pmatrix} = \mathrm{A}$$

$$\Rightarrow a = \overline{a},\ d = \overline{d} \text{ and hence real,}$$

$$\text{also } b = \overline{c},\ \overline{b} = c.$$

An example is

$$\mathrm{A} = \begin{pmatrix} 1 & -\mathrm{i} \\ \mathrm{i} & 2 \end{pmatrix}$$

$$\mathrm{A}^* = \overline{\begin{pmatrix} 1 & -\mathrm{i} \\ \mathrm{i} & 2 \end{pmatrix}'} = \begin{pmatrix} 1 & -\mathrm{i} \\ \mathrm{i} & 2 \end{pmatrix} = \mathbf{A}.$$

K: I know what you are going to say, what has this got to do with queries and users?

N, B: How did you guess, so what has it got to do with them?

K: Bear with me a little longer. The notion of representation is a little indirect here. In quantum mechanics the idea is that the value of an observable is given by the eigenvalues of the matrix.[2] The beauty is that the eigenvalues of a self-adjoint matrix are always *real*, even though the entries in the matrix may be complex. So here we come back to the fact that our representation may involve complex numbers but when we make a measurement, that is interact, we only get real results.

B: Hang on a bit, you said that the value of an observable is an eigenvalue, any eigenvalue? So, how do I know which one? Let me take a simple

[2] More correctly, this should say that the outcome of a measurement of the observable is given by an eigenvalue. See Appendix II.

example, when the observable has just two values, 1 and 0. How do I know which? Is this the right question to ask?

K: We are now getting to the meat of it. If your observable represents a two-valued question, '1' means 'yes' and '0' means 'no', then determining which answer is a matter of *probability*. For example, if your observable was to determine whether an object was about the concept 'house', then there would be two eigenvalues, one corresponding to 'house' and one corresponding to 'not-house'. The probability of each of these answers would be derived from the *geometry* of the space.

N: You have lost me . . . again. Where do the concepts 'house' and 'not-house' come from? One minute we have an observable which corresponds to a query about 'houseness', next we have concepts, presumably represented in the space, how?

K: Yes, that is right. I need to tell you about the idea of *eigenvectors*.

B: (With some despair) Oh no, not more algebra, is there no end to it?

K: (Soothingly) We are almost there. Corresponding to each eigenvalue is an eigenvector. So, for a self-adjoint operator (that is, an observable) you get a number of eigenvectors corresponding to the concepts underlying the observable. It so happens that these eigenvectors make up a basis for the space and so generate a point of view.[3] It is as if we have found a set of concepts, one corresponding to each eigenvector, with respect to which we can observe each document in the space.

B: What about this relationship between probability and the geometry of the space?

K: I will come to that in a minute.

N: (Somewhat grimly) I am glad to hear it, these algebraic considerations are starting to give me a headache. I thought all this was for IR? Anyway, proceed.

K: For the simple case where the observable represents a Yes/No question, the linear operator is a particularly simple, and important one: a projection operator. It is a theorem in linear algebra that any self-adjoint linear operator can be resolved into a linear combination of projection operators. In other words, any observable can be resolved in to a combination of yes/no questions. Although a projector may be represented by a matrix in n dimensions, it only has two eigenvalues. In general you would expect an n-dimensional matrix to have n eigenvalues.

[3] There is an issue of 'degeneracy': when an eigenspace corresponds to an eigenvalue, its dimension is equal to the degeneracy of the eigenvalue.

Projectors have two. The effect of this is that there is a certain amount of degeneracy, which means that corresponding to each eigenvalue we have an eigenspace, and together these two eigenspaces span the entire space.

B: What about the basis? If the space is n-dimensional, we need n basis vectors to make up the basis.

K: That is still so, except that within each subspace you can choose an arbitrary set of basis vectors spanning the *sub*space. Adding these two sets will give a set of basis vectors spanning the whole space. This finishes the geometry.

N: (Deliberately obtuse) What geometry? I only see vectors, subspaces, bases, and operators. Where is the geometry?

K: You are right to be suspicious, the geometry is implied, and it is used to give us both a logic and a probability measure. To calculate the probability of a particular eigenvalue we project orthogonally the state-vector down onto its eigenspace and measure the size of that projection in some way to get the probability. Probability measures have to satisfy some simple constraints, like for example that the sum of the measures of mutually orthogonal subspaces, that together exhaust the space, must sum to one. The geometry of the space through Pythagoras' Theorem ensures that this is indeed the case. Remember that theorem – (K quickly sketches it)

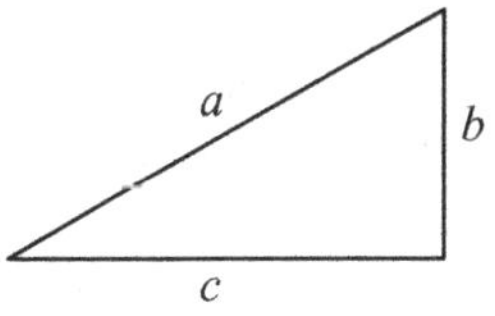

$$a^2 = b^2 + c^2$$

B: So a^2 has the value 1, where b^2 and c^2 are the measures of the corresponding subspaces. You slipped in the idea of probability rather neatly, but why should I accept that way of calculating probability as being useful, or meaningful? You seem to be simply replacing the inner product calculation with a probability. Why?

K: A good question and a hard one. First let me emphasise that we use 'probability' because we find it intuitive to talk of the probability that an object has a certain property, or that is about something. Of course, in quantum mechanics this is shorthand for saying that if one attempted to measure such a property or aboutness then a result would be returned with a probability, possibly with a probability of one or zero. The problem is how to connect that probability with the geometric structure of the space in which the objects reside. I will need to develop the abstract view a little further before I can totally convince you that this is worth doing.

N: Oh, no, not more mathematics.

B: Perhaps you can give us little more intuition about how to make this connection between the geometry and probability.

K: OK. But for further details I will have to refer you to a paper by William Wootters (1980a) and one by R. A. Fisher (1922), who were the first to moot the intuition I am about to describe. In fact Wootters developed a simple example in a very different context, which I will follow transposed to an IR context. But first let me go back to the pioneering work of Maron. Remember he developed a theory of probabilistic indexing in the sixties.

N: Yes, so he did, but as a model it never really took off, although the way of thinking in those early papers was very influential.

K: I agree, and it will serve here to interpret how the probability arises out of the geometry. Imagine that a document is designed (by the author, artist, photographer, . . .) to transmit the information that it is about a certain concept. One way to ascertain this information is to ask a large set of users to judge whether it is about that concept or not. A specific user answers either yes (Y) or no (N). Thus a long sequence, YNNYNY . . . , is obtained. We have assumed that our document is represented by a vector in a space, and that a concept is represented by a basis vector in the same space, the eigenvector of the observable representing the concept.[4] And so, geometrically, the extent to which that document is about the concept in question is given by the angle θ the document vector makes with the concept vector. We assume (following Wootters) that we are able to ask the users indefinitely, and that we cannot use the order in which the answers occur. You will agree that the probability, P, that a document is about the concept is given by the frequency of the Ys in the limit of the sequence, the size of sequence must not play a role. Now it turns out that the function $P = \cos^2 \theta$ is the best code for transmitting a Y or N in the sense of maximising information that will tell us what θ is. One could describe this as a *content hypothesis*: 'The optimal way of displaying the content of a document in a vector space is to define the probability of a concept as the square of the modulus of projection of the state-vector on the concept vector'. This is a little

[4] The idea of representing documents and concepts in the same space is not new, Deerwester *et al.* (1990) discussed this at some length.

more general than warranted by the example because it allows for complex numbers.

N: Oh no, not another C-hypothesis, haven't we already got enough of these?

K: I am afraid not, I want to highlight that the connection between the content and the vector is in the way of a hypothesis, which of course should be testable. Anyway, I now turn to the connection with logic. Earlier I said that the language I was proposing would handle logic and probability. It turns out that given the notion of subspace we now have, we can claim that the lattice of subspaces, where *meet* is the intersection, and *join* is the subspace containing the linear span of all the vectors in both subspaces, form a non-Boolean lattice which is equivalent to a non-classical logic. All this is spelt out in some detail in Chapter 5 of my book. This result was probably first elaborated by Birkhoff and von Neumann (1936). In fact, von Neumann foresaw very early on the intimate connection between logic and probability when formulated in Hilbert space. Theoreticians in computing science have not shown much interest in this until very recently; for example, Engesser and Gabbay (2002) have been investigating belief revision in the context of quantum logics. In IR, we wish to go further and explore the connection between geometry, logic and probability.

B: So what? You have a way of arranging the *subspaces* of a Hilbert space. And, just like the *subsets* of a set make up a Boolean lattice, which is isomorphic to a classical logic, we now have these subspaces and get a non-Boolean lattice and logic. Then what?

K: Well, remember that a query may be represented as a subspace, in the simplest case a 1-dimensional subspace and therefore a vector, and that we would want to calculate the probability that the subspace induces on the entire space.

N: Wow, you now want us to grasp the notion of a subspace inducing a probability on a space. Does it get any freakier?

K: Yes. This is one of the ideas that quantum mechanics brings into play, namely, that the state-vector is a measure of the space, meaning that each subspace has a probability associated with it induced by the state-vector. This generalises.

B: (Impatiently) How?

K: For this we need to return to these observables that I spoke of. I told you about a particularly simple one that was a projection operator, that is one that is idempotent ($\mathbf{P}^2 = \mathbf{P}$) and self-adjoint ($\mathbf{P}^* = \mathbf{P}$). It has the eigenvalues 1 and 0. Another way of looking at it is that it projects onto a subspace corresponding to eigenvalue 1, and that it and the complementary subspace corresponding to 0 span the space. Now it is perfectly easy to define a projector onto a 1-dimensional subspace, that is onto a ray, or onto the subspace that contains all the scalar multiples of a vector. In the Dirac notation this becomes especially easy to denote. If $\underline{x}$ is a unit vector then $\mathbf{P} = |\underline{x}\rangle\langle\underline{x}|$.[5] The point is that **P** is a member of a dual space to the vector space. It is the dual space of self-adjoint linear operators.

N: OK, now we have two spaces, the vector space and its dual. What good is that?

K: It turns out that we can name things in the dual space more easily. For example, we can name the projector onto a vector $\underline{x}$ by $|\underline{x}\rangle\langle\underline{x}|$. We can name the projector onto the subspace spanned by $\underline{x}$ and $\underline{y}$ by $\mathbf{P} = |\underline{x}\rangle\langle\underline{x}| + |\underline{y}\rangle\langle\underline{y}|$. In fact, any superposition of states or mixture of states can be named by an operator in the dual space through what is known as a *density operator*. I realise that I have gone a bit fast here, but I wanted to get the point where I can talk about density operators.

B: It seems to me that you are now shifting your emphasis from the vector space to the space of operators, why?

K: Well spotted, I am doing exactly that, and the reason is that I want to introduce you to Gleason's Theorem. His theorem makes the important connection between geometry and probability that I have been alluding to. But, his theorem is expressed in terms of density operators.

N: All right, but for heaven's sake tell me quickly what a density operator is before I lose the thread completely.

K: A density operator is a self-adjoint linear operator that belongs to a certain sub-class of self-adjoint operators (or if you like observables) such that its eigenvalues are positive and the *trace* of it is one. The trace of an operator is the sum of is eigenvalues. The technical definition is: **D** is a density operator if **D** is a trace class operator and $\mathrm{tr}(\mathbf{D}) = 1$.

K: I can now give you Gleason's Theorem, and I am afraid there is no easy or simple way to do this other than by giving the full and correct statement. So here it is: (Hughes, 1989)

'Let μ be any measure on the closed subspaces of a separable (real or complex) Hilbert space **H** of dimension at least 3. There exists a positive self-adjoint operator **D** of trace-class such that, for all closed subspaces of **H**, $\mu(L) = \mathrm{tr}(\mathbf{DP}_L)$.'[6]

[5] For the Dirac notation see Appendix I.
[6] This theorem is discussed in some detail in Chapter 6.

If μ is a *probability* measure thus requiring that $\mu(\mathbf{H}) = 1$, then $\text{tr}(\mathbf{D}) = 1$, that is, **D** is a density operator. There are many versions of this theorem, this is the one given in Hughes.

N: You had better say more about this, for this is about as opaque as it gets. I guess I would like to see how this will help us in designing an algorithm for retrieval.

B: Yes, let's have it. All this mumbo jumbo has got to be good for something. Although, I must admit it is neat and I like the way you have encoded probability in the geometry.

K: Is it that way round? In fact it is both ways round. If you start with **D**, and $\mathbf{P}_L$ the projection onto the subspace L, then is easy to show that $\mu(L)$ is a probability measure. Gleason's Theorem tells us that if we have a measure μ on the subspaces then we can encode that measure as a linear operator (density operator) to calculate that probability through $\text{tr}(\mathbf{DP}_L)$.

N: So what?

K: Well it is a sort of 'comfort theorem' ensuring that if we assume that these probability judgments can be made then we can represent those judgements through an algebraic calculation. I suppose you could say it is a sort of representation theorem. Just like a classical logic can reflect the relationships between subsets, here we have relationships between subspaces reflected through an algebraic calculation.

B: I am still not sure what extra we get through this theorem. How would you apply it?

K: (Getting enthusiastic again) Now it gets more interesting. The simplest way of thinking of a density operator is as follows:

$$\mathbf{D} = a_1\mathbf{P}_1 + \cdots + a_n\mathbf{P}_n,$$

where the a_i are weights such that $\Sigma a_i = 1$ and the $\mathbf{P}_i$ are projections onto (for simplicity let us say) a 1-dimensional vector space, a ray, so that $\mathbf{P}_i = |\underline{x}_i\rangle\langle\underline{x}_i|$ where $\underline{x}_i$ is a normalised vector. These vectors do not have to be mutually orthogonal. These vectors could represent concepts, that is, base vectors, in which case **D** is a form of weighted query. Also, **D** could represent a weighted mixture of documents like these in a cluster, or a path of documents through a space of documents like in ostensive retrieval. In all cases $\text{tr}(\mathbf{DP}_L)$ gives a probability value to the subspace L. If L is a 1-dimensional subspace, e.g. $\mathbf{P}_L = |\underline{y}\rangle\langle\underline{y}| = \mathbf{P}_y$, things become very simple indeed. That is (sorry about the algebra,

I will scribble it on the whiteboard):

$$\begin{aligned}\mu(L) &= \mathrm{tr}[(a_1\mathbf{P}_1 + \cdots + a_n\mathbf{P}_n)|\underline{y}\rangle\langle\underline{y}|] \\ &= \mathrm{tr}[(a_1|\underline{x}_1\rangle\langle\underline{x}_1| + \cdots + a_n|\underline{x}_n\rangle\langle\underline{x}_n|)|\underline{y}\rangle\langle\underline{y}|] \\ &= a_1\mathrm{tr}[|\underline{x}_1\rangle\langle\underline{x}_1 \mid \underline{y}\rangle\langle\underline{y}|] + \cdots + a_n\mathrm{tr}[|\underline{x}_n\rangle\langle\underline{x}_n \mid \underline{y}\rangle\langle\underline{y}|] \\ &= a_1\langle\underline{x}_1 \mid \underline{y}\rangle\langle\underline{y} \mid \underline{x}_1\rangle + \cdots + a_n\langle\underline{x}_n \mid \underline{y}\rangle\langle\underline{y} \mid \underline{x}_n\rangle \qquad \text{(believe me)} \\ &= a_1|\langle\underline{x}_1 \mid \underline{y}\rangle|^2 + \cdots + a_n|\langle\underline{x}_n \mid \underline{y}\rangle|^2 \text{ (using complex numbers),}\end{aligned}$$

which in a real vector space is a weighted sum of the squares of cos θ_i, where θ_i is the angle that $\underline{y}$ makes with concept or vector i. This takes us right back to the intuition based on Maron's probabilistic indexing.

B: Very neat.

N: But does it work?

K: Well, as always that is a matter for experimentation. The nearest to demonstrating that it works was the work on the Ostensive Model by Campbell and Van Rijsbergen (1996). They had a primitive ad hoc form for this way of calculating the probabilities and using them to navigate the document space. The great thing is that we now have a formalism that allows us to reason sensibly about that underlying mechanism and it applies to objects or documents in any media. It is not text specific. No assumptions are made about the vectors in the space other then that they participate in the geometry and that they can be observed for answers in the way I have been explaining.

[B and N are contemplating the algebra on the whiteboard gloomily]

B: It will never catch on. It's much too hard.

N: (Suddenly cheerful) Shall we have some coffee?

1

Introduction

This book is about underlying ideas and theory. It is about a way of looking, and it is about a formal language that can be used to describe the objects and processes in Information Retrieval. It is not about yet another model for IR, although perhaps some will want to find such an interpretation in it.

Why do we need another way of looking at things? There are some good reasons. *Firstly*, although there are several IR models, for example vector space, probabilistic, logical to name the most important, they cannot be discussed within a single framework.[1] This book, The Geometry of Information Retrieval (GIR), is a first attempt to construct a unifying framework. *Secondly*, although many of us pay lip-service to the conceptual depth of some of the fundamental notions in IR such as relevance, we rarely analyse these notions formally to any bedrock. This is not because we are lazy, it is rather because our theoretical tools have made it very difficult to do so. What follows will, it is hoped, aid such formal analysis. And *thirdly*, there is a need to support the formal specification or expression of IR processes so that we can formally reason about them. For example, we need to be able to lay down mathematical constructs that will direct us in the design of some new algorithms for IR. This is especially important if we wish to extend the boundaries of current research. *Finally*, a fourth reason is that IR research has now embraced the analysis of objects in any medium, that is, text, image, audio, etc., and it has become apparent that existing IR models apply to all of these media. In other words, IR models are not media specific, but sometimes the language that we have used has implied that they are so restricted. Here is an attempt to formulate the foundations of IR in a formal way, and at a level of abstraction, so that the results apply to any object in any medium, and to a range of modes of interaction.

[1] See the Further reading section at the end of the chapter for standard introductory references to information retrieval and quantum mechanics.

We want to consider the way *relevance* can be discussed in the context of information spaces. We begin by thinking of an information space as an abstract space in which objects of interest are represented, and within which a user can interact through observation and measurement with objects. Later such a space will be a Hilbert space. For the moment we assume that the objects are documents, and that each document is represented by a vector of finite dimensions in the space.

Relevance, like information, has proved to be a slippery notion. Conventionally, an object (usually referred to as a document but it can be an image or a sound sequence, etc.) is thought of as relevant to a user's information need, thus the ultimate arbiter of relevance is the user. Relevance is therefore a subjective notion, and the relevance of a document will vary from user to user. Even though two users may submit the same query to an IR system, their assessments of which documents are relevant may differ. In fact the relevance of a document for one user will change as the user interacts with the system. One way of describing this is to assume that relevance depends on the state of the user, and that as the user acquires more information, his or her state changes, implying that a document, potentially relevant before an interaction, may not be so afterwards. Modelling this extremely complicated process has been part of the inspiration for the search for a formal basis for IR.[2]

For the most part, computing or estimating relevance has been handled quite simply. It is generally assumed that relevance is 2-valued, a document being either relevant or not. Algorithms and models were developed to estimate the probability of relevance of any document with respect to a user need. Most simply, this is done by assuming that a query can be a reasonable representation, or expression, of a user's information need. A calculation is made estimating the similarity of the query to a document reflecting the probability of its relevance. The probability of relevance is not conceived to be the same as the degree of relevance of the document, because relevance is 2-valued at every stage (Robertson, 1977). By finding the probability of relevance for each document it is implied that there is a residual probability of non-relevance for that document.

Let us begin by visualising the assessment of relevance in a 2-dimensional space. In it each document is represented by a 2-dimensional vector. Of course the structure of the space could be ignored completely and we could simply assert that the position of one document close to another tells us nothing about potential relevance. We do not do so because IR has been extremely successful in exploiting spatial structure. We make the underlying assumption everywhere

[2] See Saracevic (1975) and Mizzaro (1997) for a detailed discussion on the nature of relevance.

in this book that the geometry of the information space is significant and can be exploited to enhance retrieval.

So, the question that remains is how do we represent the idea of relevance in the structure of such spaces. The motivation comes from quantum mechanics, where the state of a system is represented by a vector, the *state vector*, in a finite or infinite dimensional Hilbert space. *Observables*, that is quantities to be measured, are represented by self-adjoint linear operators which themselves are represented as matrices with respect to a given basis for the Hilbert space. The subtle thing is that a measurement of an observable gives a result which is one of the eigenvalues of the corresponding operator with a probability determined by the geometry of the space. In physics the interpretation[3] can be that the state vector of the system collapses onto the eigenvector of the operator corresponding to the resulting measured value, that is the corresponding eigenvalue.[4] This collapse ensures that if the measurement were repeated immediately then the same value (eigenvalue) would be measured with probability 1. What may be useful for IR about this interpretation is the way the geometric structure is exploited to associate probabilities with measurements. This is a view of measurement, which is quite general and can be applied to infinite as well as finite systems.

We want to apply the quantum theoretic way of looking at measurement to the finding of relevance in IR. We would initially be interested in *finite* systems, although this could change when thinking about measurements applied to images. It is possibly not controversial to assume that relevance is an observable. It may be controversial to assume that it corresponds to a self-adjoint linear operator, or a Hermitian operator, acting on the space of objects – which we are going to assume is a Hilbert space. Instead of the conventional assumption that the observation of relevance results in one of two values, we can easily represent a multi-valued relevance observable by simply extending the number of different eigenvalues for the relevance operator. Let us call the operator **R**. In the binary case there will be exactly two eigenvalues $\lambda_1 = 1, \lambda_2 = 0$ corresponding to the result of measuring the value of **R** for any document.

In a high-dimensional space $n > 2$, the eigenvalues, if there are just two eigenvalues, are what is called degenerate, meaning that at least one of the eigenspaces corresponding to λ_i has dimension greater than 1. This is a slightly troublesome feature because it becomes difficult to illustrate the ideas geometrically. If we take the simple example of a 3-dimensional Hilbert space – that is, each document is represented as a 3-dimensional vector, and we assume that

[3] There are other interpretations (DeWitt and Graham, 1973, Albert, 1994, Barrett, 1999).
[4] In the non-degenerate case where there is one unique eigenvector per eigenvalue.

relevance is 3-valued, then **R** will have three distinct eigenvalues $\lambda_1 \neq \lambda_2 \neq \lambda_3$ (that is, no degeneracy). To measure **R** for any document in this space is to get one of the values λ_i with a certain probability. Geometrically, we can illustrate thus:

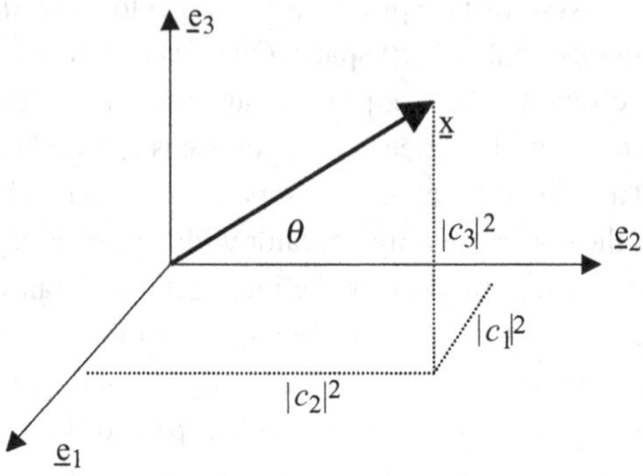

$\{\underline{e}_1, \underline{e}_2, \underline{e}_3\}$ is an orthonormal basis for the 3-space. Let $\underline{x}$ be a unit vector representing a document, let $\{\underline{e}_1, \underline{e}_2, \underline{e}_3\}$ be the eigenvectors corresponding to the three different eigenvalues $\lambda_1 \neq \lambda_2 \neq \lambda_3$. If $\underline{x} = c_1\underline{e}_1 + c_2\underline{e}_2 + c_3\underline{e}_3$ then quantum mechanics dictates that the probability that measuring **R** for $\underline{x}$ will result in λ_1, λ_2 or λ_3 is given by $|c_1|^2$, $|c_2|^2$ or $|c_3|^2$, which by Pythagoras' Theorem indeed sum to one. The obvious question to ask is why should we interpret things this way? The answer is quite technical and will emerge in the sequel, but first an intuitive explanation will be given.

We began by making the assumption that the observable **R** was representable by a Hermitian operator, or in matrix terms one for which the matrix is equal to its conjugate transpose. This is *not* an intuitive assumption. Fortunately there is a famous theorem from Gleason (Hughes, 1989, p. 147) which connects measures on the subspaces of a Hilbert space with Hermitian operators. The importance of the theorem is that it helps us interpret the geometric description; later in the book this connection will be made precise. If we assume that each subspace, in particular each 1-dimensional subspace corresponding to an individual document, can have a measure associated with it, then Gleason's Theorem tells us that there is an algorithm based on a Hermitian operator that will consistently give that measure for each closed subspace. If that measure is a probability measure then the Hermitian operator will be one of an important kind, namely a *density operator*. A definition and description of a density operator can be found in Appendix III and Chapter 6.

This relationship is quite general; it connects a consistent probability assignment to documents in space with a self-adjoint linear operator on that space. In other words there is a density operator that for each subspace will give the probability measure of that subspace. Now accepting that relevance judgments (Maron, 1965) are a matter of probability, we have established that some of the most successful retrieval engines are based on attempts to estimate probability of relevance for each document. Thus it is reasonable to represent the observable relevance as a linear operator of the kind specified by Gleason's Theorem. It is important to realise that we are by no means ruling out that the probabilities may be subjective, that is that each user, or even the same user in a different context, can hypothetically have a different probability assignment in mind. Without any further interaction we do not yet know what they are. The whole point of an IR system is to estimate (or compute) the probabilities. However, we are now in a position to reason about relevance as a first class object, namely as an observable, as applied to the space of objects.

The Hermitian operator beautifully encapsulates the uncertainty associated with relevance. If the relevance operator has k eigenvalues λ_k, then the probability of observing λ_k, one of the relevance values, for any particular document $\underline{x}$ is given by the size of the projection of $\underline{x}$ onto the eigenspace corresponding to λ_k. The reason we have an eigenspace and not an eigenvector is because the eigenvalues may be *degenerate*,[5] more about that later. All this simplifies enormously if the eigenvalues are non-degenerate, for relevance, since we usually have a bi-valued relevance, typically there will be two eigenvalues only, which means that we have two eigen*spaces*.

The analysis we have given above can be applied to any observable, and providing that we are convinced that there is a probability measure reflecting consistently some uncertainty on the space of objects, we can represent that observable by a density operator. It brings with it the added bonus that the eigenvectors (eigenspaces) of a particular operator give a particular perspective on the information space. Since the eigenvectors of a density operator make up an orthonormal basis for the space, each observable and corresponding operator will generate its own basis. In the space all calculations are done with respect to a particular basis, and if the basis is different then of course the probabilities will be different. So we see how it can follow that a difference in a relevance operator can be reflected in the probabilities.

A second, different observable, important in IR, and quite distinct from relevance is 'aboutness' (Sober, 1985, Bruza, 1993, Huibers, 1996). Philosophically, it is not clear at all whether 'aboutness' is a well-defined concept for IR, but we will simply assume that it is. It arises from an attempt to reason abstractly about the properties of documents and queries in terms of index terms.

[5] This means that there is more than one eigenvector for the same eigenvalue (Hughes, 1989, p. 50).

The approach taken in this book is that these objects like documents do *not have* or *possess* properties or attributes.[6] The properties represented by an index term exist by virtue of applying an observable to an object and thereby making a measurement resulting in a value. It is as if the properties emerge from an interacton. The simplest case would be for a single-term observable resulting in a *Yes* or *No* answer. We can consider a entire query to be an observable and its constituent index terms to be the possible results of a measurement. There are various abstract ways of modelling this. The important idea is that we do not assume objects to have the properties a priori. In discussing aboutness we come from the opposite direction from that of relevance. In the case of aboutness we come from the very concrete notion that index terms represent properties of documents, which we are making more abstract, whereas with relevance we have a very abstract notion that we are making more concrete. The result is that both relevance and aboutness can be analysed formally in the same abstract Hilbert space in a comparable way.

One reason for looking at 'aboutness' with textual documents is that it may be obvious that an index term belongs to a document because it occurs in the document as a token and therefore can act as a semantics for it. But, consider an image, which may be represented by a bunch of signals, maybe mathematical functions, and their obvious properties such as for example spatial frequencies cannot be related simply to a semantics.[7] So, we need to tackle 'aboutness' differently and more abstractly, and our proposal is that properties are modelled as observables by self-adjoint linear operators which when applied to an object (image) produce results with probabilities depending on the geometry of the space within which the objects are represented.

Having described how an aboutness operator can be handled just like a relevance operator, we can now face the problem of describing the nature of their interaction. One way of formally interpreting the IR problem is that our representation of the information need (via a query) is intended to reflect relevance as closely as possible. Thus, when we rank documents with respect to a query, ideally the ranking would be in decreasing order of probability of relevance (Robertson, 1977). But, in the case where relevance and aboutness are both represented as observables, ideally the observables would be the same. Of course, in practice, this is rarely the case, and so we are left with the situation where the eigenvectors for **R** and **A** (aboutness) are at an angle to each other.

6 Sustaining this is quite difficult since we are so used to talking in terms objects having properties. There is a profound debate about this issue in quantum mechanics, see for example Wheeler (1980): 'No elementary phenomenon is a phenomenon until it is an observed (registered) phenomenon.'

7 Sometimes referred to as the 'semantic gap' in the literature.

We can illustrate this situation in two dimensions:

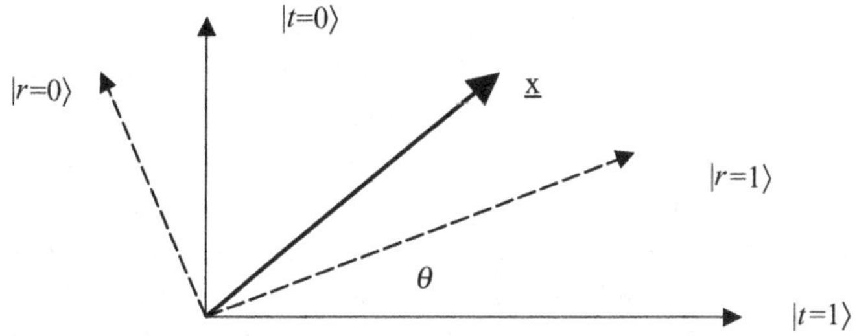

$|t = 1\rangle$ and $|t = 0\rangle$ are the two eigenvectors associated with **A**, and $|r = 1\rangle$ and $|r = 0\rangle$[8] are those associated with **R**. A document is represented by the vector $\underline{x}$. (All the vectors are normalised, that is, of unit length.) If we have an inner product[9] on this space then the geometry dictates that $\mathbf{R}\underline{x} = 1\underline{x}$ with probability $|\langle\underline{x}|r = 1\rangle|^2$ and $\mathbf{A}\underline{x} = 1\underline{x}$ with probability $|\langle\underline{x}|t = 1\rangle|^2$.[10] These probabilities arise because we wish to interpret the inner product in this way. If the eigenvectors for these two observables were to coincide then of course the probabilities would be the same. This would mean that the probability of being about t would be the same as the probability of being relevant a priori. But once having observed that $\underline{x}$ is about t, then the probability of its relevance would be 1 and its probability of non-relevance would be 0. This is the simple case.

Now take the case where the eigenvectors are at an angle to each other. We still have the a-priori probabilities, but what if we observe $\underline{x}$ to be about t, then a subsequent observation of its relevance will depend on two probabilities $|\langle r = 1|t = 1\rangle|^2$ and $|\langle\underline{x}|t = 1\rangle|^2$. If we are in a real Hilbert space then these are simply the squares of the cosines of the corresponding angles.

The really interesting effect occurs when we have the following sequence of observations: $\mathbf{A} \rightarrow \mathbf{R} \rightarrow \mathbf{A}$.

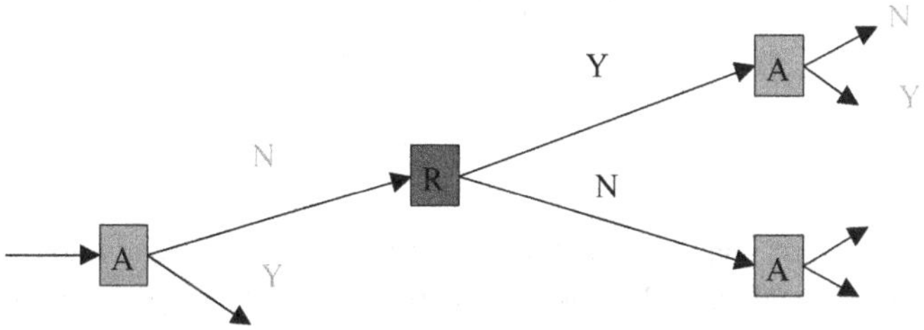

8 We are using the Dirac notation here for 'kets', however, for the moment read these as labels. The reader can find more details about the notation in Appendix I.

9 See Appendix I for a brief example of an inner product.

10 See Appendices II and III for how these probabilities are derived.

In the above diagram we assume that a document (represented by a state vector $\underline{x}$) enters the observation box **A** at the left. **A** represents an observable which corresponds to the property of 'aboutness', and to be concrete, it corresponds to whether a document is about a particular term, *t*, which might be a term such as, for example, 'money', 'bank', etc. One can view **A** as representing a question, which has the answer either yes or no. A measurement is made to establish whether $\underline{x}$ is about *t* or not, this is a yes or no decision. After that the observable **R** is applied to $\underline{x}$ assuming that $\underline{x}$ is *not* about *t*. Again a measurement is made to establish whether $\underline{x}$ is relevant or not, again a yes/no decision. Similarly this may be viewed as asking the question, 'is $\underline{x}$ relevant?' If the interaction between **A** and **R** was classical then any subsequent measurement of *t* should result in the same result as the first measurement, namely, that the answer to the question 'is $\underline{x}$ about *t*?' is still no. However, in the representation developed in this book there is an interaction between **A** and **R** such that when **R** is measured after **A** a subsequent measurement of **A** can once again give either result. This depends on whether the observables **A** and **R** have different eigenbases or, to put it more precisely, whether **A** and **R** commute. The assumption made here is that **A** and **R** do not necessarily commute, that is, determining the aboutness followed by determining relevance, is not the same as determining relevance followed by aboutness. In mathematical terms the operators **A** and **R** do not commute: **AR** ≠ **RA**. This simple example illustrates the basis for the *interaction protocol*[11] we propose between users and information spaces, leading to the development of what one might term an *interaction logic* for IR.[12]

Here is a simple example of two non-commuting observables represented by their corresponding matrices.

$$A = \begin{pmatrix} 0 & 1 \\ 1 & 0 \end{pmatrix} \quad R = \begin{pmatrix} 1 & 0 \\ 0 & -1 \end{pmatrix}$$

$$AR = \begin{pmatrix} 0 & -1 \\ 1 & 0 \end{pmatrix}$$

$$RA = \begin{pmatrix} 0 & 1 \\ -1 & 0 \end{pmatrix}$$

$$AR \neq AR.$$

We can extend this analysis to the interaction between different index terms. It is usual and convenient in IR to assume that index terms are independent. In the geometrical picture being described, term independence means that separate observables corresponding to the different terms will commute. If they are not

[11] I thank Robin Milner for suggesting this term.
[12] The reader is encouraged to read the little gem of a book by Jauch (1973) where a similar example is worked using polarising filters for light.

independent then the 2-dimensional eigenbases are different for each term, the angle between each pair of bases reflecting the dependence. In fact it is convenient to assume that a query operator has a set of eigenvectors as a basis, each vector corresponding to a concept and independent from each other concept. This is very similar to the representation adopted by Latent Semantic Indexing (Deerwester *et al.*, 1990).

The foregoing has given a simple description of the conceptual basis of what we describe mathematically in the chapters that follow. This just leaves me to explain the general approach and structure of the rest of the book. A quote from John von Neumann to some extent expresses the spirit of the endeavour. Of course he was talking about quantum mechanics and not information retrieval. I quote at length with grammatical mistakes and all (Rédei and Stöltzner, 2001, pp. 244–245):[13]

> If you take a classical mechanism of logics, and if you exclude all those traits of logics which are difficult and where all the deep questions of the foundations come in, so if you limit yourself to logics referred to a finite set, it is perfectly clear that logics in that range is equivalent to the theory of all sub-sets of that finite set, and that probability means that you have attributed weights to single points, that you can attribute a probability to each event, which means essentially that the logical treatment corresponds to set theory in that domain and that a probabilistic treatment corresponds to introducing measure. I am, of course, taking both things now in the completely trivialized finite case.
>
> But it is quite possible to extend this to the usual infinite sets. And one also has this parallelism that logics corresponds to set theory and probability theory corresponds to measure theory and that given a system of logics, so given a system of sets, if all is right, you can introduce measures, you can introduce probability and you can always do it in very many different ways.
>
> In the quantum mechanical machinery the situation is quite different. Namely instead of the sets use the linear sub-sets of a suitable space, say of a Hilbert space. The set theoretical situation of logics is replaced by the machinery of projective geometry, which in itself is quite simple.
>
> *However, all quantum mechanical probabilities are defined by inner products of vectors. Essentially if a state of a system is given by one vector, the transition probability in another state is the inner product of the two which is the square of the cosine of the angle between them. In other words, probability corresponds precisely to introducing the angles geometrically. Furthermore, there is only one way to introduce it. The more so because in the quantum mechanical machinery the negation of a statement, so the negation of a statement which is represented by a linear set of vectors, corresponds to the orthogonal complement of this linear space.*[14]
>
> And therefore, as soon as you have introduced into the projective geometry the ordinary machinery of logics, you must have introduced the concept of

[13] This is a reprint of an unpublished paper by John von Neumann, 'Unsolved problems in mathematics', delivered as an address September 2–9, 1954.

[14] Italics by the author of this book (GIR).

> orthogonality. This actually is rigorously true and any axiomatic elaboration of the subject bears it out. So in order to have logics you need in this set of projective geometry with a concept of orthogonality in it.
>
> In order to have probability all you need is a concept of all angles, I mean angles other than 90°. Now it is perfectly quite true that in a geometry, as soon as you can define the right angle, you can define all angles. Another way to put it is that if you take the case of an orthogonal space, those mappings of this space on itself, which leave orthogonality intact, leave all angles intact, in other words, in those systems which can be used as models of the logical background for quantum theory, it is true that as soon as all the ordinary concepts of logics are fixed under some isomorphic transformation, all of probability theory is already fixed.
>
> What I now say is not more profound than saying that the concept of a priori probability in quantum mechanics is uniquely given from the start. You can derive it by counting states and all the ambiguities which are attached to it in classical theories have disappeared. This means, however, that one has a formal mechanism, in which logics and probability theory arise simultaneously and are derived simultaneously. I think that it is quite important and will probably [shed] a great deal of new light on logics and probably alter the whole formal structure of logics considerably, if one succeeds in deriving this system from first principles, in other words from a suitable set of axioms. All the existing axiomatisations of this system are unsatisfactory in this sense, that they bring in quite arbitrarily algebraical laws which are not clearly related to anything that one believes to be true or that one has observed in quantum theory to be true. So, while one has very satisfactorily formalistic foundations of projective geometry of some infinite generalizations of it, of generalizations of it including orthogonality, including angles, none of them are derived from intuitively plausible first principles in the manner in which axiomatisations in other areas are.
>
> *(John von Neumann, 1954.)*

The above is a pretty good summary of how by starting with simple set theory to model retrieval we are progressively pushed into more structure on the set of objects, which brings with it different logics and theories of probability. In the end we have a representation where objects are embedded in Hilbert space, observations are achieved by applying linear operators to objects as vectors. The logic is determined by the collection of linear subspaces and a probability measure is generated through a consistent measure on the set of linear subspaces, as specified by Gleason's Theorem (Gleason, 1957).

Before proceeding to the next chapter it may be useful to highlight two technical issues which will have profound implications for any attempts to develop further this theoretical approach. The first is concerned with the use of complex numbers (Accardi and Fedullo, 1982). In what follows there is no restriction placed on the scalars for the Hilbert space. In other words in general we assume all scalars to be complex numbers of which the reals are a special case. For example, the complex combination of two vectors $\underline{x}$ and

$\underline{y}$ giving rise to $\alpha\underline{x} + \beta\underline{y}$, where α and β are complex numbers, is allowed. Now it is not immediately obvious how this use should be interpreted or indeed exploited. The thing to realise is that it is a question of *representation*. In the entire theory that follows, the *results* of measurements are and always will be real. That is, even if a document is represented by a vector in a complex space, the result of applying a linear self-adjoint operator to it, whose matrix entries may be complex, will give rise to a real with a given probability. Thus, although the representation is in terms of complex numbers, the result of an interaction is always real. For text retrieval this may prove useful if we wish, for example, to use both term frequency and document frequency associated with a given term as part of a matching algorithm expressed as an operation in Hilbert space. Thus if *tf* is the term frequency and we use *idf* to represent the document frequency, then this information can be carried by a complex number c, where $c = idf + \mathrm{i}tf$.[15] In this way the identity of the two different frequencies could be preserved until some later stage in the computation when an explicit instruction is carried out to combine the two into a real number (or weight). How to do this explicitly is not clear yet, but there is no need to cut off the generality provided by complex numbers. Of course, when the objects represent images we have absolutely no idea what the best representation is and it may be that in the same way as we need complex numbers when we do Fourier transforms of signals, when specifying operations on images we may find a use for the extra representation power afforded by complex numbers.[16]

This leaves us with the intriguing question of the inherent nature of the probability that we have developed here following the lines in which it is used in quantum mechanics. Traditionally, probabilities are specified as measures on sets, and if the sets are subsets of a multi-dimensional space they have the properties of volume. Thus, the volume of subset V_i is given as a relative volume with respect to the entire set's volume V by $|V_i| \;/\; |V|$.[17] The volume numbers behave like relative frequencies, and indeed two disjoint (relative) volumes can be added to give the relative volume of the union. This is all familiar, for example see any standard text on probability such as Feller (1957), and the Kolmogorov axioms (see his book, 1950) capture this kind of probability very neatly.

In quantum mechanics things are different and the basis for the probability assignment is Pythagoras' Theorem. In the diagram below $\underline{x}$ and $\underline{y}$ are the eigenvectors of an observable $\mathbf{A}$, and make up a 2-dimensional orthonormal

[15] $\mathrm{i} = \sqrt{-1}$.

[16] The argument made here for complex numbers is not unlike the argument made by Feynman for *negative* probabilities (Hiley and Peat, 1987, Chapter 13).

[17] $|\cdot|$ gives the volume of a set.

basis for a 2-dimensional space. The projection of c onto $\underline{x}$ is a, and b is the projection of c onto $\underline{y}$. In two dimensions we have

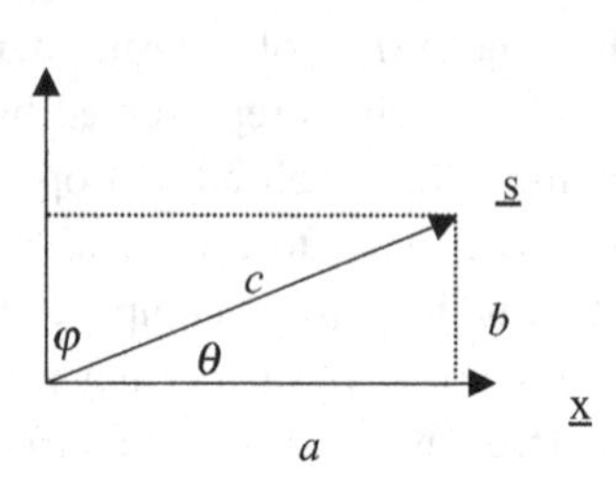

and we all know that

$$\begin{aligned} a^2 + b^2 &= c^2 \\ \left(\frac{a}{c}\right)^2 + \left(\frac{b}{c}\right)^2 &= 1 \\ \text{or} \quad \cos^2\theta + \cos^2\varphi &= 1, \quad 0 \leq \cos\theta \leq 1, \quad 0 \leq \cos\varphi \leq 1. \end{aligned}$$

This gives a way of interpreting a probability of observing the result of an observable **A** with two outcomes a_1, a_2, where a_1 is the eigenvalue corresponding to the eigenvector $\underline{x}$, and a_2 is the eigenvalue corresponding to the eigenvector $\underline{y}$. In our earlier discussion a_1 would represent yes and a_2 would represent no to a question represented by **A**. The state of the system (or the document) is represented by the vector $\underline{s}$, and if normalised its length $c = 1$. So we can assign a probability p_1 to be the probability that we get a_1 for observable **A** given the state $\underline{s}$, where $p_1 = \text{Prob}(\mathbf{A} = a_1 | \underline{s}) = \cos^2\theta$ and $p_2 = \text{Prob}(\mathbf{A} = a_2 | \underline{s}) = \cos^2\varphi$. The state $\underline{s}$ can vary throughout the space but $p_1 + p_2 = 1$ for any $\underline{s}$. In particular $p_1 = 1$ and $p_2 = 0$, if $\underline{s}$ lies along $\underline{x}$ and vice versa if $\underline{s}$ lies along $\underline{y}$.

This way of assigning probabilities generalises readily to n dimensions, indeed to infinite dimensions, and handles complex numbers without any difficulty. In one sentence, we can summarise the purpose of this book by saying that it is an attempt to show that this kind of probability assignment in Hilbert space is a suitable way of describing interaction for information retrieval.

Further reading

There are now some good introductions to information retrieval that cover the foundations of the subject from different points of view. The most recent is Belew (2000) which takes a cognitive perspective. A more traditional approach is taken by Kowalski and Maybury (2000), and Korfhage (1997). The texts by Baeza-Yates and Ribeiro-Neto (1999), and Frakes and Baeza-Yates (1992) emphasise algorithmic and implementation issues. Before these more recent textbooks were published, one was mostly dependent on research monographs, such as Fairthorne (1961), Salton (1968) and Van Rijsbergen (1979a). These are worth consulting since many of the research ideas presented in them are still of current interest. The monograph by Blair (1990) is unique for its emphasis on the philosophical foundations of IR. Dominich (2001) has given a very mathematical account of the foundations of IR. In Sparck Jones and Willett (1997) one will find a collection of some of classic papers in IR, to this it is worth adding the paper by Fairthorne (1958) which is perhaps one of the earliest paper on IR ever published in the computer science literature. A still much cited text book is Salton and McGill (1983) as it contains a useful elementary introduction to the vector space approach to IR.

The main body of this book draws heavily on the mathematics used in quantum mechanics. The preceding chapter makes clear that the motivation for viewing and modelling IR formally in the special way just described is also drawn from quantum mechanics. To gain a better understanding of quantum mechanics and the way it uses the appropriate mathematics one can consult a number of introductory (sometimes popular) texts. The bibliography lists several, together with annotations indicating their relevance and significance. One of the simplest and clearest popular introductions is Albert (1994), which does not shy away from using the appropriate mathematics when needed, but always gives an intuitive explanation of its use.[18] An excellent and classical account of the mathematical foundations is Jauch (1968), he also in 1973 published a delightful dialogue on the reality of quanta. For the philosophically minded, Barrett (1999) is worth reading. There are several good popular introductions to quantum mechanics, for example Penrose (1989, 1994), Polkinghorne (1986, 2002), Rae (1986). Wick (1995) is a well-written semi-popular account, whereas Gibbins (1987) contains a nice potted history of QM before dealing with the paradoxes of QM as Wick does. A useful dictionary, or glossary, of the well known terms in QM can be found in Gribbin (2002). There are many more entries in the annotated bibliography at the end of the book, and it may be worth scanning and reading the entries if one wishes to tackle some of the more technical literature before proceeding to the rest of this book.

[18] It is also good for getting acquainted with the Dirac notation.

2

On sets and kinds for IR

In this chapter an elementary introduction to simple information retrieval is given using set theory. We show how the set-theoretic approach leads naturally to a Boolean algebra which formally captures Boolean retrieval (Blair, 1990). We then move onto to assume a slightly more elaborate class structure, which naturally leads to an algebra which is non-Boolean and hence reflects a non-Boolean logic (see Aerts *et al.*, 1993, for a concrete example). The chapter finishes by giving a simple example in Hilbert space of the failure of the distribution law in logic.

Elementary IR

We will begin with a set of objects; these objects are usually documents. A document may have a finer-grained structure, that is, it may contain some structured text, some images and some speech. For the moment we will not be concerned with that internal structure. We will only make the assumption that for each document it is possible to decide whether a particular attribute or property applies to it. For example, for a text, we can decide whether it is about 'politics' or not; for images we might be able to decide that an image is about 'churches'. For human beings such decisions are relatively easy to make, for machines, unfortunately, it is very much harder. Traditionally in IR the process of deciding is known as indexing, or the assigning of index terms, or keywords. We will assume that this process is unproblematic until later in the book when we will discuss it in more detail. Thus we have a set of attributes, or properties (index terms, keywords) that apply to, or are true of, an object, or not, as the case may be. Formally the attributes may be thought of as predicates, and the objects for which a predicate is true are said to *satisfy* that predicate. Given a set of objects $\{x, y, z, \ldots\} = \Omega$ and a set of predicates

$\{P, Q, R, \ldots\}$ we can now illustrate a simple model for IR using naïve set theory.

Picture Ω as a set thus:

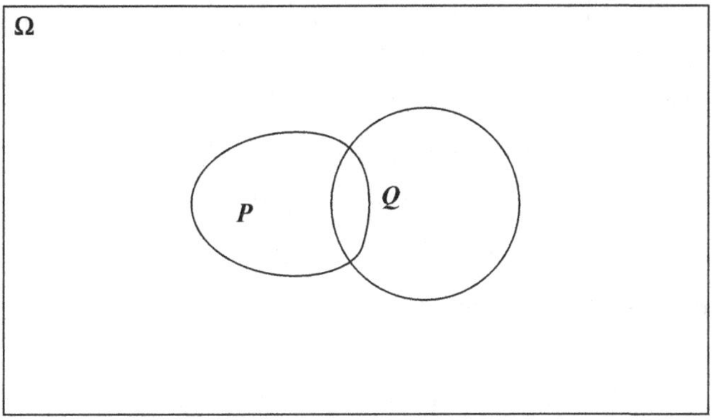

we can describe the set of objects that satisfy P as $[\![P]\!] = \{x \mid P(x) \text{ is true}\}$ and the set of objects satisfying Q as $[\![Q]\!] = \{x \mid Q(x) \text{ is true}\}$. This notation is rather cumbersome and usually, in the diagram, and discussion, $[\![P]\!]$ is simply referred to as P, that is the set of of objects satisfying a predicate P is also referred to as P. There is a well-known justification for being able to make this identification which is known as the Stone Representation Theorem (see Marciszewski, 1981, p. 9). Hence given any subset in the set Ω it represents a property shared by all the objects in the subset. That in general we can do this in set theory is known as the 'comprehension axiom', a detailed definition and discussion can be found in Marciszewski.

Now with this basic set-up we can specify and formulate some simple retrieval. We can ask the question $\{x \mid P(x) \text{ is true}\}$, that is we can request to retrieve all objects that satisfy P. Similarly, we can request to retrieve all objects that satisfy Q. How this is done is a non-trivial issue of implementation about which little will be said in this book (but see *Managing Gigabytes* by Witten *et al.*, 1994). The next obvious step is to consider retrieving all objects that satisfy both P and Q, that is,

$$[\![P \wedge Q]\!] = \{x \mid \text{`}P(x)\text{ is true' and `}Q(x)\text{ is true'}\}.$$

Here we have slipped in the predicate $P \wedge Q$, whose meaning (or extension) is given by the intersections of the sets satisfying P and Q. In other words we have extended the language of predicates to allow connectives. Similarly, we can define

$$[\![P \vee Q]\!] = \{x \mid \text{`}P(x)\text{ is true' or `}Q(x)\text{ is true'}\}$$

and

$$[\![\neg Q]\!] = \{x \mid \text{It is not the case that '}Q(x)\text{ is true'}\}.$$

What we have now is a formal language of basic predicates and simple logical connectives $\wedge$ (and), $\vee$ (or) and $\neg$ (not). The meaning of any expression in that language, for example $(P \wedge Q) \vee (\neg R)$, is given by the set-theoretic operations on the 'meaning' of the individual predicates. That is

$$[\![P \wedge Q]\!] = [\![P]\!] \cap [\![Q]\!],$$
$$[\![P \vee Q]\!] = [\![P]\!] \cup [\![Q]\!] \text{ and}$$
$$[\![\neg P]\!] = \Omega - [\![P]\!],$$

and where '$\cap$' is set intersection, '$\cup$' is set union, and '$-$' is set complementation. Hence

$$[\![(P \wedge Q) \vee \neg R]\!] = ([\![P]\!] \cap [\![Q]\!]) \cup [\![\neg R]\!].$$

The fact that we can do this thus, that is make up the meaning of an expression in terms of the meanings of the component expressions, without taking into account the context, is known as the Principle of Compositionality. (Dowty *et al.*, 1981, Thomason,1974).

In retrieval terms, if a query Q is given by $(R \wedge B) \wedge \neg M$, where

$R =$ rivers
$B =$ banks
$M =$ money,

then Q is a request for information for documents about 'river banks' and not about 'money'. It amounts to requesting the set $[\![Q]\!]$ given by $\{x \mid Q(x) \text{ is true}\}$, that is we are looking for the set of all x where each x satisfies P and Q but not M. Pictorially it looks like this:

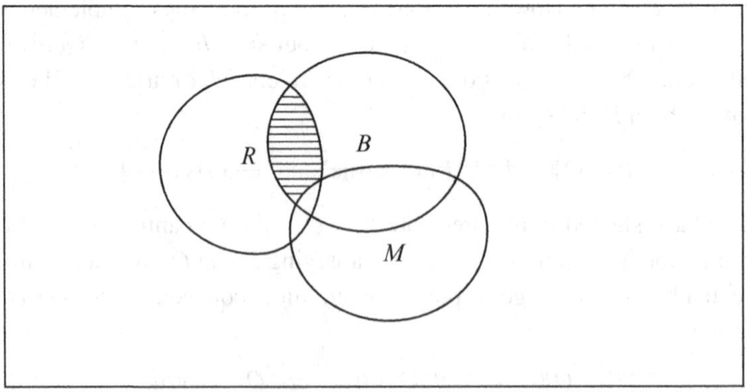

What has been described so far are the basics of Boolean retrieval (Kowalski and Maybury, 2000, Korfhage, 1997). 'Boolean' because the logic used to express the retrieval request, such as Q, is Boolean (Marciszewski, 1981).

The beauty of this approach is that we do not have to say anything about the structure of the set Ω. There is no information about whether an object x is similar or dissimilar to an object y. The only information that is used is whether an object x possesses a predicate P, whether any two objects share a predicate P, and whether the same objects satisfy one or more predicates.[1] We need to know no more, we simply have to be able to name the objects $\{x, y, z, \ldots\}$ and be able to decide whether any predicate (attribute) $\{P, Q, R, \ldots\}$ applies to it.

Unfortunately experience and experiment have shown that IR based on this simple model does not deliver the required performance (Blair, 1990). The performance of a retrieval system is usually defined in terms of the ability to retrieve the 'relevant' objects (precision) whilst at the same time retrieving as few of the 'non-relevant' ones as possible (recall).[2] This is not a simple issue. There is a vast literature on what determines a relevant and a non-relevant object (Saracevic, 1975, Mizzaro, 1997). We return to aspects of this decision-making later. What is worth saying here is that it is not straightforward to formulate a request such as Q and to retrieve $[\![Q]\!]$. There is no guarantee that $[\![Q]\!]$ will contain all the relevant objects and only the relevant ones, that is, no non-relevant ones. Typically $[\![Q]\!]$ will contain some of each. The challenge is to define retrieval strategies that will enable a user to formulate and reformulate Q so that the content of $[\![Q]\!]$ is optimal.

In order to introduce the standard effectiveness measures of retrieval we are required to extend the structure of the set Ω with the counting measure, so that we can tell what the size of each subset is. If we assume that the subset of relevant documents in Ω is A, then the number of relevant documents is given by $|A|$, where $|\cdot|$ is the counting measure. The most popular and commonly used effectiveness measures are *precision* and *recall*. In set-theoretic terms, if B is the set of retrieved documents then

$$\text{precision} = |A \cap B|/|B|, \text{ and recall} = |A \cap B|/|A|.$$

A well-known composite effectiveness measure is the E-measure;[3] a special case is given by

$$E = |A \,\Delta\, B|/(|A| + |B|) = (|A \cup B| - |A \cap B|)/(|A| + |B|),$$

[1] We will ignore predicates such as x is similar to y.
[2] This kind of performance is normally referred to as retrieval effectiveness; we will do the same, see below.
[3] A formal treatment of the foundation of the E-measure may be found in Van Rijsbergen (1979c).

where Δ is known as the symmetric difference.[4] It calculates the difference between the union and intersection of two sets. Another special case is $F = 1 - E$, which is now commonly used instead of E when measuring effectiveness. Both E and F can be expressed in terms of precision and recall.

It is tempting to generalise the counting measure $|\cdot|$ to some general (probabilistic) measure, but at this stage there are no grounds for doing that (but see Van Rijsbergen, 1979b). Beyond being able to tell what size a set is, unless we know more about the detailed structure of each object in Ω, we cannot say much more.

Returning to our general set-theoretic discussion about the correspondence between subsets and predicates, it would appear that A and B are the extension of predicates, properties attributable to the members of A and B. With a thorough abuse of notation one might express this as $A = [\![\text{relevant}]\!]$ and $B = [\![\text{retrieved}]\!]$. However, they are strange predicates because they are not known in advance. Let us take the predicate *retrieved* first. This is usually specified algorithmically, and indeed in the case of Boolean retrieval is the set satisfying a Boolean expression Q, whatever that may turn out to be. The second predicate *relevance* is user dependent, because only a user can determine whether an object $x \in \Omega$ is relevant to her or his information need. The impression given by the definitions of precision and recall is slightly misleading because they appear to have asserted that the set A is known in advance and static, neither of which in practice is the case. As a first approximation in designing models and implementations for IR we assume that such a set exists and can be found by generating a series of subsets B_i which together will somehow end up containing A, the set of all relevant documents. That is, a user attempts to construct $\cup_i B_i$ such that $A \subseteq \cup_i B_i$. This process can be broken down into a number of steps such that $|A \cap B_i|$ is as large as possible and $B_i \neq B_j$, so that at each stage, new members of A may be found. Unfortunately, without a file-structure on Ω it is difficult to see how to guide a user towards the discovery of A. Of course each B_i may give hints as to how to formulate the next Q_{i+1} corresponding to B_{i+1} but such a process is fairly random.

What is more interesting is to consider the interaction between the various predicates. Let us concentrate on the two kinds, one to connect with 'aboutness', these predicates I have called $\{P, Q, R, \ldots\}$; and the kind for 'relevance' which for convenience I will call predicate X. We will consider how the observation of one predicate followed by the observation of another may affect the judgement about the first. Perhaps it would be best to begin with a simple example. Let Q stands for 'banks', that is

$$[\![Q]\!] = \{x \mid x \text{ is about banks}\}$$

4 This is like a Hamming distance for sets.

and

$$[\![\neg Q]\!] = \{x \mid x \text{ is not about banks}\}.$$

In our set-theoretic account we have assumed that 'aboutness' is a bivalent property, that is

$$x \in [\![Q]\!] \text{ or } x \in [\![\neg Q]\!] \text{ for all } x \in \Omega.$$

Many models for IR assume this,[5] they assume that whether an object is about Q or not Q can be established objectively once and for all by some computation. This assumption may be challenged, and in fact it is more natural to assume that an object is about neither, or both, until an observation by a user forces it to be about one or the other, from the point of view of the user.

Now let us bring predicate X (relevance) into play. Once object x has been observed to be about banks (Q) and the relevance is established, a subsequent repeat observation of whether x is about banks may lead to a different result. The intuitive explanation is that some cognitive activity has taken place between the two observations of Q that will change the state of the observer from one measurement moment to the next (see for example Borland, 2000, p. 25).[6] The same phenomenon can occur when two aboutness predicates P and Q are observed in succession. The traditional view is that we can treat P and Q independently and that the observation of P followed by Q will not affect the subsequent observation of P. Once again observing Q in between two observations of P involves some cognitive activity and may have an effect. Of course we are assuming here that aboutness, like relevance, is established through the interaction between the user and the object under observation.

What we have described above is a notion of *compatibility* between predicates or subsets. Technically, this can be expressed as

$$P = (P \wedge Q) \vee (P \vee \neg Q),$$

when P and Q are compatible, or

$$X = (X \wedge Q) \vee (X \vee \neg Q),$$

where X is the relevance predicate. In the latter case, if Q stands for a simple index term like 'banks', then the expression means that relevance can be separated into two distinct properties 'relevance and bankness' and 'relevance and non-bankness'. When predicates are incompatible the relationship does

[5] There are notable exceptions, for example Maron (1965), and the early work of Goffman (1964).

[6] 'That is the relevance or irrelevance of a given retrieved document may affect the user's current state of knowledge resulting in a change of the user's information need, which may lead to a change of the user's perception/interpretation of the subsequent retrieved documents . . .'

not hold. There is a well known law of logic, *distribution*, which enables us to rewrite X as follows:

$$X = (X \wedge Q) \vee (X \wedge \neg Q) = X \wedge (Q \vee \neg Q) \text{ if } X \text{ and } Q \text{ are compatible.}^7$$

In our Boolean model the distributive law holds, and all predicates (subsets) are treated as compatible. If, on the other hand, we wish to model a possible incompatibility between predicates, because of interaction, then the Boolean Model is too strong, because it forces compatibility.

Before moving on to other structures there is one more aspect of the set-theoretic (Boolean) approach that needs to be clarified. One of the most difficult things in modelling IR is to deal with the interplay between sets, measures and logic. The element of logic that is central, and most troublesome, is the notion of implication. In Boolean logic the connective '$\rightarrow$' is defined for two propositions A and B by setting $A \rightarrow B = \neg A \vee B$. Using the notation introduced earlier, the semantics may be given as

$$[\![A \rightarrow B]\!] = \{x | x \in [\![\neg A]\!] \cup [\![B]\!]\}.$$

This connective is important because it enables us to perform inference. For us to prove an implication such as $A \rightarrow B$ it suffices to deduce the consequent B from the antecedent (according to some fixed rules). This can be strengthened into a full-blown Deduction Theorem that for classical logic states

$$A \wedge B \models C \text{ if and only if } A \models B \rightarrow C;$$

in words this says that if C is semantically entailed by A and B, then A semantically entails $B \rightarrow C$, and if A semantically entails $B \rightarrow C$ then C is semantically entailed by A and B. Of course A may be empty, in which case we have

$$B \models C \text{ if and only if } \models B \rightarrow C.$$

Much of classical inference is based on this result. When later we introduce more structure into our object space Ω we will discover that the lack of distribution in the logic means we have to sacrifice the full-blown Deduction Theorem but retain its special case.[8]

We now move on from considering just sets, subsets, and the relationships between them to a slightly more elaborated class structure, which inevitably

[7] See Holland (1970) for extensive details.
[8] For a deeper discussion about this see Van Rijsbergen (2000).

leads to a non-boolean logic. We motivate this class structure by first looking at a primitive form of it, namely, an inverted file, which itself is used heavily in IR.

Inverted files and natural kinds

Inverted files have been used in information retrieval almost since the very beginning of the subject (Fairthorne, 1958). Most introductions to IR contain a detailed description and definition of this file-structure (see for example Van Rijsbergen, 1979a, Salton and McGill, 1983 and Witten *et al.*, 1994). Here we use it in order to motivate a discussion about classes of objects, their properties and their associated kinds. In particular we demonstrate how these considerations lead to a weak logic that is not distributive and of course, therefore, not Boolean. All we need for our discussion is classes of objects taken from Ω and a notion of attribute, property or trait associated with objects. To begin with we must determine whether objects share attributes in common or not. The kind of class S that will interest us is one where the members share a number of attributes and only those attributes. Thus any object not in S does not share all the properties. At the most primitive level this is true of the buckets of an inverted file. For example, the class of objects about mammals is indexed by 'mammals' and the inverted file will have a bucket (a class!) containing all and only those objects indexed by 'mammals'. Similarly, 'predators' indexes the class of objects about predators. These classes may of course overlap, an object may be indexed by more than one attribute.

Definition D1[9]

A set T of attributes *determine* a set A of individuals if and only if the following conditions are satisfied:

(1) every individual in A *instantiates* every attribute in T;
(2) no individual not in A *instantiates* every attribute in T.

If T is a singleton set then the As are the buckets of an inverted file.

Definition D2

A set of individuals is an *artificial* class if there is a corresponding set tr(A) of attributes that determine A.

[9] The formal treatment that follows owes much to Hardegree (1982).

Please notice that we are using a contrary terminology from the philosophical literature (Quine, 1969, Lakoff, 1987) by defining artificial classes instead of natural classes. We prefer to follow the *Numerical Taxonomy* literature (Sneath and Sokal, 1973, p. 20).

Formally, we can define the attributes of a class A and the individual instantiating the attributes as follows (where V is the set of possible attributes, and Ω the universe of objects).

Definition D3

$$\text{tr}(A) = \{t \in V \mid a \,\Delta\, t \text{ for all } a \in A\}.$$

Definition D4

$$\text{in}(T) = \{a \in \Omega \mid a \,\Delta\, t \text{ for all } t \in T\},$$

where Δ is a relation on $\Omega \times V$, the cross product of the universe of objects with the universe of attributes.

Let us consider an example:

(1) H is the set of objects about humans;
(2) L is the set of objects about lizards;
(3) $H \cup L$ is the set of objects about humans or lizards.

If we now think of tr(.) as an indexing operation, then it would generate the set of attributes that defines a set of objects. Similarly, in(.) is an operation that generates a set of objects that share a given set of attributes. Thus tr(H) generates the attributes, or index terms, for H, and tr(L) does the same thing for L. What is more interesting is to consider tr($H \cup L$). Its definition is given by

$$\text{tr}(H \cup L) = \{t \in V | a \,\Delta\, t \text{ for all } a \in H \cup L\},$$

that is, it is the set of attributes shared by all the members of H and L. A question now arises. Is $H \cup L$ an artificial class? For this to be the case tr($H \cup L$) would need to determine $H \cup L$, which it probably does not. For in(tr($H \cup L$)) the objects sharing all the attributes in tr($H \cup L$) is more likely to be the class of objects about vertebrates which properly includes $H \cup L$ (and some others, e.g. fish). Thus

$$H \cup L \subset \text{in}(\text{tr}(H \cup L).$$

And here we have the nub of the problem. Whereas in naïve set theory one would expect equality between $H \cup L$ and in(tr($H \cup L$), in normal use the latter set of objects in general includes $H \cup L$. One can salvage the situation by insisting that a class must satisfy certain conditions in order that it counts as a class, this inevitably leads to a non-Boolean logic.

Before we extend our example any further we will define the notion of monothetic kinds (which philosophers call natural kinds). In terms of the example it comes down to ensuring that tr(in(.)) and in(tr(.)) are closure operations. Let us begin by defining the mathematical nature of tr and in. They are a Galois connection (see Hardegree, 1982, Davey and Priestley, 1990 and Ganter and Wille, 1999).

Definition D5

Let $(P, \leq_1)$ and $(Q, \leq_2)$ be two partially ordered sets. Then a Galois connection between these two posets is, by definition, a pair of functions (f, g) satisfying the following conditions:

(1) f maps P into Q; g maps Q into P;
(2) for all a, b in P, if $a \leq_1 b$ then $f(a) \geq_2 f(b)$;
(3) for all x, y in Q, if $x \leq_2 y$ then $g(x) \geq_1 g(y)$;
(4) for all $a \in P$, $a \leq_1 g[f(a)]$;
(5) for all $x \in Q$, $x \leq_2 f[g(x)]$.

One can easily show that (tr, in) as defined in D3 and D4 is a Galois connection between $\wp(\Omega)$ and $\wp(V)$, the power sets of Ω and V respectively.

We can now define a closure operation on a Galois connection. For this we need the definition of a *closure* operation c on a poset, say $(R, \leq)$, where for all $a, b \in R$ we have

(1) $a \leq c(a)$;
(2) if $a \leq b$ then $c(a) \leq c(b)$;
(3) $c[c(a)] = c(a)$;

Now let us look at the operations on the structure defined by Ω, V and the relation Δ which are used to define tr and in. We say that a subset of A of Ω is *Galois closed* if and only if in[tr(A)] $= A$; a subset of T of V is *Galois closed* if and only if tr[in(T)] $= T$. This is not automatic, for the earlier example where $H \cup L \subset$ in(tr($H \cup L$) showed that $H \cup L$ is *not* Galois closed. So, with this new machinery we can now say that the Galois closed subsets of Ω are the artificial classes. We can now go on to define the monothetic kinds.

Definition D6

Let Ω, V and Δ be as defined before and let (tr, in) be the associated Galois connection. A *monothetic* kind is defined as an ordered pair (A, I) satisfying

1. $A \subseteq \Omega$;
2. $I \subseteq V$;
3. $\mathrm{tr}(A) = T$;
4. $\mathrm{in}(T) = A$;

In other words, T determines A and A determines T. This is a very strong requirement. For example, most classification algorithms do not produce such classes but instead produce *polythetic* kinds (see Van Rijsbergen, 1979a). The nearest thing to an algorithm producing monothetic kinds is the L* algorithm described in (Van Rijsbergen, 1970, Sibson, 1972).

Hardegree (1982) in his paper goes on to develop a logic based on these kinds, and we will return to this when we discuss logics on a more abstract space, a Hilbert space.

Let us now return to the example about humans and lizards and let us see how a non-standard logic arises. Let H, L and B be three kinds (possibly human, lizard and bird), and assuming that we have a logic for kinds, conjunction and disjunction are given by

$$K_1 \wedge K_2 = (A_1 \cap A_2, \mathrm{tr}(A1 \cap A2)),$$
$$K_1 \vee K_2 = (\mathrm{in}(T_1 \cap T_2), T_1 \cap T_2),$$

where $K_1 = (A_1, T_1)$ and $K_2 = (A_2, T_2)$ are monothetic kinds. The sets of monothetic kinds make up a complete lattice where conjunction (join) and disjunction (meet) are defined in the usual way. Returning to the simple example, consider $B \wedge (H \vee L)$ and $(B \wedge H) \vee (B \wedge L)$: if the distributive law were to hold then these expressions would be equal, but $H \vee L$ is by definition (lattice theory) the smallest kind that includes both H and L, which is probably the vertebrate kind, call it U. And so $B \wedge (H \vee L) = B \wedge U$; if B is thought of as the bird kind then $B \wedge U = B$. But now consider the other expression, $(B \wedge H) \vee (B \wedge L)$. It is straightforward to argue that $B \wedge H = B \wedge L =$ empty (the null kind), hence $(B \wedge H) \vee (B \wedge L)$ is empty, *and the distributive law fails*. In classical logic (Boolean logic) the distributive law holds, and so Boolean logic cannot be an appropriate logic for monothetic kinds. Or to put it differently: Boolean logic is classless.

The obvious question to ask is, does this matter? Well, it does, especially if one is interested in defining classes in an abstract space, such as a vector space. Here is a geometric demonstration.

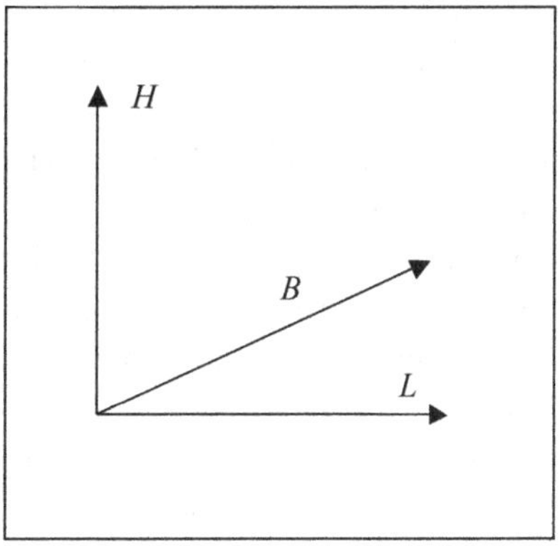

In this 2-dimensional space[10] the class of documents about humans is given by the subspace H, the class about birds by B, and the class about lizards by L. (This is a very crude example.) Now define $H \vee L$ by the subspace spanned by H and L, $H \wedge L$ as the intersection of the subspace corresponding to H and the subspace corresponding to L. Similarly for the join and meet of the other classes. The subspace corresponding to $H \vee L$ will be the entire 2-dimensional plane, and thus $B \wedge (H \vee L) = B$, whereas geometrically $(B \wedge H) \vee (B \wedge L)$ will again be empty, the null space. Once again the distribution law fails. If one intends to introduce logical reasoning within a vector space then this issue has to be confronted.

The problem also has to be avoided when the Galois connection is interpreted as an inverted file relation. Intersection of the posting lists (buckets) of index terms works without any problems, so does the union of lists, and indeed this is how Boolean retrieval is implemented. But the operations intersection and union do not necessarily correspond to the equivalent logical notions for artificial classes. They are simple convenient ways of talking logically about set-theoretic operations relying on the Stone Representation Theorem. This is convenient and comfortable in the context of retrieving textual objects, but consider now the case of retrieving from a set of image objects where retrieval is based on the contents (a largely unsolved problem). The attributes, more accurately thought of as features, are not conveniently available as index terms (no visual keywords!). In general the attributes are generated through quite complex and sophisticated processing, and the assumption that the conjunction (or disjunction) of two attributes is representable by the intersection (or union) of lists of objects does not seem as intuitive as it is for text. Much more likely is that the language of features to describe image objects will have a logic which will be different from

[10] The details of this representation will be made more precise later.

a Boolean logic. Earlier on we saw an example, showing how incompatibility of features and user-dependent assessment of features led to a non-classical logic. Similar arguments apply when interacting with images, even more strongly.

Finally, there is a very interesting structural issue that has to do with duality. The definition of an artificial class is given in terms of necessary and sufficient conditions by definition D1. A consequence of this is that one could equally well talk about artificial classes in the attributes which correspond to the object classes. Without going into the details, it can be understood that the logic for object classes is reflected as a logic in the attribute classes and also vice versa. This symmetry is often referred to as *duality*, a notion that will recur. Later on we will illustrate how subspaces in an abstract space correspond to projectors into the space, more precisely the set of projectors are in 1:1 correspondence with the subspaces of the abstract space. This is important and significant because in many ways the logic associated with the attribute space is more natural to deal with than the one on the object space. In IR terms, a logic capturing the relations between index terms is more intuitive than one concerned with subsets of documents. But more about this later.

Further reading

This chapter uses only elementary concepts from set theory and logic, and summary details for these concepts can be found in Marciszewski (1981). The elements of lattice theory and order on classes are readily accessible in the classic textbook by Birkhoff and MacLane (1957). Holland (1970) contains material on lattices with an eye to its application in Hilbert space theory and hence ready for use in quantum theory. For more background on non-classical logic and, in particular, conditionals, Priest (2001) is recommended. The book by Barwise and Seligman (1997), especially Chapter 2, makes good complementary reading as it also draws on the work of Hardegree (1982).

3

Vector and Hilbert spaces

The purpose of this chapter is to lay the foundations for a logic on a vector space, or a Hilbert space (see Appendix I), and for a specification of an algebraic realisation. We will begin by introducing the basics of vector spaces, which of course may be found in many textbooks.[1] We will introduce elementary finite-dimensional vectors through their realisation as n-dimensional vectors in a *real* Euclidean space (Halmos, 1958, p. 121). For most practical purposes this will be sufficient, and has the great attraction of being quite rigorous and also very intuitive. When we move to more general spaces the extension will be noted; for example, sometimes we will allow the scalars to be complex.

The set of all n-dimensional vectors $\underline{x}$, displayed as follows,

$$\underline{x} = \begin{pmatrix} x_1 \\ \cdot \\ \cdot \\ \cdot \\ x_n \end{pmatrix} = |\underline{x}\rangle,$$

make up the vector space. Here we have a number of notations that need clarifying. Firstly, we can simply refer to a vector by $\underline{x}$, or by a particular realisation using what is called a *column vector*, or through the Dirac notation $|\underline{x}\rangle$ which

[1] Readers familiar with elementary vector space theory can speed directly to Chapter 4. Halmos (1958), Finkbeiner (1960), Mirsky (1990), and Sadun (2001) are all good texts to start with. For the moment we will only be interested in finite-dimensional vector spaces (but see Halmos, 1951, Jordan, 1969). It is possible to introduce vector spaces without considering any particular realisation, proceeding by defining the properties of addition between vectors, and multiplication between vectors and scalars; we will not do this here, but readers can find the relevant material in Appendix II. Those interested wanting to know more should consult the excellent book by Halmos (1958). A word of caution: his book is written with deceptive simplicity, Halmos assumes a fairly sophisticated background in mathematics, but he is always rewarding to study.

is known as a *ket*.[2] It is now easy to represent addition and multiplication.

If
$$\underline{x} = \begin{pmatrix} x_1 \\ \cdot \\ \cdot \\ \cdot \\ x_n \end{pmatrix} \quad \text{and} \quad \underline{y} = \begin{pmatrix} y_1 \\ \cdot \\ \cdot \\ \cdot \\ y_n \end{pmatrix}$$

then

$$\underline{x} + \underline{y} = |\underline{x}\rangle + |\underline{y}\rangle = \begin{pmatrix} x_1 + y_1 \\ \cdot \\ \cdot \\ \cdot \\ x_n + y_n \end{pmatrix},$$

addition is done component by component, or as is commonly said, componentwise. Multiplication by a scalar α is

$$\alpha\underline{x} = \alpha|\underline{x}\rangle = \begin{pmatrix} \alpha x_1 \\ \cdot \\ \cdot \\ \cdot \\ \alpha x_n \end{pmatrix}$$

A linear combination of a set of vectors $\{\underline{x}_1, \ldots, \underline{x}_n\}$ is defined as

$$\underline{y} = c_1\underline{x}_1 + \cdots + c_n\underline{x}_n,$$

where $\underline{y}$ is another vector generated in the vector space.

These vectors $\{\underline{x}_1, \ldots, \underline{x}_n\}$ are *linearly dependent* if there exist constant scalars $c_1, \ldots, c_n$, not all zero, such that

$$c_1\underline{x}_1 + \cdots + c_n\underline{x}_n = \underline{0},$$

that is, they generate the *zero vector*, which we will normally write as 0 without the underscore. Intuitively this means that if they are dependent, then any vector can be expressed as a linear combination of some of the others. Thus vectors $\{\underline{x}_1, \ldots, \underline{x}_n\}$ are *linearly independent* if $c_1\underline{x}_1 + \cdots + c_n\underline{x}_n = \underline{0}$, if and only if $c_1 = c_2 = \cdots = c_n = 0$.

A set of n linearly independent vectors in an n-dimensional vector space V_n form a *basis* for the space. This means that every arbitrary vector $\underline{x} \in V_n$ can be expressed as a unique linear combination of the basis vectors,

$$\underline{x} = c_1\underline{x}_1 + \cdots + c_n\underline{x}_n,$$

[2] The Dirac notation is explained in Dirac (1958) and related to modern algebraic notation in Sadun (2001), there is also a brief summary and explanation in Appendix I.

where the c_i are called the co-ordinates of $\underline{x}$ with respect to the basis set $\{\underline{x}_1, \ldots, \underline{x}_n\}$. To emphasise the origin of the co-ordinates $\underline{x}$ is usually written as $\underline{x} = x_1\underline{x}_1 + \cdots + x_n\underline{x}_n$. There is a set of standard basis vectors which are conventionally used unless an author specifies the contrary, these are

$$\underline{e}_1 = \begin{pmatrix} 1 \\ 0 \\ \cdot \\ \cdot \\ 0 \end{pmatrix}, \underline{e}_2 = \begin{pmatrix} 0 \\ 1 \\ \cdot \\ \cdot \\ 0 \end{pmatrix}, \ldots, \underline{e}_n = \begin{pmatrix} 0 \\ 0 \\ \cdot \\ \cdot \\ 1 \end{pmatrix}.$$

The $\underline{e}_i$ are linearly independent, and $\underline{x}$ is written conventionally as

$$\underline{x} = x_1\underline{e}_1 + \cdots + x_n\underline{e}_n = \begin{pmatrix} x_1 \\ x_2 \\ \cdot \\ \cdot \\ \cdot \\ x_{n-1} \\ x_n \end{pmatrix}.$$

Notice that the zero vector using this new notation comes out as a vector of all zeroes:

$$\underline{x} = 0\underline{e}_1 + \cdots + 0\underline{e}_n = \begin{pmatrix} 0 \\ 0 \\ \cdot \\ \cdot \\ \cdot \\ 0 \\ 0 \end{pmatrix}.$$

The *transpose* of a vector $\underline{x}$ is $\underline{x}^{\mathrm{T}} = (x_1, \ldots, x_n)$, which is called a *row vector*. In the Dirac notation this denoted by $\langle \underline{x}|$, the so-called *bra*.

Let us now define an *inner product* (dot product) on a vector space V_n where the scalars are real.[3] The inner product is a real-valued function on the cross product $V_n \times V_n$ associating with each pair of vectors $(\underline{x}, \underline{y})$ a unique real number. The function (. , .) has the following properties:

I(1) $(\underline{x}, \underline{y}) = (\underline{y}, \underline{x})$, symmetry;
I(2) $(\underline{x}, \lambda\underline{y}) = \lambda(\underline{x}, \underline{y})$;
I(3) $(\underline{x}_1 + \underline{x}_2, \underline{y}) = (\underline{x}_1, \underline{y}) + (\underline{x}_2, \underline{y})$;
I(4) $(\underline{x}, \underline{x}) \geq 0$, and $(\underline{x}, \underline{x}) = 0$ when $\underline{x} = \underline{0}$.

[3] This definition could have been relegated to Appendix I, but its occurrence is so ubiquitous in both IR and QM that it is reproduced here.

Some obvious properties follow from these, for example,

$$(\underline{x}, \alpha_1 \underline{y}_1 + \alpha_2 \underline{y}_2) = \alpha_1(\underline{x}, \underline{y}_1) + \alpha_2(\underline{x}, \underline{y}_2)$$

thus the inner product is linear in the second component, and because of symmetry it is also linear in the first component.[4]

There will be times when the vector space under consideration will have as its field of scalars the complex numbers. In that case the n-dimensional vectors are columns of complex numbers:

$$\underline{x} = \begin{pmatrix} z_1 \\ \cdot \\ \cdot \\ \cdot \\ z_n \end{pmatrix}, \text{ where } z_j = a_j + \mathrm{i}b_j, \text{ and } a_j, b_j \text{ are real numbers but } \mathrm{i} = \sqrt{-1}.$$

In the complex case the inner product is modified slightly because the mapping (. , .) now maps into the set of complex numbers; Halmos (1958) in Section 60 gives an interesting discussion about complex inner products. All the properties above hold except for I(1), which now reads

$$(\underline{x}, \underline{y}) = \overline{(\underline{y}, \underline{x})}, \text{ where } \overline{a + ib} = a - ib \text{ is the complex conjugate,}$$

and of course affects some of the consequences. Whereas a real inner product was linear in both its components, a complex inner product is only linear in the second component and *conjugate* linear in the first. This is easy to show,

$$\begin{aligned}(\alpha_1 \underline{x}_1 + \alpha_2 \underline{x}_2, \underline{y}) &= \overline{(\underline{y}, \alpha_1 \underline{x}_1 + \alpha_2 \underline{x}_2)} \\ &= \overline{\alpha_1(\underline{y}, \underline{x}_1)} + \overline{\alpha_2(\underline{y}, \underline{x}_2)} \\ &= \overline{\alpha_1}(\underline{x}_1, \underline{y}) + \overline{\alpha_2}(\underline{x}_2, \underline{y}),\end{aligned}$$

where α_1, α_2 are complex numbers and we have used the the properties of complex numbers to derive the transformation. Should α_1, α_2 be real, then the expression reverts to one for a real inner product.

A standard inner product (there are many, see e.g. Deutsch, 2001) is given by

$$\begin{aligned}(\underline{x}, \underline{y}) &= \sum_{i=1}^{n} \overline{x}_i y_i \\ &= \sum_{i=1}^{n} x_i y_i \text{ when the vector space is real.}\end{aligned}$$

[4] Caution: mathematicians tend to define linearity in the first component, physicists in the second, we follow the physicists here (see Sadun, 2001).

Using the column and row vector notation, this inner product is representable as

$$(\overline{x}_1, \ldots, \overline{x}_n)\begin{pmatrix} y_1 \\ \cdot \\ \cdot \\ \cdot \\ y_n \end{pmatrix} \quad \text{and} \quad (x_1, \ldots, x_n)\begin{pmatrix} y_1 \\ \cdot \\ \cdot \\ \cdot \\ y_n \end{pmatrix},$$

the sum is obtained by matrix multiplication, doing a component-wise multiplication of a row by a column. A more condensed notation is achieved by setting

$$\underline{x}^{\mathrm{T}} = (x_1, \ldots, x_n), \text{ the transpose,}$$
$$\underline{x}^{*} = (\overline{x_1}, \ldots, \overline{x_n}), \text{ the adjoint.}$$

We can thus write the inner product $(\underline{x}, \underline{y})$ as $\underline{x}^{\mathrm{T}}\underline{y}$ or $\underline{x}^{*}\underline{y}$, a row matrix times a column matrix; and in the Dirac notation we have $\langle \underline{x} \mid \underline{y} \rangle$.[5]

We now return to considering real vector spaces until further notice, and proceed to defining a *norm* induced by an inner product. Its geometric interpretation is that it is the length of a vector. It is a function $\|.\|$ from V_n to the reals. One such norm is

$$\|\underline{x}\| = \sqrt{(\underline{x}, \underline{x})},$$

which by property I(4) is always a real number. When we have the standard inner product, we get

$$\|\underline{x}\| = \sqrt{\sum_{i=1}^{n} x_i^2} = \left(x_1^2 + \cdots + x_n^2\right)^{1/2}.$$

With this norm we can go on to define a distance between two vectors $\underline{x}$ and $\underline{y}$,

$$d(\underline{x}, \underline{y}) = \|\underline{x} - \underline{y}\| = \sqrt{(\underline{x} - \underline{y}, \underline{x} - \underline{y})} = ((x_1 - y_1)^2 + \cdots + (x_n - y_n)^2)^{1/2}.$$

A vector $\underline{x} \in V_n$ is a *unit vector*, or *normalised*, when $\|\underline{x}\| = 1$, that is when it has length one. The basic properties of a norm are

N(1) $\|\underline{x}\| \geq 0$ and $\|\underline{x}\| = 0$ if and only if $\underline{x} = 0$;
N(2) $\|\alpha\underline{x}\| = |\alpha|\,\|\underline{x}\|$ for all α and $\underline{x}$;
N(3) $\forall \underline{x}, \underline{y}, |(\underline{x}, \underline{y})| \leq \|\underline{x}\|\,\|\underline{y}\|$.

[5] Hence the bra(c)ket name for it. It is also sometimes denoted as $\langle \underline{x} \parallel \underline{y} \rangle$.

Property N(3) is known as the Cauchy–Schwartz inequality and is proved in most introductions to linear algebra (e.g. Isham, 1989). One immediate consequence of property N(3) is that we can write

$$-1 \leq \frac{(\underline{x}, \underline{y})}{\|\underline{x}\| \|\underline{y}\|} \leq 1, \text{ and therefore we can express it as}$$

$$(\underline{x}, \underline{y}) = \|\underline{x}\| \|\underline{y}\| \cos \varphi, \qquad 0 \leq \varphi \leq \pi,$$

where φ is the angle between the two vectors $\underline{x}$ and $\underline{y}$. We can now formally write down the cosine coefficient (correlation) that is so commonly used in IR to measure the similarity between two documents vectors,

$$\cos \varphi = \frac{(\underline{x}, \underline{y})}{\|\underline{x}\| \|\underline{y}\|} = \frac{\sum_{i=1}^{n} x_i y_i}{\sqrt{\sum x_i^2} \times \sqrt{\sum x_i^2}}.$$

If the vectors $\underline{x}$, $\underline{y}$ are unit vectors $\|\underline{x}\| = 1 = \|\underline{y}\|$, that is normalised, then

$$\cos \varphi = \sum_{i=1}^{n} x_i y_i = (\underline{x}, \underline{y}).$$

Having defined the distance $d(\underline{x}, \underline{y})$ between two vectors (the metric on the space), we can derive its basic properties. They are

D(1)	$d(\underline{x}, \underline{x}) \geq 0$ and $d(\underline{x}, \underline{x}) = 0$	if and only if $\underline{x} = \underline{y}$;
D(2)	$d(\underline{x}, \underline{y}) = d(\underline{y}, \underline{x})$	symmetry;
D(3)	$d(\underline{x}, \underline{y}) \leq d(\underline{x}, \underline{z}) + d(\underline{z}, \underline{y})$	triangle inequality.

An important property, *orthogonality*, of a pair of vectors $\underline{x}$, $\underline{y}$ is defined as follows:

$$\underline{x} \text{ and } \underline{y} \text{ are orthogonal if and only if } (\underline{x}, \underline{y}) = 0.$$

Geometrically this means that the two vectors are perpendicular. With this property we can define an *orthonormal* basis. A set of linearly independent vectors $\{\underline{x}_1, \ldots, \underline{x}_n\}$ constitutes an orthonormal basis for the space V_n if and only if

$$(\underline{x}_i, \underline{x}_j) = \delta_{ij} = \begin{pmatrix} 1 & \text{if} & i = j \\ 0 & \text{if} & i \neq j \end{pmatrix}.$$

So, for example, the standard basis $\{\underline{e}_1, \ldots, \underline{e}_n\}$ makes up just such an orthonormal basis.

An important notion is the concept of *subspace*, which is a subset of a vector space that is a vector space itself. A set of vectors *spans* a vector space if every vector can be written as a linear combination of some of the vectors in the set. Thus we can define the subspace spanned by a set of vectors $S = \{\underline{x}_1, \ldots, \underline{x}_m\} \subset V_n$ as the set of linear combinations of vectors of S, that is

$$\text{span}[S] = \{\alpha_1 \underline{x}_1 + \cdots + \alpha_m \underline{x}_m \mid \underline{x}_i \in V_n \quad \text{and} \quad \alpha_i \in \Re\}.^6$$

Clearly, subspaces can be related through subset inclusion, intersection and union. Inclusion is intuitive. The intersection of a set of subspaces is a subspace, but the union of a set of subspaces is not normally a subspace. Remember that we are considering finite-dimensional vector spaces here; in the infinite case *closure* of the subspace becomes an issue (Simmons, 1963). We will have more to say about the union of subspaces later. For the moment it is sufficient to think of 'a union operation' as the smallest subspace containing the span of the set-theoretic union of a collection of subspaces. Interestingly, this harks back to the question of whether the union of two artificial classes makes up a class.[7]

In abstract terms notice what we have done. In the first place we have defined an inner product on a vector space. The inner product has induced a norm, and the norm has induced a metric.[8] Norms and metrics can be defined independently, that is they do not necessarily have to be induced, but in practice we tend to work with induced norms and metrics.

One of the important applications of the theory thus far is the generation of an orthonormal basis for a space or subspace, given a set of p linearly independent vectors $\{\underline{a}_i \mid i = 1, 2, \ldots, p, p \le n, \underline{a}_i \in V_n\}$. The task is to find a basis of p orthonormal vectors $\underline{b}_i$ for the subspace spanned by the p vectors $\underline{a}_i$. The method that will be described next is a well-known version of the Schmidt Orthogonalisation Process. (Schwarz *et al.*, 1973).

Step 1

Choose any arbitary vector, say $\underline{a}_1$, and normalise it to get $\underline{b}_1$,

(1) $r_{11} = \sqrt{(\underline{a}_1, \underline{a}_1)}$;
(2) $\underline{b}_1 = \underline{a}_1 / r_{11}$.

[6] $\Re$ is used for the set of real numbers.
[7] At this point it may be worth rereading the end of Chapter 2, where an example of classes in a vector space is given.
[8] There is a delightful illustration of how these concepts fit together in the chapter on the Hahn–Banach Theorem in Casti (2000).

Step 2

Let $\underline{b}_1, \ldots, \underline{b}_{k-1}$ be the orthonormal vectors found thus far using the linearly independent vectors $\underline{a}_1, \ldots, \underline{a}_{k-1}$, that is

$$(\underline{b}_i, \underline{b}_j) = \delta_{ij} \quad \text{for} \quad i, j = 1, 2, \ldots, k-1.$$

We now construct a vector $\underline{x}$ with the help of $\underline{a}_k$ and the $\underline{b}_1, \ldots, \underline{b}_{k-1}$ generated so far:

$$\underline{x} = \underline{a}_k - \sum_{j=1}^{k-1} r_{jk}\underline{b}_j.$$

We can interpret this as constructing a vector $\underline{x}$ normal to the subspace spanned by the $\{\underline{b}_1, \ldots, \underline{b}_{k-1}\}$, or, which is the same thing, an $\underline{x}$ orthogonal to each $\underline{b}_i$ in turn:

$$(\underline{b}, \underline{x}) = (\underline{b}_i, \underline{a}_k) - \sum_{j=1}^{k-1} r_{jk}(\underline{b}_i, \underline{b}_j) = 0.$$

This reduces to

$$\begin{aligned} (\underline{b}_i, \underline{a}_k) - r_{ik} &= 0, \\ r_{ik} &= (\underline{b}_i, \underline{a}_k). \end{aligned}$$

Since the $\underline{b}_i$ are normalised, these r_{ik} are the projections of $\underline{a}_k$ onto each $\underline{b}_i$ in turn. The new basis vector $\underline{b}_k$ is now given by

$$\underline{b}_k = \frac{\left(\underline{a}_k - \sum_{j=1}^{k-1} r_{jk}\,\underline{b}_j\right)}{r_{kk}},$$

$$\text{where } r_{kk} = \left(\underline{a}_k - \sum_{j=1}^{k-1} r_{jk}\,\underline{b}_j, \underline{a}_k \sum_{j=1}^{k-1} r_{jk}\,\underline{b}_j\right)^{1/2},$$

$$\text{normalising} \quad \underline{b}_k : (\underline{b}_k, \underline{b}_k) = 1.$$

One of the beauties of this normalisation process is that we can dynamically grow the basis incrementally without having to re-compute the basis constructed so far. To compute $[\underline{b}_1, \ldots, \underline{b}_k]$ we compute $\underline{b}_k$ and simply add it to $\{\underline{b}_1, \ldots, \underline{b}_{k-1}\}$ forming the new basis for the enlarged subspace. Of course a prior requirement is that the $\underline{a}_i$ are linearly independent. An obvious application of this process is the construction of a *user-specified* subspace based on document vectors identified incrementally by a user during a browsing process.

We are now ready for an introduction to operators that act on a vector or Hilbert space, the topic of the next chapter.

Further reading

For an immediate example of how the vector space representation is used in document retrieval see Salton and McGill (1983) and Belew (2000); both these textbooks give nice concrete examples. Appendix I gives a brief definition of Hilbert space. One of the most elementary introductions to vector, or Hilbert, spaces may be found in Hughes (1989). Cohen (1989) gives a precise and short introduction to Hilbert space as a lead in to the presentation of quantum logics. Another good introduction to Hilbert spaces is given by Lomonaco (2002), Chapter I, in the context of Quantum Computation. This latter introduction is beautifully presented. More references can be found in Appendix I.

4

Linear transformations, operators and matrices

We now introduce the idea of a linear transformation (or operator) from one vector space V_n to another W_m. We can see that W_m might be the same space as V_n, and it often is, but need not be so. Loosely speaking, such a transformation is a function from one space to another preserving the vector space operations. Thus, if T is such an operator then[1]

$$\mathrm{T}(\alpha \underline{\mathrm{x}}) = \alpha \mathrm{T}(\underline{\mathrm{x}}), \text{ and}$$
$$\mathrm{T}(\underline{\mathrm{x}} + \underline{\mathrm{y}}) = \mathrm{T}(\underline{\mathrm{x}}) + \mathrm{T}(\underline{\mathrm{y}}), \text{ or, equivalently,}$$
$$\mathrm{T}(\alpha \underline{\mathrm{x}} + \beta \underline{\mathrm{y}}) = \alpha \mathrm{T}(\underline{\mathrm{x}}) + \beta \mathrm{T}(\underline{\mathrm{y}}), \text{ for all scalars } \alpha, \beta \text{ and vectors } \underline{\mathrm{x}}, \underline{\mathrm{y}}.$$

For a transformation to satisfy these requirements is for it to be linear. In general $\underline{\mathrm{y}}$ $(= \mathrm{T}(\underline{\mathrm{x}}))$ is a vector in the image space W_m, whereas $\underline{\mathrm{x}}$ is a vector in the domain space V_n. For now we are going to restrict our considerations to the case $V_n = W_m (m = n)$, that is, linear transformations from a vector space onto itself.

The subject of linear transformations and operators both for finite and infinite vector spaces is a huge subject in itself (Halmos, 1958, Finkbeiner, 1960, Riesz and Nagy, 1990, Reed and Simon, 1980). Here we will concentrate on a small part of the subject, where the transformations are represented by finite matrices. Every linear transformation on a vector space V_n can be represented by a square matrix, where the entries in the matrix depend on the particular basis used for the space. Right from the outset this is an important point to note: a transformation can be represented by many matrices, one corresponding to each

[1] In the sequel operators and matrices will be in a bold typeface except for here, the beginning of Chapter 4, where we wish to distinguish temporarily between operators and matrices, so operators will be in normal typeface whereas matrices will be in bold. We drop this distinction later when it becomes unnecessary, after which both will be in bold.

basis, but the transformation thus represented is the same. The effect of a transformation on a vector is entirely determined by the effect on the individual basis vectors.

$$\begin{aligned} \mathrm{T}(\underline{\mathrm{x}}) &= \mathrm{T}(\alpha_1 \underline{\mathrm{b}}_1 + \cdots + \alpha_n \underline{\mathrm{b}}_n) \\ &= \alpha_1 \mathrm{T}(\underline{\mathrm{b}}_1) + \cdots + \alpha_n \mathrm{T}(\underline{\mathrm{b}}_n). \end{aligned}$$

Thus to know $\mathrm{T}(\underline{\mathrm{x}})$ we need to know $\underline{\mathrm{x}}$ in terms of $\{\underline{\mathrm{b}}_1, \ldots, \underline{\mathrm{b}}_n\}$, that is, $\underline{\mathrm{x}} = \alpha_1 \underline{\mathrm{b}}_1 + \cdots + \alpha_n \underline{\mathrm{b}}_n$, and the effect of T on each $\underline{\mathrm{b}}_i$, namely $\mathrm{T}(\underline{\mathrm{b}}_i)$ for all i. The same is true for its representation in matrix form. To make the relationship between matrices and basis vectors explicit, let us assume that a transformation T is represented by a square matrix **A**.

$$\mathbf{A} = \begin{pmatrix} a_{11} & . & . & . & a_{1n} \\ . & . & . & . & . \\ . & . & . & . & . \\ . & . & . & . & . \\ a_{n1} & . & . & . & a_{nn} \end{pmatrix} = (a_{ik}).$$

This matrix has n rows and n columns. If $\{b_1, \ldots, b_n\}$ is the basis for V_n, then it is standard to assume that the kth column contains the co-ordinates of the transformed vector $\mathrm{T}(\underline{\mathrm{b}}_k)$, referred to the basis $\{b_1, \ldots, b_n\}$.

$$\mathrm{T}(\underline{\mathrm{b}}_k) = \sum_{i=1}^{n} a_{ik} \underline{\mathrm{b}}_i.$$

Now if $\underline{\mathrm{x}} = \sum_{k=1}^{n} x_k \underline{\mathrm{b}}_k$ and $\underline{\mathrm{y}} = \sum_{i=1}^{n} y_i \underline{\mathrm{b}}_i$,

and $\mathrm{T}(\underline{\mathrm{x}}) = \underline{\mathrm{y}}$, we have

$$\begin{aligned} \mathrm{T}(\underline{\mathrm{x}}) &= \sum_{k=1}^{n} x_k \mathrm{T}(\underline{\mathrm{b}}_k) = \sum_{k=1}^{n} x_k \sum_{i=1}^{n} a_{ik} \underline{\mathrm{b}}_i \\ &= \sum_{i=1}^{n} \left(\sum_{k=1}^{n} a_{ik} x_k \right) \underline{\mathrm{b}}_i \\ &= \sum_{i=1}^{n} y_i \underline{\mathrm{b}}_i = y, \end{aligned}$$

from which we deduce that $y_i - \sum_k a_{ik} x_k = 0$, for all i, because the $\underline{\mathrm{b}}_i$ are linearly independent. In terms of the representation of both the transformation T and vectors in the space with respect to the basis $\underline{\mathrm{b}}_i$, we have now a computation rule for deriving $\underline{y}$ from the effect of the matrix **A** on the representation of $\underline{x}$. When

$$\mathbf{A} = (a_{ik}), \quad \underline{y} = \begin{pmatrix} y_1 \\ \cdot \\ \cdot \\ \cdot \\ y_n \end{pmatrix}, \underline{x} = \begin{pmatrix} x_1 \\ \cdot \\ \cdot \\ \cdot \\ x_n \end{pmatrix},$$

to calculate the *i*th component of $\underline{y}$ we multiply the *i*th row component-wise with $\underline{x}$, thus

$$\begin{pmatrix} y_1 \\ \cdot \\ y_i \\ \cdot \\ y_n \end{pmatrix} = \begin{pmatrix} a_{11} & \cdot & \cdot & \cdot & a_{in} \\ \cdot & \cdot & \cdot & \cdot & \cdot \\ a_{i1} & \cdot & a_{ik} & \cdot & a_{in} \\ \cdot & \cdot & \cdot & \cdot & \cdot \\ a_{n1} & \cdot & \cdot & \cdot & a_{nn} \end{pmatrix} \begin{pmatrix} x_1 \\ \cdot \\ \cdot \\ \cdot \\ x_n \end{pmatrix}.$$

(There is a sort of cancellation rule that must hold for the dimensions,

$$(n \times 1) = (n \times \not{n})(\not{n} \times 1) = (n \times 1).)$$

If the transformation T for $\underline{y} = \mathrm{T}(\underline{x})$ can be inverted, denoted T^{-1}, which means that $\underline{x} = \mathrm{T}^{-1}(\underline{y})$, then it is *non-singular*, otherwise it is *singular*. The same is true for matrices, $\underline{x} = \mathbf{A}^{-1}(\underline{y})$, where $\mathbf{A}^{-1}$ is the inverse matrix and exists if the corresponding transformation is non-singular; the terminology transfers to the representations, and so we speak of non-singular matrices.

The arithmetic operations on matrices are largely what we would expect. Addition is simply component-wise for matrices of matching dimensions, and the same for subtraction. To multiply a matrix by a scalar, every component is multiplied by the scalar. Multiplication of matrices is exceptional as being more complex.

The product of two transformations $\mathrm{T}_1\mathrm{T}_2$ is defined through the effect it has on a vector, so

$$\mathrm{T}_1\mathrm{T}_2(\underline{x}) = \mathrm{T}_a(\underline{x}), \text{ where } \mathrm{T}_a = \mathrm{T}_1\mathrm{T}_2,$$
$$\mathrm{T}_2\mathrm{T}_1(\underline{x}) = \mathrm{T}_b(\underline{x}), \text{ where } \mathrm{T}_b = \mathrm{T}_2\mathrm{T}_1,$$

and in general the product is not commutative, that is, $\mathrm{T}_1\mathrm{T}_2 \neq \mathrm{T}_2\mathrm{T}_1$. The same applies to matrices, $\mathbf{AB} = \mathbf{C}_a$ and $\mathbf{BA} = \mathbf{C}_b$, are calculated through their effects of **B** followed by **A**, or **A** followed by **B**, on vectors,

$$\underline{y}_1 = \mathbf{C}_a\underline{x} = \mathbf{AB}\underline{x},$$
$$\underline{y}_2 = \mathbf{C}_b\underline{x} = \mathbf{BA}\underline{x},$$

and again, in general $\underline{y}_1 \neq \underline{y}_2$. The rule for matrix multiplication is derived similarly to the rule for multiplying a matrix by a column vector (Mirsky, 1990). It is

$$\begin{pmatrix} c_{11} & . & * & . & c_{1n} \\ . & . & * & . & . \\ . & . & c_{ij} & . & . \\ . & . & * & . & . \\ c_{n1} & . & * & . & c_{nn} \end{pmatrix} = \begin{pmatrix} a_{11} & . & . & . & a_{1n} \\ . & . & . & . & . \\ a_{i1} & * & * & * & a_{in} \\ . & . & . & . & . \\ a_{n1} & . & . & . & a_{nn} \end{pmatrix} \begin{pmatrix} b_{11} & . & b_{1j} & . & b_{1n} \\ . & . & * & . & . \\ . & . & * & . & . \\ . & . & * & . & . \\ b_{n1} & . & b_{nj} & . & b_{nn} \end{pmatrix}.$$

There are several ways of expressing this product in a abbreviated form:

$$(c_{ij}) = (a_{ik})(b_{kj}),$$

$$c_{ij} = \sum_{k=1}^{n} a_{ik} b_{kj},$$

$$c_{ij} = a_{ik} b_{kj}.$$

The last of the three lines uses the convention that when an index is repeated it is to be summed over. To compute the (i, j)th entry in $\mathbf{C}$ we multiply the ith row with the jth column component by component and add the results. It is like the Euclidean inner product between two vectors.

Example 1

$$\begin{pmatrix} 1 & 1 \\ 1 & 1 \end{pmatrix} \begin{pmatrix} 1 & -1 \\ -1 & 1 \end{pmatrix} = \begin{pmatrix} 1-1 & -1+1 \\ 1-1 & -1+1 \end{pmatrix} = \begin{pmatrix} 0 & 0 \\ 0 & 0 \end{pmatrix}.$$

Example 2

$$\begin{pmatrix} \cos\varphi & -\sin\varphi \\ \sin\varphi & -\cos\varphi \end{pmatrix} \begin{pmatrix} 1 & 0 \\ 0 & 0 \end{pmatrix} = \begin{pmatrix} \cos\varphi & 0 \\ \sin\varphi & 0 \end{pmatrix}.$$

Example 3

$$\begin{pmatrix} 1 & 0 \\ 0 & 0 \end{pmatrix} \begin{pmatrix} \cos\varphi & -\sin\varphi \\ \sin\varphi & \cos\varphi \end{pmatrix} = \begin{pmatrix} \cos\varphi & -\sin\varphi \\ 0 & 0 \end{pmatrix}.$$

Just as there are special vectors, e.g. $\underline{e}_i$, all zeroes except for a 1 in the ith position, there are special matrices. In particular we have the *identity* matrix, all 1s down the diagonal and zeroes everywhere else,

$$\mathbf{I} = \begin{pmatrix} 1 & 0 & 0 & 0 & 0 \\ 0 & 1 & 0 & 0 & 0 \\ 0 & 0 & 1 & 0 & 0 \\ 0 & 0 & 0 & 1 & 0 \\ 0 & 0 & 0 & 0 & 1 \end{pmatrix}.$$

The identity matrix plays a special role, for example to define the inverse of a matrix (if it exists), we set $\mathbf{AB} = \mathbf{I} = \mathbf{BA}$, from which it follows that $\mathbf{B} = \mathbf{A}^{-1}$, or $\mathbf{A} = \mathbf{B}^{-1}$, or in other words that $\mathbf{B}$ is the inverse of $\mathbf{A}$ and vice versa. $\mathbf{I}$ is the matrix that maps each vector into itself.

Another special matrix is the zero matrix, a matrix with all zero entries, which maps every vector into the zero vector.

It is interesting (only once!) to see what happens to a matrix of a transformation when there is a change of basis. Let us say that the basis is changed from $\{\underline{b}_1, \ldots, \underline{b}_n\}$ to $\{\underline{b}'_1, \ldots, \underline{b}'_n\}$, then

$$\underline{b}'_k = \underline{c}_{1k}\, \underline{b}_1 + \cdots + \underline{c}_{nk}\, \underline{b}_n, \qquad k = 1, \ldots, n,$$

because any vector can be expressed as a linear combination of the basis vectors. Any vector $\underline{x}$ referred to the new basis is

$$\underline{x} = \sum_{k=1}^{n} x'_k\, \underline{b}'_k,$$

which when expressed with respect to the old basis

$$\begin{aligned} \underline{x} &= \sum_{k=1}^{n} x'_k \sum_{i=1}^{n} c_{ik} \underline{b}_i \\ &= \sum_{i=1}^{n} \sum_{k=1}^{n} c_{ik} x'_k \underline{b}_i. \end{aligned}$$

Thus $x_i = \sum_{k=1}^{n} c_{ik} x'_k$, which gives us the rule for doing the co-ordinate transformation corresponding to the basis change:

$$\underline{x} = \mathbf{C}\underline{x}';$$

$\mathbf{C}$ is a non-singular matrix, uniquely invertible.

We can now calculate the effect of a co-ordinate transformation on a matrix. Let $\underline{x}$, $\underline{y}$ be the co-ordinates in one basis and $\underline{x}'$, $\underline{y}'$ the co-ordinates of the same vectors in another basis. Let $\mathbf{A}$ be the matrix representing a transformation in the first system, and **B** represent the same transformation in the second system. Then

$$\begin{aligned}
&\underline{y} = \mathbf{A}\underline{x} \quad \text{and} \quad \underline{y}' = \mathbf{B}\underline{x}',\\
&\underline{x} = \mathbf{C}\underline{x}' \quad \text{and} \quad \underline{y} = \mathbf{C}\underline{y}',\\
&\underline{y} = \mathbf{C}\underline{y}' = \mathbf{A}\underline{x} = \mathbf{A}(\mathbf{C}\underline{x}') = \mathbf{AC}\underline{x}'\\
&\Rightarrow \underline{y}' = \mathbf{C}^{-1}\mathbf{AC}\underline{x}\\
&\Rightarrow \mathbf{B} = \mathbf{C}^{-1}\mathbf{AC}.
\end{aligned}$$

The two matrices **A** and **B** are related in this way through what is called a *similarity transformation* **C**, and are said to be *similar*. Many important properties of matrices are invariant with respect to similarity transformations. For example, the *eigenvalues* of a matrix are invariant; more about which later.

Another important class of special transformations (or matrices)[2] is the class of *projectors*. To define them we must first define the *adjoint* of a matrix. The defining relation is

$$(\mathbf{A}^*\underline{x}, \underline{y}) = (\underline{x}, \mathbf{A}\underline{y}).$$

When the set of scalars is complex, the matrix $\mathbf{A}^*$ is the complex conjugate of the transpose of **A**: $\overline{\mathbf{A}^{\mathrm{T}}}$. The transpose of **A** is simply the matrix derived by interchanging the rows with the columns.

Example 1 – the real case, given that *a*, *u*, *x*, *c* are real numbers

$$\begin{pmatrix} a & x \\ u & c \end{pmatrix}^* = \begin{pmatrix} a & u \\ x & c \end{pmatrix}.$$

Example 2 – the complex case

$$\begin{pmatrix} a+ib & x-\mathrm{i}y \\ u-\mathrm{i}v & c+\mathrm{i}d \end{pmatrix}^* = \begin{pmatrix} a-ib & u+\mathrm{i}v \\ x+\mathrm{i}y & c-\mathrm{i}d \end{pmatrix}.$$

In the real case, which we are mostly concerned with, $\mathbf{A}^* = \mathbf{A}^{\mathrm{T}}$. Operators can be *self-adjoint* (or *Hermitian*) that is,

$$(\mathbf{A}\underline{x}, \underline{y}) = (\underline{x}, \mathbf{A}\underline{y}) \text{ for all } \underline{x}, \underline{y} \text{ implies that } \mathbf{A} = \mathbf{A}^*.$$

In a real inner product space the self-adjoint matrices are the same as the symmetric matrices. In a complex space the complex conjugate of the transpose must be equal to **A**. These matrices play an important role in many applications,

[2] From now on we will use matrices and transformations interchangeably, that is, they will be printed in bold.

for example the Hermitian matrices have real eigenvalues which are exploited as the results of measurements in quantum mechanics.

Some properties of adjoints are

$$\begin{aligned}(\mathbf{A}+\mathbf{B})^* &= \mathbf{A}^*+\mathbf{B}^*,\\ (\alpha\mathbf{A})^* &= \overline{\alpha}\mathbf{A}^*,\\ (\mathbf{A}^*)^* &= \mathbf{A},\\ \mathbf{I}^* &= \mathbf{I},\\ (\mathbf{AB})^* &= \mathbf{B}^*\mathbf{A}^*,\end{aligned}$$

Projectors

On a vector space V_n the projectors[3] are idempotent, self-adjoint linear operators. An operator $\mathbf{E}$ is idempotent if $\mathbf{E}^2\underline{x} = \mathbf{E}\underline{x}$ for all $\underline{x}$, that is $\mathbf{E}^2 = \mathbf{E}$, by self-adjointness we require $\mathbf{E} = \mathbf{E}^*$. Hence projection operators are both Hermitian and idempotent.

Example

$\frac{1}{2}\begin{pmatrix}+1 & -i\\ +i & +1\end{pmatrix}$ is both Hermitian[4] and idempotent, because

$$\begin{aligned}\tfrac{1}{2}\begin{pmatrix}+1 & -i\\ +i & +1\end{pmatrix}\times\tfrac{1}{2}\begin{pmatrix}+1 & -i\\ +i & +1\end{pmatrix} &= \tfrac{1}{4}\begin{pmatrix}1+1 & -i-i\\ i+i & +1+1\end{pmatrix}\\ &= \tfrac{1}{4}\begin{pmatrix}+2 & -2i\\ +2i & +2\end{pmatrix} = \tfrac{1}{2}\begin{pmatrix}+1 & -i\\ +i & +1\end{pmatrix}.\end{aligned}$$

Projectors are operators that project onto a subspace. In fact the set of projectors on a vector space is in one-to-one correspondence with the subspaces of that space. They include the zero operator $\mathbf{E}_0$ that projects every vector $\underline{x}$ to the empty subspace, $\mathbf{E}_0\underline{x} = \underline{0}$ for all $\underline{x}$, and the identity operator $\mathbf{I}$ which maps every vector onto itself, $\mathbf{I}\underline{x} = \underline{x}$ for all $\underline{x}$. We will use projection operators extensively in the sequel, especially ones that project onto 1-dimensional spaces. For each basis vector, there is a subspace generated by it, and corresponding to it there is a projector which projects all the vectors in the space onto it. These projectors make up a collection of orthogonal projectors, because any vector orthogonal to a subspace projected onto will project to $\underline{0}$, and any vector already in the space will be projected to itself. Also, any vector in the space can be represented as

[3] The words 'projectors' and 'projection operators' are used interchangeably.
[4] Take the conjugate transpose to show that it is Hermitian.

the sum of two vectors, one a vector in a subspace and another vector in the subspace orthogonal to it.

Let us now do an example calculation using some of these ideas. If the space is spanned by a basis $\{\underline{b}_1, \ldots, \underline{b}_n\}$, and it constitutes an orthonormal set, then for any normalized $\underline{x}(\|\underline{x}\| = 1)$, $\underline{x} = c_1\underline{b}_1 + \cdots + c_n\underline{b}_n$, we would have $\sum_{i=1}^{n} |c_i|^2 = 1$ (c_i may be complex[5]). Now let $\mathbf{P}_i$ be the projector corresponding to the subspace spanned by $\underline{b}_i$, then

$$\begin{aligned}\mathbf{P}_i\underline{x} &= c_1\mathbf{P}_i\underline{b}_1 + \cdots + c_i\mathbf{P}_i\underline{b}_i + \cdots + c_n\mathbf{P}_i\underline{b}_n \\ &= 0 + \cdots + c_i\mathbf{P}_i\underline{b}_i + \cdots 0 \\ &= c_i\underline{b}_i.\end{aligned}$$

If we calculate

$$\begin{aligned}(\underline{x}, \mathbf{P}_i\underline{x}) &= (\underline{x}, \mathbf{P}_i\mathbf{P}_i\underline{x}) \text{ because } \mathbf{P}_i^2 = \mathbf{P}_i \\ &= (\mathbf{P}_i\underline{x}, \mathbf{P}_i\underline{x})\ [= |\mathbf{P}_i\underline{x}|^2] \\ &= (c_i\underline{b}_i, c_i\underline{b}_i) \\ &= c_i^*(\underline{b}_i, c_i\underline{b}_i) \\ &= c_i^*c_i(\underline{b}_i, \underline{b}_i) \\ &= c_i^*c_i \\ &= |c_i|^2.\end{aligned}$$

Now remember that $\sum_{i=1}^{n} |c_i|^2 = 1$, hence the vector $\underline{x}$ has generated a probability distribution on the subspaces corresponding to the $\mathbf{P}_i$s. This is an interesting result because, depending on how we choose our $\{\underline{b}_1, \ldots, \underline{b}_n\}$, we get a different probability distribution. This is like taking a particular point of view, a perspective from which to view the space.

We can formalise the idea of a probability associated with a vector $\underline{x}$ more precisely, specifically, for each normalized vector $\underline{x} \in V_n$ define a function $\mu_{\underline{x}}$ on the set of subspaces of V_n as follows:

$$\mu_{\underline{x}}(L_i) = (\mathbf{P}_i\underline{x}, \mathbf{P}_i\underline{x}) = |\mathbf{P}_i\underline{x}|^2.$$

It has the usual properties:

(a) $\mu_{\underline{x}}(\underline{0}) = 0$;
(b) $\mu_{\underline{x}}(V_n) = 1$;
(c) for subspaces L_i and L_j, $\mu_{\underline{x}}(L_i \oplus L_j) = \mu_{\underline{x}}(L_i) + \mu_{\underline{x}}(L_j)$ provided that $L_i \cap L_j = \Phi$, where $L_i \oplus L_j$ the smallest subspace containing L_i and L_j.

[5] $c_i = a_i + ib_i$, then $|c_i|^2 = a_i^2 + b_i^2$.

The relationship between vectors, subspaces and probability measure will be a recurring theme, culminating in the famous theorem of Gleason (Gleason, 1957).

Eigenvalues and eigenvectors

We now come to one of the more important concepts associated with linear transformations and matrices. We introduce it in terms of matrices, but of course it could equally well be discussed in terms of transformations.

We define the *eigenvector* $\underline{x}$ of a matrix $\mathbf{A}$ as a non-zero vector satisfying $\mathbf{A}\underline{x} = \lambda\underline{x}$, where λ is a scalar. The value λ is called an *eigenvalue* of $\mathbf{A}'$ associated with the eigenvector $\underline{x}$. This apparently simple equation has a huge literature associated with it (e.g. Halmos, 1958, Wilkinson, 1965), and a detailed discussion of its theoretical significance can be found in many a book on linear algebra (some references can be found in the bibliography).

Example

$$\mathbf{A} = \begin{pmatrix} 0 & 2 \\ 2 & 0 \end{pmatrix} \text{ and } \underline{v} = \begin{pmatrix} 3 \\ 3 \end{pmatrix};$$

$$\begin{pmatrix} 0 & 2 \\ 2 & 0 \end{pmatrix}\begin{pmatrix} 3 \\ 3 \end{pmatrix} = \begin{pmatrix} 6 \\ 6 \end{pmatrix} = 2\begin{pmatrix} 3 \\ 3 \end{pmatrix}.$$

Hence $\binom{3}{3}$ is an eigenvector of $\mathbf{A}$ and 2 is an eigenvalue of $\mathbf{A}$.

Example

$$\underline{u} = \begin{pmatrix} -3 \\ 0 \end{pmatrix};$$

$$\begin{pmatrix} 0 & 2 \\ 2 & 0 \end{pmatrix}\begin{pmatrix} 3 \\ 0 \end{pmatrix} = \begin{pmatrix} 0 \\ 6 \end{pmatrix} \neq \lambda\begin{pmatrix} 3 \\ 0 \end{pmatrix} \text{ for any } \lambda.$$

Hence $\underline{u}$ is not an eigenvector.

Example

$$\underline{w} = \begin{pmatrix} -3 \\ 3 \end{pmatrix};$$

$$\begin{pmatrix} 0 & 2 \\ 2 & 0 \end{pmatrix}\begin{pmatrix} -3 \\ 3 \end{pmatrix} = \begin{pmatrix} 6 \\ -6 \end{pmatrix} = -2\begin{pmatrix} -3 \\ 3 \end{pmatrix}.$$

Hence $\underline{w}$ is an eigenvector and its eigenvalue is -2.

In general a matrix can have complex numbers as its entries, and the field of scalars may also be complex. Despite this we will mostly be interested in matrices that have real *eigenvalues*. For example, Hermitian matrices have eigenvalues that are all real. This means that for real matrices, symmetric matrices have real eigenvalues. Notice that it is possible for real matrices to have complex eigenvalues. Another important property of Hermitian and symmetric matrices is that if the eigenvalues are all distinct, that is *non-degenerate*, then the eigenvectors associated with them are mutually orthogonal.

Let $\mathbf{A}\underline{x}_1 = \lambda_1\underline{x}$, $\mathbf{A}\underline{x}_2 = \lambda_2\underline{x}$, and since $\mathbf{A}$ is Hermitian, $\lambda_1 \neq \lambda_2$, $\underline{x}_1 \neq \underline{x}_2$, and we have

$$\begin{aligned}\lambda_1(\underline{x}_1, \underline{x}_2) = (\mathbf{A}\underline{x}_1, \underline{x}_2) = (\underline{x}_1, \mathbf{A}\underline{x}_2) = \lambda_2(\underline{x}_1, \underline{x}_2)\\ 0 = (\lambda_1 - \lambda_2)(\underline{x}_1 - \underline{x}_2)\\ \Rightarrow (\underline{x}_1, \underline{x}_2) = 0, \text{ that is } \underline{x}_1 \text{ and } \underline{x}_2 \text{ are orthogonal.}\end{aligned}$$

Hence for an n-dimensional matrix $\mathbf{A}$, for which $\lambda_1 \neq \lambda_2 \neq \cdots \neq \lambda_n$, we have the eigenvectors $\underline{x}_i$ satisfying

$$(\underline{x}_i, \underline{x}_j) = \delta_{ij} = \begin{cases} 1, & i = j, \\ 0, & i \neq j. \end{cases}$$

We are now a position to present one of the major results of finite-dimensional vector spaces: the Spectral Theorem (Halmos, 1958). The importance of this theorem will become clearer as we proceed, but for now it may be worth saying that if an observable is seen as a question, the spectral theorem shows how such a question can be reduced to a set of yes/no questions.

Spectral theorem

To any self-adjoint transformation $\mathbf{A}$ on a finite-dimensional inner product space V_n there correspond real numbers $\alpha_1, \ldots, \alpha_r$ and orthogonal projections $\mathbf{E}_1, \ldots,$ $\mathbf{E}_r$, $r \leq n$, so that

(1) the α_j are pairwise distinct,
(2) the $\mathbf{E}_j$ are pairwise orthogonal $(\perp)$[6] and different from 0,
(3) $\sum_{j=1}^{r} \mathbf{E}_j = \mathbf{I}$, and
(4) $\mathbf{A} = \sum_{j=1}^{r} \alpha_j \mathbf{E}_j$.

The proof of this theorem may be found in Halmos (1958). We will restrict ourselves to some comments. The α_i are the distinct eigenvalues of $\mathbf{A}$ and

[6] A symbol commonly used to indicate orthogonality, $\mathbf{E}_i \perp \mathbf{E}_j$, if and only if $\mathbf{E}_i\mathbf{E}_j = \mathbf{E}_j\mathbf{E}_i = 0$.

the projectors $\mathbf{E}_i$ are those corresponding to the subspaces generated by the eigenvectors. If there are n distinct eigenvalues each of these subspaces is 1-dimensional, but if not then some of the eigenvalues are *degenerate*, and the subspace corresponding to such a degenerate eigenvalue will be of higher dimensionality than 1. Also notice that we have only needed an inner product on the space, there was no need to call on its induced norm or metric. Many calculations with Hermitian matrices are simplified because to calculate their effects we only need to consider the effects of the set of projectors $\mathbf{E}_i$.

Look how easy it is to prove that each α_i is an eigenvalue of $\mathbf{A}$. By (2) $\mathbf{E}_i \perp \mathbf{E}_j$, now choose a vector $\underline{x}$ in the subspace onto which $\mathbf{E}_j$ projects, then $\mathbf{E}_j\underline{x} = \underline{x}$, and $\mathbf{E}_i\underline{x} = 0$ for all $i \neq j$, thus

$$\mathbf{A}\underline{x} = \sum_i \alpha_i \mathbf{E}_i \underline{x} = \alpha_j \mathbf{E}_j \underline{x} = \alpha_j \underline{x}.$$

Hence α_j is an eigenvalue.

In the Dirac notation[7] these projectors take on a highly informative, but condensed, form. Let φ_i be an eigenvector and α_i the corresponding eigenvalues of $\mathbf{A}$, then $\mathbf{E}_i$ is denoted by

$$\begin{aligned} \mathbf{E}_i &= |\varphi_i\rangle\langle\varphi_i|, \text{ or} \\ &= |\alpha_i\rangle\langle\alpha_i|, \end{aligned}$$

where the φ_i and α_i are used as labels.

Remember that $|.\rangle$ indicates a column vector and $\langle.|$ a row vector. This notation is used to enumerate the $\mathbf{E}_i$ explicitly in terms of the projectors corresponding to the orthonormal basis given by the eigenvectors of $\mathbf{A}$. Its power comes from the way it facilitates calculation, for example,

$$\mathbf{E}_i\underline{x} = |\varphi_i\rangle\langle\varphi_i|\underline{x}\rangle,$$

but $\langle\varphi_i|\underline{x}\rangle$is the projection of $\underline{x}$ onto the unit vector φ_i, so

$$\mathbf{E}_i = x_i|\varphi_i\rangle, \text{ where } x_i = \langle\varphi_i|\underline{x}\rangle,$$

The spectral representation, or spectral form, of $\mathbf{A}$ is written as

$$\mathbf{A} = \sum_{i=1}^{n} \alpha_i |\varphi_i\rangle\langle\varphi_i|$$

if $\mathbf{A}$ has n non-degenerate eigenvalues.

[7] Consult Appendix I for a brief introduction to the Dirac notation.

Becoming familiar with the Dirac notation is well worth while. It is used extensively in the classical books on quantum mechanics, but rarely explained in any detail. The best sources for such an explanation are Dirac (1958), the master himself, Sadun (2001), which makes the connection with normal linear algebra, and Griffiths (2002), which introduces the notation via its use in quantum mechanics. There is also a crash course in Appendix I.

This completes the background mathematics on vector spaces and operators that will take us through the following chapters.

Further reading

In addition to the standard texts referenced in this chapter, the books by Fano (1971) and Jordan (1969) are good introductions to linear operators in Hilbert space. A very clear and simple introduction can be found in Isham (1989) and Schmeidler (1965). Sometimes the numerical and computational aspects of linear algebra become important, for that the reader is advised to consult Wilkinson (1965), Golub and Van Loan (1996), Horn and Johnson (1999) and Collatz (1966). The most important result in this chapter is the Spectral Theorem, for further study Arveson (2000), Halmos (1951) and Retherford (1993) are recommended. Recent books on advanced linear algebra and matrix theory are, respectively, Roman (1992) and Zhang (1999).

5
Conditional logic in IR

We have established that the subspaces in a Hilbert Space are in 1:1 correspondence with the projectors onto that space, that is, to each subspace there corresponds a projection and vice versa. In the previous chapters we have shown how subsets and artificial classes give us a semantics for rudimentary retrieval languages. What we propose to do next is to investigate a semantics based on subspaces in a Hilbert space and see what kind of retrieval language corresponds to it. In particular we will be interested in the nature of conditionals.

To appreciate the role and value of conditionals in IR we look a little more closely at how they arise in the application of logic to IR. When retrieval is modelled as a form of inference it becomes necessary to be explicit about the nature of conditionals. It is simplest to illustrate this in terms of textual objects. A document is seen as a set of assertions or propositions and a query is seen as a single assertion or proposition. Then, a document is considered relevant to a query if it implies the query. The intuition is that when, say, q is implied by document Δ, then Δ is assumed to be about q. Although retrieval based on this principle is possible, it is not enough. Typically, a query is not implied by any document leading to failure as in Boolean retrieval. To deal with this a number of things can be done. One is to weaken the implication, another is to attach a measure of uncertainty to implication. There is now a considerable literature on this starting with Van Rijsbergen (1986), culminating in Crestani *et al.* (1998). It is especially worth looking at Nie and Lepage (1998), which gives a broader introduction to the 'logic in IR', but nevertheless is in the same spirit as this chapter.

Let us begin with the class of projectors (projection operators, or simply projections) on a Hilbert space **H**. These are self-adjoint linear operators which are idempotent,[1] that is,

$$\mathbf{E} = \mathbf{E}^* = \mathbf{E}^2.$$

With each projector **E**, is associated the subspace

$$[\![\mathbf{E}]\!] = \{\underline{x} \mid \mathbf{E}\underline{x} = \underline{x}, \underline{x} \in \mathbf{H}\}.$$

Any projector **E** has exactly two eigenvalues, namely 1 and 0. These can be interpreted as the truth values of the proposition **E**, or $[\![\mathbf{E}]\!]$, whichever is more convenient. If any self-adjoint transformation is now seen as a generalised question, or *observable*, then it can be decomposed through the Spectral Theorem into a linear combination of questions,

$$\mathbf{A} = \alpha_1\mathbf{E}_1 + \alpha_2\mathbf{E}_2 + \cdots + \alpha_k\mathbf{E}_k, \text{ where } \mathbf{E}_i\mathbf{E}_j = 0 \text{ for } i \neq j.$$

It is well known that the class of projectors on a Hilbert space make up an orthomodular lattice (or modular if finite) (Holland, 1970). The order relation is given by

$$\mathbf{E} \leq \mathbf{F} \text{ if and only if } \mathbf{FE} = \mathbf{E},$$

that is,

$$\forall \underline{x} \in \mathbf{H} \text{ we have that } \mathbf{FE}\underline{x} = \mathbf{E}\underline{x}.$$

What we have done here is give $\mathbf{E} \leq \mathbf{F}$ an algebraic characterisation, namely $\mathbf{FE} = \mathbf{E}$. We can similarly characterise algebraically, when **E** and **F** commute ($\mathbf{EF} = \mathbf{FE}$),

$$\begin{aligned} \mathbf{E}^{\perp} &= \mathbf{I} - \mathbf{E}, \\ \mathbf{E} \wedge \mathbf{F} &= \mathbf{EF}, \\ \mathbf{E} \vee \mathbf{F} &= \mathbf{E} + \mathbf{F} - \mathbf{EF}, \end{aligned}$$

where $\perp$, $\wedge$, $\vee$ are the usual lattice operations complement, meet and join (Davey and Priestley, 1990). In general **E** and **F** will not commute.

Our main concern is to develop an algebraic characterisation of the conditional $\mathbf{E} \to \mathbf{F}$ and to study its properties. Given the entailment relation $\mathbf{E} \leq \mathbf{F}$ defined by $\mathbf{FE} = \mathbf{E}$ (Herbut, 1994), we define a new proposition $\mathbf{E} \to \mathbf{F}$, the conditional of **E** and **F** by (Hardegree, 1976)

$$\begin{aligned} [\![\mathbf{E} \to \mathbf{F}]\!] &= \{\underline{x} \mid \mathbf{FE}\underline{\mathbf{x}} = \mathbf{E}\underline{\mathbf{x}}, \underline{\mathbf{x}} \in \mathbf{H}\} \\ &= \{\underline{x} \mid (\mathbf{F} - \mathbf{I})\,\mathbf{E}\underline{x} = 0, \underline{x} \in \mathbf{H}\} \\ &= \{\underline{x} \mid \mathbf{F}^{\perp}\mathbf{E}\underline{x} = 0, \underline{x} = \mathbf{H}\}; \end{aligned}$$

[1] Just a reminder that we are not distinguishing between operators and their representative matrices, both are given in a bold type-face.

we will call this the Subspace conditional (S-conditional). It is easy to show that $[\![\mathbf{E} \to \mathbf{F}]\!]$ is in fact a subspace (Hardegree, 1976). It remains to investigate its properties and whether it has the character of an implication. First notice that when $\mathbf{E} \leq \mathbf{F}$, $\mathbf{E}$ entails $\mathbf{F}$, then $\mathbf{F}\mathbf{E}\underline{x} = \mathbf{E}\underline{x}$ for all $\underline{x} \in \mathbf{H}$; hence $[\![\mathbf{E} \to \mathbf{F}]\!] = \mathbf{H}$, or lattice-theoretically $\mathbf{E} \to \mathbf{F} = \mathbf{I}$ since $[\![\mathbf{I}]\!] = \mathbf{H}$. This corresponds to a well-known result in classical logic:

$$\models \mathbf{A} \supset \mathbf{B} \text{ if and only if } \mathbf{A} \models \mathbf{B},$$

or lattice-theoretically

$$\mathbf{A} \to \mathbf{B} = \mathbf{I} \text{ if and only if } \mathbf{A} \leq \mathbf{B}.$$

Thus the conditional $\mathbf{A} \to \mathbf{B}$ is valid only in the case that $\mathbf{A}$ entails $\mathbf{B}$. We can interpret $\mathbf{A} \to \mathbf{B}$ as the material conditional.

Classically the Deduction Theorem also holds:

$$\mathbf{A} \,\&\, \mathbf{B} \models \mathbf{C} \text{ if and only if } \mathbf{A} \models \mathbf{B} \supset \mathbf{C},$$
$$\mathbf{A} \wedge \mathbf{B} \leq \mathbf{C} \text{ if and only if } \mathbf{A} \leq \mathbf{B} \to \mathbf{C}.$$

From this follows the distribution law, that is,

$$\mathbf{A} \wedge (\mathbf{B} \vee \mathbf{C}) = (\mathbf{A} \wedge \mathbf{B}) \vee (\mathbf{A} \wedge \mathbf{C}).$$

But the lattice of subspaces is not necessarily distributive and so the Deduction Theorem cannot hold for $\mathbf{E} \to \mathbf{F}$.

Van Fraassen (1976) laid down some minimal conditions for any self-respecting connective '$\to$' to satisfy

C_1: $\mathbf{A} \leq \mathbf{B} \Rightarrow \mathbf{A} \to \mathbf{B} = \mathbf{I}$,
C_2: $\mathbf{A} \wedge (\mathbf{A} \to \mathbf{B}) \leq \mathbf{B}$ (modus ponens).

Note that

$$\mathbf{A} \to \mathbf{B} = \mathbf{I} \Rightarrow \mathbf{A} \leq \mathbf{B} \text{ by } C_2,$$

and so

$$\mathbf{A} \leq \mathbf{B} \Leftrightarrow \mathbf{A} \to \mathbf{B} = \mathbf{I}.$$

In their earlier work, Nie and others have made a strong case that counterfactual conditionals are the appropriate implication connectives to use in IR (Nie *et al.*, 1995). In the standard account of counterfactual conditionals (Lewis, 1973), the implication connective '$\to$' does not satisfy the strong versions of transitivity, weakening and contraposition (Priest, 2001). These are

ST: $(\mathbf{A} \to \mathbf{B}) \wedge (\mathbf{B} \to \mathbf{C}) \leq (\mathbf{A} \to \mathbf{C})$,
SW: $\mathbf{A} \to \mathbf{C} \leq (\mathbf{A} \wedge \mathbf{B}) \to \mathbf{C}$,
SC: $\mathbf{A} \to \mathbf{B} = \mathbf{B}^{\perp} \to \mathbf{A}^{\perp}$.

However, the weak versions are usually satisfied:

WT: $\mathbf{A} \to \mathbf{B} = \mathbf{I}$ and $\mathbf{B} \to \mathbf{C} = \mathbf{I} \Rightarrow \mathbf{A} \to \mathbf{C} = \mathbf{I}$,
WW: $\mathbf{A} \to \mathbf{C} = \mathbf{I} \Rightarrow (\mathbf{A} \wedge \mathbf{B} \to \mathbf{C}) = \mathbf{I}$,
WC: $\mathbf{A} \to \mathbf{B} = \mathbf{I}$ if and only if $\mathbf{B}^\perp \to \mathbf{A}^\perp = \mathbf{I}$.

The strong and weak forms of these laws are distinguished by statements concerning truth and validity. The weak form of transitivity says that if $\mathbf{A} \to \mathbf{B}$, $\mathbf{B} \to \mathbf{C}$ are *valid* then so is $\mathbf{A} \to \mathbf{C}$. This is not the same as claiming that if $\mathbf{A} \to \mathbf{B}$, $\mathbf{B} \to \mathbf{C}$ are *true* that $\mathbf{A} \to \mathbf{C}$ is. Not surprisingly, the S-conditional satisfies the weak laws but not the strong ones. Any connective satisfying C_1 and C_2 can be shown to satisfy the weak forms WT, WW and WC. So, what about the S-conditional? It satisfies

C_1: $\mathbf{E} \leq \mathbf{F} \Rightarrow \mathbf{E} \to \mathbf{F} = \mathbf{I}$,
C_2: $\mathbf{E} \wedge (\mathbf{E} \to \mathbf{F}) \leq \mathbf{F}$.

Proof:

C_1: Suppose $\mathbf{E} \leq \mathbf{F}$; then for all $\underline{x}$, $\mathbf{FE}\underline{x} = \mathbf{E}\underline{x}$ by definition, also by definition we have that $[\![\mathbf{E} \to \mathbf{F}]\!] = \mathbf{H}$, which implies that $\mathbf{E} \to \mathbf{F} = \mathbf{I}$.
C_2: Suppose $\underline{x}$ satisfies $\mathbf{E}$ and $\mathbf{E} \to \mathbf{F}$, that is $\underline{x} \in [\![\mathbf{E}]\!]$, or $\mathbf{E}\underline{x} = \underline{x}$, similarly $(\mathbf{E} \to \mathbf{F})\underline{x} = \underline{x}$, but the latter is true if and only if $\mathbf{FE}\underline{x} = \mathbf{E}\underline{x}$ by definition. But we already have that $\mathbf{E}\underline{x} = \underline{x}$, therefore $\mathbf{F}\underline{x} = \underline{x}$ and $\underline{x}$ satisfies $\mathbf{F}$, hence $\mathbf{E} \wedge (\mathbf{E} \to \mathbf{F}) \leq \mathbf{F}$. QED.

Thus $\mathbf{E} \to \mathbf{F}$ is one of those conditionals that does not satisfy the strong versions of transitivity, weakening or contraposition but it does satisfy the weak forms.

Let us summarise the situation thus far. The set of subspaces of a Hilbert space form a special kind of lattice (complete, atomic, orthomodular) which is not *distributive*. The logical structure of this lattice is not Boolean or classical. The logical connectives $\perp$, $\wedge$, $\vee$ and $\to$ in terms of subspace operations are defined as:

$[\![\mathbf{E} \wedge \mathbf{F}]\!] = [\![\mathbf{E}]\!] \cap [\![\mathbf{F}]\!]$, a set-theoretic intersection which is again a subspace.
$[\![\mathbf{E}^\perp]\!] = [\![\mathbf{E}]\!]^\perp$, the set of vectors which is orthogonal to $\mathbf{E}$ which form a subspace.
$[\![\mathbf{E} \vee \mathbf{F}]\!] = [\![\mathbf{E}]\!] \oplus [\![\mathbf{F}]\!]$, the closure of all linear combinations of $\underline{x} \in [\![\mathbf{E}]\!]$ and $\underline{y} \in [\![\mathrm{F}]\!]$ which again forms a subspace.
$[\![\mathbf{E} \to \mathbf{F}]\!] = \{\mathrm{x} \mid \mathbf{FE}\underline{x} = \mathbf{E}\underline{x}, \underline{x} \in \mathbf{H}\}$.

It turns out that an example of $\mathbf{E} \to \mathbf{F}$ can be given in closed form, namely

$$\mathbf{E} \to \mathbf{F} = \mathbf{E}^\perp \vee (\mathbf{E} \wedge \mathbf{F}),$$

which is known as the Sasaki hook; and there are many others, see Mittelstaedt (1972)). With this interpretation the semantics of $\mathbf{E} \to \mathbf{F}$ is given by

$$[\![\mathbf{E} \to \mathbf{F}]\!] = [\![\mathbf{E}]\!]^{\perp} \oplus ([\![\mathbf{E}]\!] \cap [\![\mathbf{F}]\!]).$$

The connectives introduced are not truth-functional. This is easy to see for negation and disjunction. Clearly $[\![\mathbf{E}^{\perp}]\!] \oplus [\![\mathbf{E}]\!] = \mathbf{H}$. This means that there are vectors $\underline{x} \in \mathbf{H}$ which satisfy neither $\mathbf{E}^{\perp}$ nor $\mathbf{E}$, but do satisfy $\mathbf{E}^{\perp} \vee \mathbf{E}$, making $\perp$ a 'choice negation'. Similarly, since $[\![\mathbf{E} \vee \mathbf{F}]\!]$ is the closure of $\underline{x} + \underline{y}$, where $\underline{x} \in [\![\mathbf{E}]\!]$ and $\underline{y} \in [\![\mathbf{F}]\!]$, it describes a 'choice disjunction'.

Compatibility

To see how the non-classical S-conditional relates to the classical material implication we need to re-introduce the notion of compatibility. Remember that we previously defined the compatibility of two projectors **E** and **F** by $\mathbf{EF} = \mathbf{FE}$. This time we take a general lattice-theoretical approach. On any orthomodular lattice we can define

$$\mathbf{A} \to \mathbf{B} = \mathbf{A}^{\perp} \vee (\mathbf{A} \wedge \mathbf{B}).$$

It is easy to prove that (see Hardegree, 1976) that the minimal conditions C_1 and C_2 are satisfied. Moreover C_2, modus ponens, is equivalent to the *orthomodular law* for lattices:

$$\mathbf{A} \leq \mathbf{B} \Rightarrow \mathbf{B} \wedge (\mathbf{B}^{\perp} \wedge \mathbf{A}) \leq \mathbf{A}.$$

We are now ready to define our relation K of compatibility:

$$\mathbf{A}K\mathbf{B} \text{ if and only if } \mathbf{A} = (\mathbf{A} \wedge \mathbf{B}) \vee (\mathbf{A} \wedge \mathbf{B}^{\perp}).$$

Any orthocomplemented lattice is orthomodular if the relation K is symmetric: $\mathbf{A}K\mathbf{B} = \mathbf{B}K\mathbf{A}$. The lattice is Boolean if the relation K is universal, that is, 'compatibility rules OK'. The S-conditional

$$\begin{aligned} \mathbf{A} \to \mathbf{B} &= \mathbf{A}^{\perp} \vee (\mathbf{A} \wedge \mathbf{B}) \\ &= \mathbf{A}^{\perp} \vee \mathbf{B} \end{aligned}$$

when $\mathbf{A}K\mathbf{B}$. In other words, the S-conditional defaults to the material conditional when the two elements of the lattice are compatible. Since the lattice of subspaces of a Hilbert space form an orthomodular lattice this holds for $\mathbf{E} \to \mathbf{F}$, where **E** and **F** are projectors. To prove the default result is non-trivial (see Holland, 1970), and depends on the connection between compatibility and distributivity:

$$\mathbf{A}K\mathbf{B} \text{ and } \mathbf{A}K\mathbf{C} \Rightarrow \{\mathbf{A}, \mathbf{B}, \mathbf{C}\} \text{ isdistributive.}$$

(Remember that the lattice of Hilbert subspaces is not distributive.) Now since $\mathbf{A}K\mathbf{A}^{\perp}$ and if $\mathbf{A}K\mathbf{B}$, then

$$\begin{aligned} \mathbf{A} \to \mathbf{B} &= \mathbf{A}^{\perp} \wedge (\mathbf{A} \wedge \mathbf{B}) \\ &= (\mathbf{A}^{\perp} \vee \mathbf{A}) \wedge (\mathbf{A}^{\perp} \vee \mathbf{B}) \\ &= \mathbf{I} \wedge (\mathbf{A}^{\perp} \vee \mathbf{B}) \\ &= \mathbf{A}^{\perp} \vee \mathbf{B}. \end{aligned}$$

The main reason for examining the conditions for compatibility and distribution is that if IR models are to be developed within a general vector (Hilbert) space frame-work, then without further empirical evidence to the contrary it has to be assumed that the subspace logic will be non-classical and in general fails the law of distribution. The failure can be seen as coming about because of the lack of compatibility between propositions, to be represented by subspaces in a Hilbert space. Accepting that subspaces are 'first class objects', we interpret the class of objects about something, as a subspace, and similarly, the class of relevant objects at any point in time is seen as a subspace. So we have moved from considering 'subsets', via 'artificial classes' to subspaces as first class objects whose relationships induce logics.

If **R** is the projector on the subspace of relevant objects, and **E** is the projector onto the subspace of objects about the observable **E** (a yes/no property) then compatibility means that

$$\mathbf{R} = (\mathbf{R} \wedge \mathbf{E}) \vee (\mathbf{R} \wedge \mathbf{E}^{\perp}).$$

Here is the nub of our non-classical view, namely that the disjunction is not necessarily classical. In simple IR terms an object may be about some topic or its negation once observed, but before observation it may be neither. Interpreting the compatibility, or lack of it, we assumed that $\mathbf{RE} \neq \mathbf{ER}$, which means that observing relevance followed by topicality is not the same as observing topicality followed by relevance.

Compatibility for projectors about topicality may also fail. If we have two projectors $\mathbf{E}_1$ and $\mathbf{E}_2$ that are not compatible then

$$\mathbf{E}_2 \neq (\mathbf{E}_2 \wedge \mathbf{E}_1) \vee (\mathbf{E}_2 \wedge \mathbf{E}_1^{\perp}).$$

Or we can say that $\mathbf{E}_1\mathbf{E}_2 \neq \mathbf{E}_2\mathbf{E}_1$, that is observing that an object is about $\mathbf{E}_1$ followed by $\mathbf{E}_2$ is not the same as observing $\mathbf{E}_2$ followed by $\mathbf{E}_1$. With the assumption of stochastic independence in Bayesian updating, the observation of $\mathbf{E}_1$ followed by $\mathbf{E}_2$ has the same impact on computing the posterior probability as the reverse. But, in general one would expect $P(H \mid \mathbf{E}_1, \mathbf{E}_2) \neq P(H \mid \mathbf{E}_2, \mathbf{E}_1)$, as is of course the case in Jeffrey conditionalisation (Jeffrey, 1983).

Stalnaker conditional

There is a well-known conditional in the philosophical literature which fails to satisfy ST, SW and SC, and this is the Stalnaker conditional (Stalnaker, 1970, Lewis, 1976, Van Fraassen, 1976 and Harper *et al.*, 1981). It was the motivation behind a series of papers that explored its application in information retrieval (Crestani *et al.*, 1998). We next show that the S-conditional is a Stalnaker conditional, an important connection to make since it links much of the analysis in the previous pages with previous work in IR.

To show it we need to introduce possible world analysis (Priest, 2001). Remember that our propositions are subspaces in a Hilbert space and that corresponding to each subspace is a projector onto it. A world in this setup is identified with a vector $\underline{x} \in \mathbf{H}$. On this Hilbert space we have a distance function between any two vectors $\underline{x}$ and $\underline{y}$ given by the inner product

$$d(\underline{x}, \underline{y}) = \sqrt{(\underline{x} - \underline{y}, \underline{x} - \underline{y})} = \|\underline{x} - \underline{y}\|.$$

Now the definition of a Stalnaker conditional goes as follows. We define a family of selection functions on $\mathbf{H}$, called Stalnaker selection functions. If S_A is such a function for proposition $\mathbf{A}$, then $S_A(\underline{x})$ denotes the 'nearest' world to $\underline{x}$ in which $\mathbf{A}$ is satisfied. Intuitively a counterfactual $\mathbf{A} > \mathbf{B}$ is true in world $\underline{x}$ only when the nearest $\mathbf{A}$-world to $\underline{x}$ is also a $\mathbf{B}$-world. By an $\mathbf{A}(\mathbf{B})$-world we of course mean the world at which $\mathbf{A}(\mathbf{B})$ is true. We have used '>' for our implication because we do not have a semantics for it yet. This is given by

$$\underline{x} \in [\![\mathbf{A} > \mathbf{B}]\!] \text{ if and only if } S_A(\underline{x}) \in [\![\mathbf{B}]\!].$$

To ensure that '>' is a respectable implication satisfying C_1 and C_2 a number of technical restrictions (mostly obvious) are placed on it (see Stalnaker, 1970, or Lewis, 1976, for details).

R_1: $S_A(\underline{x}) \in [\![\mathbf{A}]\!]$,

R_2: $\underline{x} \in [\![\mathbf{A}]\!] \Rightarrow S_A(\underline{x}) = \underline{x}$,

R_3: $S_A(\underline{x}) \in [\![\mathbf{B}]\!]$ and $S_B(\underline{x}) = [\![\mathbf{A}]\!] \Rightarrow S_A(\underline{x}) = S_B(\underline{x})$.

A technical convenience condition requires that whenever $S_A(\underline{x})$ does not exist, that is, there is no nearest **A**-world to $\underline{x}$, then $S_A(\underline{x}) = \theta$, the absurd world.

Hardegree (1976) introduced what he called the 'canonical selection function' by interpreting the foregoing entirely within a Hilbert space. The most important aspect of his interpretation is that

$$S_A(\underline{x}) = \mathbf{A}\underline{x},$$

where **A** is the proposition corresponding to, or the projection from **H** onto, the subspace $[\![\mathbf{A}]\!]$. The claim is made that within a Hilbert space the nearest vector $\underline{y} \in [\![\mathbf{A}]\!]$ to any vector $\underline{x} \in \mathbf{H}$ is given by $\mathbf{A}\underline{x}$ with respect to the distance function $d(\underline{x}, \underline{y}) = \|\underline{x} - \underline{y}\|$ defined previously. It is instructive to set out the proposition and see a proof. To be proved is that for all $\underline{y}$ for which $\mathbf{A}\underline{y} = \underline{y}$ ($\underline{y} \in [\![\mathbf{A}]\!]$) the nearest (unique) vector closest to $\underline{x}$ is $\mathbf{A}\underline{x}$. It is enough to show that for $\underline{y}$ such that $\mathbf{A}\underline{y} = \underline{y}$ we have

$$(\underline{x} - \mathbf{A}\underline{x}, \underline{x} - \mathbf{A}\underline{x}) < (\underline{x} - \underline{y}, \underline{x} - \underline{y}) \text{ unless } \mathbf{A}\underline{x} = \underline{y}.$$

There are many ways of proving it, but possibly the most elementary is to start with the following (by definition):

$$\text{for all } \underline{x}, (\underline{x}, \underline{x}) > 0 \text{ unless } \underline{x} = \theta,$$
$$\text{thus } (\mathbf{A}\underline{x} - \underline{y}, \mathbf{A}\underline{x} - \underline{y}) > 0 \text{ unless } \mathbf{A}\underline{x} - \underline{y} = \theta, \text{ or } \mathbf{A}\underline{x} = \underline{y}.$$

We can transform this last equation into the equation to be proved as follows:

$$(\mathbf{A}\underline{x} - \underline{y}, \mathbf{A}\underline{x} - \underline{y}) > 0,$$
$$(\mathbf{A}\underline{x}, \mathbf{A}\underline{x}) - (\mathbf{A}\underline{x}, \underline{y}) - (\underline{y}, \mathbf{A}\underline{x}) + (\underline{y}, \underline{y}) > 0,$$

Adding

$$(\underline{x}, \underline{x}) - (\underline{x}, \underline{x}) - 2(\mathbf{A}\underline{x}, \mathbf{A}\underline{x}) + (\mathbf{A}\underline{x}, \underline{x}) + (\underline{x}, \mathbf{A}\underline{x}) = 0$$

to both sides, but note that

$$(\mathbf{A}\underline{x}, \underline{x}) = (\underline{x}, \mathbf{A}\underline{x}) = (\mathbf{A}\underline{x}, \mathbf{A}\underline{x})$$
$$\text{because } \mathbf{A} = \mathbf{A}^* \text{ and } \mathbf{A} = \mathbf{A}^2,$$

we obtain

$$(\underline{x}, \underline{x}) - (\underline{x}, \mathbf{A}\underline{x}) - (\mathbf{A}\underline{x}, \underline{x}) + (\mathbf{A}\underline{x}, \mathbf{A}\underline{x}) < (\underline{x}, \underline{x}) - (\mathbf{A}\underline{x}, \underline{y}) - (\underline{y}, \mathbf{A}\underline{x}) + (\underline{y}, \underline{y}).$$
$$\text{But } (\mathbf{A}\underline{x}, \underline{y}) = (\underline{x}, \mathbf{A}\underline{y}) = (\underline{x}, \underline{y}) \text{ because } \mathbf{A}\underline{y} = \underline{y},$$
$$\text{and } (\underline{y}, \mathbf{A}\underline{x}) = (\mathbf{A}\underline{y}, \underline{x}) = (\underline{y}, \underline{x}) \text{ because } \mathbf{A}\underline{y} = \underline{y};$$

we get

$$(\underline{x}, \underline{x}) - (\underline{x}, \mathbf{A}\underline{x}) - (\mathbf{A}\underline{x}, \underline{x}) + (\mathbf{A}\underline{x}, \mathbf{A}\underline{x}) < (\underline{x}, \underline{x}) - (\underline{x}, \underline{y}) - (\underline{y}, \underline{x}) + (\underline{y}, \underline{y})$$
$$\text{unless } \mathbf{A}\underline{x} = \underline{y},$$

which is the same as

$$(\underline{x} - \mathbf{A}\underline{x}, \underline{x} - \mathbf{A}\underline{x}) < (\underline{x} - \underline{y}, \underline{x} - \underline{y}) \text{ unless } \mathbf{A}\underline{x} = \underline{y},$$

which was to be proved (Hardegree, 1976).

This establishes that our canonical selection function is a simple function indeed; to map $\underline{x}$ to the nearest **A**-world we project $\underline{x}$ onto $[\![\mathbf{A}]\!]$ using the projector **A**.

Now, drawing it together, we can write down the semantics for the S-conditional and the Stalnaker conditional as follows:

$$\begin{aligned} S_A(\underline{x}) &= \mathbf{A}\underline{x}, \\ [\![\mathbf{A} > \mathbf{B}]\!] &= \{\underline{x} \mid \mathbf{A}\underline{x} \in [\![\mathbf{B}]\!], \underline{x} \in \mathbf{H}\} \\ &= \{\underline{x} \mid \mathbf{B}\mathbf{A}\underline{x} = \mathbf{A}\underline{x}\}, \\ [\![\mathbf{A} \to \mathbf{B}]\!] &= \{\underline{x} \mid \mathbf{B}\mathbf{A}\underline{x} = \mathbf{A}\underline{x}\} \\ &= [\![\mathbf{A}^\perp \vee (\mathbf{A} \wedge \mathbf{B})]\!]. \end{aligned}$$

From this we conclude that

$$\mathbf{A} > \mathbf{B} = \mathbf{A} \to \mathbf{B} = \mathbf{A}^\perp \vee (\mathbf{A} \wedge \mathbf{B}).$$

We have shown that the Stalnaker conditional and the S-conditional are the same thing. At this point we could go on to describe how to construct the probability of a conditional. Stalnaker (1970) did this by claiming it was best modelled as a conditional probability, which was shown by Lewis (1976) to be subject to a number of triviality results. Lewis then showed how through *imaging* one could calculate the probability of a conditional that was not subject to those triviality results. Van Rijsbergen (1986) conjectured that imaging would be the correct way to handle the probability of a conditional for IR. Subsequently this was explored further by Crestani and Van Rijsbergen (1995) in a series of papers. However, given the way that a conditional can be given a semantics in a vector space, we can use our results so far to calculate the probability associated with a conditional via Gleason's Theorem using the trace function. This will be done in the next chapter.

Further reading

A formal connection is made between conditional logic and quantum logic which enables a conditional logic to be interpreted in Hilbert space (or vector space). Hitherto this has not been possible. Some of the earliest papers arguing for this connection are by Hardegree (1975, 1976, 1979) and by Lock and Hardegree (1984). In IR a recommendation for using a form of the Stalnaker conditional for counterfactual reasoning was given by Van Rijsbergen (1986), followed by a more detailed analysis by Nie and Brisebois *et al.* (1995) and Nie and Lepage (1998). It is interesting that conditional logic has emerged as an important area of research for IR. The fact that non-classical logics have been developed independently in quantum mechanics is very convenient, especially given the relationship between them and conditional logic described by Hardegree. It means that we can translate the relevant logical statements into algebraic calculations in Hilbert space, using results from quantum mechanics to guide us, and intuitions from IR to construct the appropriate algebraic form.

There is an extensive philosophical literature on conditional logic, for example, Stalnaker (1970), Lewis (1973), Putnam (1975, 1981), Friedman and Putnam (1978), Gibbins (1981), Bub (1982), Stairs (1982) and Bacciagaluppi (1993). It makes useful reading before attempting to apply conditional logic to IR problems. Research on quantum logics emerged from the seminal paper by Birkhoff and Von Neumann (1936) and has been active ever since. The quantum logics literature is important for IR because it demonstrates how to interpret such logics in vector spaces and also how to associate appropriate probability measures with them (Halpin, 1991). There are several good bibliographies on quantum logics, for example, in Suppes (1976), Pavicic (1992) and Rédei (1998). To obtain an overview of the subject it is recommended that one read parts of Beltrametti and Cassinelli (1981), Beltrametti and Van Fraassen (1981), Garden (1984) and Rédei (1998). More specialised development of such logics can be found in Kochen and Specker (1965a), Heelan (1970a,b), Mittelstaedt (1972), Greechie and Gudder (1973), Finch (1975), Piron (1977) and Pitowsky (1989).

In the light of the Spectral Theorem demonstrated in Chapter 4, it is clear that an observable can be reduced to a set of yes/no questions. This is explored in detail by Beltrametti and Cassinelli (1977) and Hughes (1982). The relationship between quantum logic and probability has been investigated in detail by Kägi-Romano (1977), Bub (1982) and Pitowsky (1989). Logicians have always be interested in non-standard logics (Priest, 2001), often with a sceptical view, see, for example, Dalla Chiara (1986, 1993). More recently computer scientists have shown an interest (Román, 1994 and Engesser and Gabbay, 2002). The relationship between classical and quantum logic is explored by Piron (1977) and Heelan (1970a).

Finally, the most thorough explanation of logics associated with Hilbert spaces remains Varadarajan (1985). There is now an interesting article by the same author describing some of the historical context (Varadarajan, 1993).

6

The geometry of IR

'Let no man enter here who is ignorant of geometry'

Plato[1]

In the previous chapters we have introduced set-theoretic, logical and algebraic notions, all of which can be used profitably in IR. We now wish to broaden the discussion somewhat and attempt to introduce a *language* and a *notation* for handling these disparate notions within a single space, viz. Hilbert space (Simmons, 1963), thereby constructing a probability measure on that space via its geometry. At first glance this appears to be a difficult task, but if we consider that much IR research has been modelled in finite vector spaces (Salton, 1968) with an inner product, many of our intuitions for the inner product can be transferred to the discussion based on Hilbert spaces. One major reason for adopting the more abstract point of view is that we wish to present a 'language' for describing and computing objects, whether text, image or speech, in a general way before considering any particular implementation.

The language introduced uses a small set of operators and functions, and the notation will be the Dirac notation (Dirac, 1958). Although at first sight the Dirac notation strikes one as confusing and indeed awkward for learning about linear algebra, its use in calculating or computing simple relationships in Hilbert space is unparalleled.[2] Its great virtues are that any calculation is simple, the meaning is transparent, and many of the 'housekeeping' rules are automatically taken care of. We will demonstrate these virtues as we progress.

So, to begin with we will assume that any object of interest, e.g. a document, an image or a video clip, is represented by a normalised vector (one

[1] The first known claim that this appeared above the entrance to Plato's academy in Athens was made by Philoponus (see Zeller, 1888).

[2] Readers may wish to consult Appendix I at this stage.

of unit length) in an abstract Hilbert space of finite dimension. Extension to an infinite-dimensional space would not be difficult but would add unnecessary complications at this point. Later it will be more convenient to represent an object by the projector on to a 1-dimensional Hilbert space, known as a ray. Unless specified otherwise, the Hilbert space will be assumed to be complex, that is, the scalars will be complex numbers. It is possible and likely that the extra representation power achieved through complex numbers may be of some use in the future. In any case measurement outcomes are always assumed to be real.

Preliminaries: D-notation

To begin with we have that each vector in space **H** is representable by a ket, thus w.r.t. the canonical basis,

$$|\underline{x}\rangle = \begin{pmatrix} x_1 \\ \cdot \\ \cdot \\ \cdot \\ x_n \end{pmatrix}.$$

On this space of vectors it is possible to define a linear function F mapping each vector into a scalar. A general result is that such linear functionals are in 1:1 correpondence with the vectors in the space (Riesz and Nagy, 1990), and that $F(|\underline{x}\rangle) = \alpha$ can be uniquely represented by

$$F(\underline{x}) = \langle \underline{y} \mid \underline{x} \rangle,$$

an inner product.[3] For example, imagine we had a linear function, mapping each document in a space into a real number, then that mapping can be represented by finding a vector $\underline{y}$ for which $\langle \underline{y} \mid \underline{x} \rangle$ is equal to the value of F at each $|\underline{x}\rangle$. Implicitly we are using this when we calculate the cosine correlation between a query vector and any document. If we had a linear function producing a value for each document, then the operation of the function is representable as an inner product between a query vector and each document.

This 1:1 correspondence between linear functionals and vectors leads to the implementation of the inner product $\langle \underline{y} \mid \underline{x} \rangle$ by representing $\langle \underline{y}|$ as the

3 We have switched here to the Dirac notation for inner product.

conjugate transpose of $|\underline{y}\rangle$, that is

$$\langle \underline{y}| = \begin{pmatrix} y_1 \\ \cdot \\ \cdot \\ \cdot \\ y_n \end{pmatrix}^* = (\bar{y}_1 \cdots \bar{y}_n).$$

Thus

$$\langle \underline{y} \mid \underline{x} \rangle = \sum_{i=1}^{n} \bar{y}_i x_i$$

w.r.t. the canonical basis.

Given the canonical basis of orthonormal vectors $\{\underline{e}_1, \underline{e}_2, \ldots, \underline{e}_n\}$ for a Hilbert space **H**, then the orthonormality condition is easily stated as $\langle \underline{e}_i \mid \underline{e}_j \rangle = \delta_{ij}$. For any set of linearly independent vectors defining a basis $\{\underline{f}_1, \underline{f}_2, \ldots, \underline{f}_n\}$ we can write $\langle \underline{f}_i \mid \underline{f}_j \rangle = g_{ij}$. This can be used to change the representation of vectors and matrices in one system $\{\underline{f}_1, \underline{f}_2, \ldots, \underline{f}_n\}$ to one in $\{\underline{e}_1, \underline{e}_2, \ldots, \underline{e}_n\}$ and vice versa (Sadun, 2001).

Having defined an *inner* product between vectors it is possible to define an *outer* product. In the Dirac notation an outer product is defined, as one might expect, as $|\underline{y}\rangle\langle\underline{x}|$. Before giving a formal definition, observe that in the matrix representation

$$|\underline{y}\rangle\langle\underline{x}| = \begin{pmatrix} y_1 \\ \cdot \\ \cdot \\ \cdot \\ y_n \end{pmatrix} (\bar{x}_1 \quad \ldots \quad \bar{x}_n)$$

$$= \begin{pmatrix} y_1\bar{x}_1 & y_1\bar{x}_2 & \cdot & \cdot & y_1\bar{x}_n \\ y_2\bar{x}_1 & \cdot & \cdot & \cdot & \cdot \\ \cdot & \cdot & \cdot & \cdot & \cdot \\ \cdot & \cdot & \cdot & \cdot & \cdot \\ y_n\bar{x}_1 & \cdot & \cdot & \cdot & y_n\bar{x}_n \end{pmatrix}.$$

For example, in a 5-dimensional space

$$|\underline{e}_i\rangle\langle\underline{e}_j| = \begin{pmatrix} 0 \\ 0 \\ 1 \\ 0 \\ 0 \end{pmatrix} (0 \quad 1 \quad 0 \quad 0 \quad 0) = \begin{pmatrix} 0 & 0 & 0 & 0 & 0 \\ 0 & 0 & 0 & 0 & 0 \\ 0 & 1 & 0 & 0 & 0 \\ 0 & 0 & 0 & 0 & 0 \\ 0 & 0 & 0 & 0 & 0 \end{pmatrix}.$$

Formally, for any two vectors $\underline{x}$, $\underline{y} \in \mathbf{H}$ we define the operator $|\underline{y}\rangle\langle\underline{x}|$ for any $\underline{w}$ by

$$(|\underline{y}\rangle\langle\underline{x}|)\underline{w} = |\underline{y}\rangle\langle\underline{x} \mid \underline{w}\rangle = \langle\underline{x} \mid \underline{w}\rangle|\underline{y}\rangle.$$

This has two interpretations, either it is the result of applying the operator $|\underline{y}\rangle\langle\underline{x}|$ to the vector $\underline{w}$, or the result of multiplying the vector $\underline{y}$ by the complex number $\langle\underline{x} \mid \underline{w}\rangle$. Both interpretations are valid, and this illustrates beautifully how the Dirac notation looks after its own 'housekeeping'.

The map $(\underline{y}, \underline{x}) \rightarrow |\underline{y}\rangle\langle\underline{x}|$ from $\mathbf{H} \times \mathbf{H}$ into the set of bounded linear operators has the following properties (Parthasarathy, 1992, p. 5):

(1) $|\underline{y}\rangle\langle\underline{x}|$ is linear in $\underline{y}$ and conjugate linear in $\underline{x}$, that is

$$|\alpha_1\underline{y}_1 + \alpha_2\underline{y}_2\rangle\langle\underline{x}| = \alpha_1|\underline{y}_1\rangle\langle\underline{x}| + \alpha_2|\underline{y}_2\rangle\langle\underline{x}|,$$
$$|\underline{y}\rangle\langle\beta_1\underline{x}_1 + \beta_2\underline{x}_2| = \overline{\beta}_1|\underline{y}\rangle\langle\underline{x}_1| + \overline{\beta}_2|\underline{y}\rangle\langle\underline{x}_2|.$$

(2) $(|\underline{y}\rangle\langle\underline{x}|)^* = |\underline{x}\rangle\langle\mathrm{x}|$.

(3) $|\underline{y}_1\rangle\langle\underline{x}_1||\underline{y}_2\rangle\langle\underline{x}_2|\cdots|\underline{y}_n\rangle\langle\underline{x}| = \left\{\prod_{i=1}^{n-1}\langle\underline{x}_i|\underline{y}_{i+1}\rangle\right\}|\underline{y}_1\rangle\langle\underline{x}_n|;$

(4) If $\underline{y} \neq 0$ and $\underline{x} \neq 0$ then the range of $|\underline{y}\rangle\langle\underline{x}|$ is the one-dimensional subspace $\{\lambda\underline{y} \mid \lambda \in C\}$.

(5) $\||\underline{y}\rangle\langle\underline{x}|\| = \|\underline{y}\|\|\underline{x}\|$.

(6) For any bounded linear operator $\mathbf{T}$,

$$\mathbf{T}|\underline{y}\rangle\langle\underline{x}| = |\mathbf{T}\underline{y}\rangle\langle\underline{x}|,$$
$$|\underline{y}\rangle\langle\underline{x}|\mathbf{T} = |\underline{y}\rangle\langle\mathbf{T}^*\underline{x}|.$$

(7) An operator is a projection with dim $R(\mathbf{T}) = 1$, that is the dimensionality of the *range* of $\mathbf{T}$ is one, if and only if $\mathbf{T} = |\underline{x}\rangle\langle\underline{x}|$ for some unit vector $\underline{x}$. In such a case $R(\mathbf{T}) = \{\lambda\underline{x}|\lambda \in \mathrm{C}\}$.

(8) If $\mathbf{P}$ is a projection and $\{\underline{e}_1, \underline{e}_2, \ldots, \underline{e}_n\}$ is any orthonormal basis for the *subspace* $R(\mathbf{P})$, then

$$\mathbf{P} = \sum_{i=1}^{n} |\underline{e}_i\rangle\langle\underline{e}_i|$$

if $R(\mathbf{P}) = \mathbf{H}$ and $\dim(\mathbf{H}) = n$, then

$$\mathbf{P} = \sum_{i=1}^{n} |\underline{e}_i\rangle\langle\underline{e}_i| = \mathbf{I}.$$

(This is the so-called *resolution of unity*, or the *completeness property*.)

The Dirac notation for the inner product $(\varphi, \mathbf{A}\psi)$ in the previous chapter can be written as $\langle\varphi|\mathbf{A}|\psi\rangle$. Using the completeness property we can derive some useful identities.

$$\underline{x} = \mathbf{I}\underline{x}\left(\sum_{i=1}^{n}|\underline{e}_i\rangle\langle\underline{e}_i|\right)\underline{x} = |\underline{e}_i\rangle\langle\underline{e}_i|\underline{x} + |\underline{e}_2\rangle\langle\underline{e}_2|\underline{x} + \cdots + |\underline{e}_n\rangle\langle\underline{e}_n|\underline{x} \qquad (\mathrm{I}_1)$$

$$= \sum_{i=1}^{n}\langle\underline{e}_i\,|\,\underline{x}\rangle\underline{e}_i.$$

In a *real* Hilbert space $\langle\underline{e}_i\,|\,\underline{x}\rangle$ is of course $||\underline{e}_i||\,||\underline{x}||\cos\theta$, where θ is the angle between the vectors $\underline{x}$ and $\underline{e}_i$, and if $||\underline{e}_i|| = 1$ then $||\underline{x}||\cos\theta$ is the size of the projection of $\underline{x}$ onto $\underline{e}_i$.

Another useful identity is

$$\langle\underline{x}\,|\,\underline{y}\rangle = \langle\underline{x}|\,\mathbf{I}\,|\underline{y}\rangle = \left\langle\underline{x}\left|\sum_{i=1}^{n}|\underline{e}_i\rangle\langle\underline{e}_i|\right|\underline{y}\right\rangle = \sum_{i=1}^{n}\langle\underline{x}\,|\,\underline{e}_i\rangle\langle\underline{e}_i|\underline{y}\rangle. \qquad (\mathrm{I}_2)$$

This is familiar because in a real Hilbert space, if $\underline{x} = (x_1, x_2, \ldots, x_n)^{\mathrm{T}}$ and $\underline{y} = (y_1, y_2, \ldots, y_n)^{\mathrm{T}}$ then $\langle\underline{x}\,|\,\underline{e}_i\rangle = x_i$ and $\langle\underline{e}_i\,|\,\underline{y}\rangle = y_i$ and so

$$\langle\underline{x}\,|\,\underline{y}\rangle = \sum_{i=1}^{n} x_i y_i,$$

a well-known form by now.

The matrix elements of an operator $\mathbf{A}$ w.r.t. a basis $\{\underline{e}_1, \underline{e}_2, \ldots, \underline{e}_n\}$ are given by $\langle\underline{e}_i|\mathbf{A}|\underline{e}_j\rangle = a_{ij}$, where a_{ij} is the matrix element in the ith row and jth column. Keeping this interpretation in mind, there are the following identities.

$$\langle\underline{e}_j|\mathbf{A}|\underline{x}\rangle = \langle\underline{e}_j|\mathbf{AI}|\underline{x}\rangle = \langle\underline{e}_j|\mathrm{A}\sum_{i=1}^{n}|\underline{e}_i\rangle\langle\underline{e}_i||\underline{x}\rangle = \sum_{i=1}^{n}\langle\underline{e}_j|\mathrm{A}|\underline{e}_i\rangle\langle\underline{e}_i|\underline{x}\rangle. \qquad (\mathrm{I}_3)$$

Another identity reflecting the process of applying a matrix (operator) to a vector is

$$\mathbf{A}\underline{e}_k = \mathbf{IA}\underline{e}_k = \sum_{i=1}^{n}|\underline{e}_i\rangle\langle\underline{e}_i|\mathbf{A}\underline{e}_k = \sum_{i=1}^{n}\langle\underline{e}_i|\mathbf{A}|\underline{e}_k\rangle\underline{e}_i. \qquad (\mathrm{I}_4)$$

If the $\underline{e}_i$ are the canonical basis and the ikth element of $\mathbf{A}$ is $\langle\underline{e}_i|\mathbf{A}|\underline{e}_k\rangle$, then in matrix notation we have

$$\mathbf{A}\underline{e}_k = \begin{pmatrix} \langle\underline{e}_1|\mathbf{A}|\underline{e}_1\rangle & . & . & . & \langle\underline{e}_1|\mathbf{A}|\underline{e}_n\rangle \\ . & . & . & . & . \\ . & . & . & . & . \\ . & . & . & . & . \\ \langle\underline{e}_n|\mathbf{A}|\underline{e}_1\rangle & . & . & . & \langle\underline{e}_n|\mathbf{A}|\underline{e}_n\rangle \end{pmatrix}\begin{pmatrix} 0 \\ . \\ 1 \\ . \\ 0 \end{pmatrix}$$

$$= \begin{pmatrix} a_{11} & . & . & . & a_{1n} \\ . & . & . & . & . \\ . & . & . & . & . \\ . & . & . & . & . \\ a_{n1} & . & . & . & a_{nn} \end{pmatrix} \begin{pmatrix} 0 \\ . \\ 1 \\ . \\ 0 \end{pmatrix}$$

$$= \begin{pmatrix} a_{1k} \\ . \\ . \\ . \\ a_{nk} \cdot \end{pmatrix}.$$

I_4 is a very compact way of describing this calculation. Of course the $\underline{e}_i$ need not be the canonical basis.

A final identity, showing a compact form of matrix multiplication, is

$$\langle \underline{e}_j | \mathbf{AB} | \underline{e}_k \rangle = \text{the } jk\text{th element of } \mathbf{AB},$$
$$\langle \underline{e}_j | \mathbf{AIB} | \underline{e}_k \rangle = \langle \underline{e}_j | \mathbf{A} \sum_{i=1}^{n} | \underline{e}_i \rangle \langle \underline{e}_i | \mathbf{B} | \underline{e}_k \rangle = \sum_{i=1}^{n} \langle \underline{e}_j | \mathbf{A} | \underline{e}_i \rangle \langle \underline{e}_i | \mathbf{B} | \underline{e}_k \rangle, \qquad (I_5)$$

which is the product rule for multiplying matrices once again in a very compact form. Observe how effectively the resolution of identity is used.

Earlier on we gave the properties of the outer product of two vectors, or dyad as it is sometimes called. Dirac (1958) has a neat way of introducing this product (see his book on p. 25). Given the identities above we can now express any linear operator as a linear combination of simple dyads.

$$\begin{aligned} \mathbf{A} &= \mathbf{IAI} \\ &= \sum_{ij} | \underline{e}_i \rangle \langle \underline{e}_i | \mathbf{A} | \underline{e}_j \rangle \langle \underline{e}_j | \\ &= \sum_{ij} \langle \underline{e}_i | \mathbf{A} | \underline{e}_j \rangle | \underline{e}_i \rangle \langle \underline{e}_j | \\ &= \sum_{ij} a_{ij} | \underline{e}_i \rangle \langle \underline{e}_j |, \text{ where } \langle \underline{e}_i | \mathbf{A} | \underline{e}_j \rangle = a_{ij}. \end{aligned}$$

An alternative derivation may be found in Nielsen and Chuang (2000) on page 67.

One additional simple, and important, result that is beautiful to express in this notation is the famous Cauchy–Schwarz inequality, namely

$$|\langle \underline{x} \mid \underline{y} \rangle|^2 \leq \langle \underline{x} \mid \underline{x} \rangle \langle \underline{y} \mid \underline{y} \rangle, \text{ or}$$
$$\frac{|\langle \underline{x} \mid \underline{y} \rangle|^2}{\langle \underline{x} \mid \underline{x} \rangle \langle \underline{y} \mid \underline{y} \rangle} \leq 1, \text{ or}$$

$$\frac{|\langle \underline{x} \mid \underline{y} \rangle|^2}{\|\underline{x}\|^2 \|\underline{y}\|^2} \leq 1.$$

To prove this result using the D-notation proceed as follows. Construct an orthonormal basis for the space such that $|\underline{y}\rangle/(\langle \underline{y} \mid \underline{y} \rangle)^{1/2}$ is the first basis vector.

$$\begin{aligned}
&\langle \underline{x} \mid \underline{x} \rangle \langle \underline{y} \mid \underline{y} \rangle \\
&= \sum_{i=1}^{n} \langle \underline{x} \mid \underline{e}_i \rangle \langle \underline{e}_i \mid \underline{x} \rangle \langle \underline{y} \mid \underline{y} \rangle \\
&\geq \frac{\langle \underline{x} \mid \underline{y} \rangle \langle \underline{y} \mid \underline{x} \rangle}{\langle \underline{y} \mid \underline{y} \rangle} \langle \underline{y} \mid \underline{y} \rangle, \text{ substituting for the first basis vector} \\
&= \langle \underline{x} \mid \underline{y} \rangle \langle \underline{y} \mid \underline{x} \rangle \\
&= |\langle \underline{x} \mid \underline{y} \rangle|^2.
\end{aligned}$$

This calculation demonstrates nicely the power of the D-notation. Readers having difficulty following this derivation are advised to read Appendix I where the derivation is repeated at the end of the crash course on linear algebra.

The trace

The *trace* of an operator is also referred by some authors as pre-probability Griffiths (2002). There are many ways of introducing it, but since we shall largely be interested in in one kind of trace, the trace of a positive self-adjoint operator, the simplest way is to define it formally and list some of its properties (see also Petz and Zemánek, 1988).

The quantity $\sum_{j=1}^{n} \langle \underline{e}_j | \mathbf{T} | \underline{e}_j \rangle$, summed over the vectors in the basis, for any **T** is known as the trace of **T**. It is independent of the choice of basis and equal to the sum of the diagonal elements of the matrix w.r.t. any orthonormal basis. The mapping $\mathbf{T} \rightarrow \mathrm{tr}(\mathbf{T})$ has the following important properties (Parthasarathy, 1992):

(1) $\mathrm{tr}(\alpha \mathbf{T}_1 + \beta \mathbf{T}_2) = \alpha \mathrm{tr}(\mathbf{T}_1) + \beta \mathrm{tr}(\mathbf{T}_2)$ (linearity).
(2) $\mathrm{tr}(\mathbf{T}_1 \mathbf{T}_2) = \mathrm{tr}(\mathbf{T}_2 \mathbf{T}_1)$, in fact $\mathrm{tr}(\mathbf{T}_1 \mathbf{T}_2 \ldots \mathbf{T}_k) = \mathrm{tr}(\mathbf{T}_2 \ldots \mathbf{T}_k \mathbf{T}_1)$. A cyclic permutation of the product of operators in the argument of tr does not change the result.
(3) $\mathrm{tr}(\mathbf{T})$ = the sum of the eigenvalues of **T** inclusive of multiplicity.
(4) $\mathrm{tr}(\mathbf{T}^*) = \overline{\mathrm{tr}(\mathbf{T})}$, the trace of the adjoint is the complex conjugate of the trace of **T**.
(5) $\mathrm{tr}(\mathbf{T}) \geq 0$ whenever $\mathbf{T} \geq 0$ (i.e. positive definite).

(6) The space of bounded linear operators $B(\mathbf{H})$ with the inner product $\langle \mathbf{T}_1, \mathbf{T}_2 \rangle = \mathrm{tr}(\mathbf{T}_1 \mathbf{T}_2)$ is a Hilbert space of dimension n^2 (see Nielsen and Chuang, 2000, p. 76).
(7) If λ: $B(\mathbf{H}) \to C$ is a linear map such that $\lambda([\mathbf{X}, \mathbf{Y}]) = 0$ for all $\mathbf{X}, \mathbf{Y} \in B(\mathbf{H})$,[4] and $\lambda(\mathrm{I}) = n$, then $\lambda(\mathbf{X}) = \mathrm{tr}(\mathbf{X})$ for all $\mathbf{X}$.

We can immediately derive some simple and important results about the traces of special operators.

The trace of a projection operator is equal to the dimension of the subspace projected on. Suppose we have $\mathbf{P} = \mathbf{E}_1 + \mathbf{E}_2 + \cdots + \mathbf{E}_k$, a projection onto a k-dimensional subspace, and $\mathbf{E}_i = |\underline{\mathrm{x}}_i\rangle\langle\underline{\mathrm{x}}_i|$, the projector onto the 1-dimensional ray represented by $\underline{\mathrm{x}}_i$, and the $\underline{\mathrm{x}}_i$ are orthonormal. Then

$$\begin{aligned}\mathrm{tr}(\mathbf{P}) &= \sum_{i=1}^{n} \langle \underline{\mathrm{e}}_i | \mathbf{P} | \underline{\mathrm{e}}_i \rangle, \text{ letting } \underline{\mathrm{e}}_i = \underline{\mathrm{x}}_i \quad 1 \le i \le k \le n \\ &= \langle \underline{\mathrm{e}}_1 \mid \underline{\mathrm{e}}_1 \rangle \langle \underline{\mathrm{e}}_1 \mid \underline{\mathrm{e}}_1 \rangle + \cdots + \langle \underline{\mathrm{e}}_k \mid \underline{\mathrm{e}}_k \rangle \langle \underline{\mathrm{e}}_k \mid \underline{e}_k \rangle + 0 + \cdots + 0 = k.\end{aligned}$$

In particular $\mathrm{tr}(|\underline{\mathrm{x}}\rangle\langle\underline{\mathrm{x}}|) = 1$, when $||\underline{\mathrm{x}}|| = 1$.

A second important result is (Penrose, 1994, p. 318),

$$\mathrm{tr}(|\underline{\mathrm{x}}\rangle\langle\underline{\mathrm{y}}|) = \langle \underline{\mathrm{y}} \mid \underline{\mathrm{x}}.\rangle$$

This is easily proved

$$\begin{aligned}\mathrm{tr}(|\underline{\mathrm{y}}\rangle\langle\underline{\mathrm{x}}|) &= \sum_{i=1}^{n} \langle \underline{\mathrm{e}}_i \mid \underline{\mathrm{x}} \rangle \langle \underline{\mathrm{y}} \mid \underline{\mathrm{e}}_i \rangle \\ &= \sum_{i=1}^{n} \langle \underline{\mathrm{y}} \mid \underline{\mathrm{e}}_i \rangle \langle \underline{\mathrm{e}}_i \mid \underline{\mathrm{x}} \rangle \\ &= \langle \underline{\mathrm{y}} | \sum_{i=1}^{n} | \underline{\mathrm{e}}_i \rangle \langle \underline{\mathrm{e}}_i || \underline{\mathrm{x}} \rangle \\ &= \langle \underline{\mathrm{y}} | \mathbf{I} | \underline{\mathrm{x}} \rangle = \langle \underline{\mathrm{y}} \mid \underline{\mathrm{x}} \rangle.\end{aligned}$$

Density operators

Our aim in this chapter is to connect probabilities with the geometry of the space. We have already alluded to this previously, where we pointed forward to a famous theorem of Gleason (1957). There are many ways of stating this theorem (Hughes, 1989, Jordan, 1969, Parthasarathy, 1992), but anticipating the discussion to follow I will give Hughes' version.

[4] $[\mathbf{X}, \mathbf{Y}] = (\mathbf{XY} - \mathbf{YX})$.

Gleason's Theorem

Let μ be any measure on the closed subspaces of a separable (real or complex) Hilbert space **H** of dimension at least 3. There exists a positive self-adjoint operator **T** of trace class such that, for all closed subspaces L of **H** we have $\mu(L) = \text{tr}(\mathbf{TP}_L)$.

In this theorem $\mathbf{P}_L$ is the projection onto L, and an operator **T** is of *trace class* provided **T** is positive and its trace is finite. We are interested in measures μ that are probability measures, that is $\mu(\mathbf{H}) = 1$, in which case $\text{tr}(\mathbf{TP}_H) = \text{tr}(\mathbf{TI}) = \text{tr}(\mathbf{T}) = 1$. In the special case where trace class operators are of trace one, they are called *density operators* (or *density matrices*).

Definition

D is said to be a density operator if **D** is a trace class operator and $\text{tr}(\mathbf{D}) = 1$.

Density operators are identified with *states*. A state can be either *pure*, in which case the density operator is a projection onto a one-dimensional ray, or it can be a *mixture* of pure states, specifically, a convex combination of k pure states, where k is the rank of the operator (Park, 1967). It is conventional to use the lower case symbol ρ for the density operator or its equivalent matrix. We will adopt the same convention. There is a large literature on *density operators* scattered throughout the quantum mechanics literature (see Penrose, 1994, Section 6.4), that usually also requires some understanding of the physics;[5] we aim to avoid that and rather link the mathematics directly to the abstract spatial structure.

Let us recapitulate the situation before applying some of our machinery to IR. We have shown that a state, either pure or mixed, induces a probability measure on the subspaces of a Hilbert space. The algorithm for computing the probability induced by a given state represented by ρ is $\mu(L) = \text{tr}(\rho\mathbf{P}_L)$. It is easy to check that we have a probability measure by using the properties of trace and deriving the properties listed for such a measure given in Appendix III. There are a number of ways of expressing this probability. For example, when ρ is a pure state represented by $|\varphi\rangle\langle\varphi|$,

$$\text{tr}(\rho\mathbf{P}_L) = \text{tr}(|\varphi\rangle\langle\varphi|\mathbf{P}_L) = \langle\varphi|\mathbf{P}_L|\varphi\rangle = \langle\mathbf{P}_L\varphi|\mathbf{P}_L\varphi\rangle = ||\mathbf{P}_L\varphi||^2,$$

or, if $\rho = \lambda_1|\varphi_1\rangle\langle\varphi_1| + \cdots + \lambda_n|\varphi_n\rangle\langle\varphi_n|$, where $\sum \lambda_i = 1$, a mixture, then

$$\begin{aligned}\text{tr}(\rho\mathbf{P}_L) &= \text{tr}([\lambda_1|\varphi_1\rangle\langle\varphi_1| + \cdots + \lambda_n|\varphi_n\rangle\langle\varphi_n|]\mathbf{P}_L)\\ &= \lambda_1\langle\varphi_1|\mathbf{P}_L|\varphi_1\rangle + \cdots + \lambda_n\langle\varphi_n|\mathbf{P}_L|\varphi_n\rangle.\end{aligned}$$

[5] An excellent introduction is Blum (1981), especially Chapter 2.

Or, if $\mathbf{P}_L = \mathbf{E}_1 + \mathbf{E}_2 + \cdots + \mathbf{E}_k$, a projector onto a k-dimensional subspace, then

$$\begin{aligned}\mathrm{tr}(\rho\mathbf{P}_L) &= \mathrm{tr}(\rho\mathbf{E}_1 + \cdots + \rho\mathbf{E}_k)\\ &= \mathrm{tr}(\rho\mathbf{E}_1) + \cdots + \mathrm{tr}(\rho\mathbf{E}_k).\end{aligned}$$

Remember that any Hermitian matrix $\mathbf{A}$ can be expressed as a linear combination of projectors $\mathbf{A} = \lambda_1\mathbf{P}_1 + \cdots + \lambda_n\mathbf{P}_n$, where we will assume that the λ_i are all different. It is a simple technical issue to deal with the situation when they are not. If we now calculate

$$\mathrm{tr}(\rho\mathbf{A}) = \lambda_1\mathrm{tr}(\rho\mathbf{P}_1) + \cdots + \lambda_n\mathrm{tr}(\rho\mathbf{P}_n),$$

then each $\mathrm{tr}(\rho\mathbf{P}_i)$ can be interpreted as the probability of obtaining the real value λ_i when we observe $\mathbf{A}$ (Hermitian) in state ρ. With this interpretation it is possible to interpret $\mathrm{tr}(\rho\mathbf{A})$ as an expectation, that is,

$$\langle\mathbf{A}\rangle = \mathrm{tr}(\rho\mathbf{A}).$$

It is simply a matter of multiplying each possible observed value by its respective probability and then summing them to obtain the expectation.

This expectation has the usual properties:

(1) $\langle c\mathbf{A}\rangle = c\langle\mathbf{A}\rangle$, where c is a constant;
(2) $\langle\mathbf{A} + \mathbf{B}\rangle = \langle\mathbf{A}\rangle + \langle\mathbf{B}\rangle$;
(3) $\langle\mathbf{I}\rangle = 1$.

In Jordan (1969) the reader will find a uniqueness theorem for the algorithm for $\langle\mathbf{A}\rangle$.

Theorem

If a finite expectation value $\langle\mathbf{A}\rangle$ with properties (1), (2), (3) and some further technical ones, is defined for all bounded operators $\mathbf{A}$, then there is a unique density matrix ρ such that $\langle\mathbf{A}\rangle = \mathrm{tr}(\rho\mathbf{A})$.

Notice also that the expectation value of a projector operator $\mathbf{P}_L$ is the probability measure of the subspace L projected onto by $\mathbf{P}_L$.

Interpreting tr(.)

We are now in a position to interpret this mathematical machinery for IR in various ways. The interpretation is mainly geometrical and will establish a crucial link between geometry and probability in vector spaces.

In information retrieval we often represent a document by a vector $\underline{x}$ in an n-dimensional space, and a query by $\underline{y}$. Similarity matching is accomplished by computing $\langle \underline{x} \mid \underline{y} \rangle$, usually assuming that $||\underline{x}|| = 1 = ||\underline{y}||$. Let us say that we are interested in the similarity between a fixed query $\underline{y}$ and any document $\underline{x}$ in the space. With our new machinery we can express the fact that the state $\rho = |\underline{y}\rangle\langle\underline{y}|$ induces a probability measure on the subspaces of **H**, and in particular on the 1-dimensional subspaces, namely vectors. Thus we attach a probability to each document vector $\underline{x}$ via the algorithm:

$$\begin{aligned} \operatorname{tr}(\rho P_{\underline{x}}) &= \operatorname{tr}(|\underline{y}\rangle\langle\underline{y}||\underline{x}\rangle\langle\underline{x}|) \\ &= \langle \underline{y} \mid \underline{x} \rangle \operatorname{tr}(|\underline{y}\rangle\langle\underline{x}|) \\ &= \langle \underline{y} \mid \underline{x} \rangle \langle \underline{x} \mid \underline{y} \rangle \\ &= \langle \underline{y} \mid \underline{x} \rangle \overline{\langle \underline{y} \mid \underline{x} \rangle} \\ &= |\langle \underline{y} \mid \underline{x} \rangle|^2. \end{aligned}$$

If the Hilbert space is a *real* Hilbert space and $||\underline{x}|| = 1 = ||\underline{y}||$, then $\langle \underline{x} | \underline{y} \rangle = \|\underline{x}\|\|\underline{y}\| \cos\theta = \cos\theta$ and so $\operatorname{tr}(\rho P_{\underline{x}}) = \cos^2\theta$, thus we end up with the square of the cosine correlation, but interpretable as a probability. So, the query has induced a probability on each document equal to the square of the cosine of the angle between the document and the query. Referring back to Gleason's Theorem, the density operator corresponding to the query may be a linear combination of a number of 1-dimensional projectors. And, the subspace L can be of a dimension greater than one.

It should be clear by now that ρ, the density operator, can represent a 1-dimensional vector, or a set of vectors, albeit a convex combination of vectors, a fact that will be exploited when we apply the theory to several examples in IR. In most applications in IR we compute a similarity to a given query and a single vector or a set of vectors. For example, when the set of interest is a cluster we compute a similarity between it, via a cluster representative, and a query. Traditionally, a cluster of documents is represented by a vector which in some (usually precise) sense summarises the documents in the cluster (Van Rijsbergen, 1979a). So, for example, if a cluster contains n documents $\{\underline{d}_1, \ldots, \underline{d}_n\}$, then some average vector of these n vectors must be calculated.

More usefully, we calculate a weighted average of the vectors. The same can be achieved by a convex mixture of vectors represented as a mixture of projectors:

$$\rho = \lambda_1 |\underline{d}_1\rangle\langle\underline{d}_1| + \cdots + \lambda_n |\underline{d}_n\rangle\langle\underline{d}_n|, \text{ where } \sum \lambda_i = 1.$$

The λ_i are chosen to reflect the relative importance of each vector in the mixture. Although the $\underline{d}_i$ do not have to be eigenvectors of ρ, it can be arranged so that they are, which is accomplished by finding the orthonormal basis for the subspace spanned by $\{\underline{d}_1, \ldots, \underline{d}_n\}$. So without loss of generality we can assume that the $\underline{d}_i$ form an orthonormal set. If the query is $\underline{q}$ ($\|\underline{q}\| = 1$) then a probabilistic matching function is naturally given by

$$\begin{aligned}
\operatorname{tr}(\rho|\underline{q}\rangle\langle\underline{q}|) &= \operatorname{tr}(\lambda_1 |\underline{d}_1\rangle\langle\underline{d}_1| + \cdots + \lambda_n |\underline{d}_n\rangle\langle\underline{d}_n|)|\underline{q}\rangle\langle\underline{q}| \\
&= \lambda_1 \operatorname{tr}(|\underline{d}_1\rangle\langle\underline{d}_1||\underline{q}\rangle\langle\underline{q}|) + \cdots + \lambda_n \operatorname{tr}(|\underline{d}_n\rangle\langle\underline{d}_n||\underline{q}\rangle\langle\underline{q}|) \\
&= \lambda_1 \operatorname{tr}(|\underline{d}_1\rangle\langle\underline{d}_1 \mid \underline{d}_1\rangle\langle\underline{q}|) + \cdots + \lambda_n \operatorname{tr}(|\underline{d}_n\rangle\langle\underline{d}_n \mid \underline{d}_n\rangle\langle\underline{q}|) \\
&= \lambda_1 \cos^2\theta_1 + \cdots + \lambda_n \cos^2\theta_n,
\end{aligned}$$

where θ_i was defined earlier as the angle between $\underline{d}_i$ and $\underline{q}$. The object ρ can also be interpreted as the centroid of $\{\underline{d}_1, \ldots, \underline{d}_n\}$, but, notice that ρ and $|\underline{q}\rangle\langle\underline{q}|$ are operators, not vectors. By working in the dual space of operators we have a framework that unifies our vector operations and probabilities.[6] If we wish to measure the probability matching function between a cluster and a query $\underline{q}$, we simply calculate

$$\operatorname{tr}(\rho|\underline{q}\rangle\langle\underline{q}|),$$

where tr(.) is a linear functional on the space of operators. It turns out that one can in fact define an inner product on that space by $\operatorname{tr}(\mathbf{A}^*\mathbf{B}) \equiv \langle\mathbf{A} \mid \mathbf{B}\rangle$, where **A** and **B** are linear operators, this is known as the Hilbert–Schmidt or trace inner product (Nielsen and Chuang, 2000).

It is worth commenting on this further level of abstraction. We have interpreted the trace function for a set of special linear operators, density operators and projectors, as giving a probability. With the definition of the trace inner product we have something more general, but nevertheless we may find it useful to interpret even this special case as an inner product. In IR we are quite familiar with the notion of inner product between objects. In some cases it may be an advantage to view the similarity between a query and, say, a cluster representative as an inner product. The trace inner product formalises this in a neat way.

[6] It also introduces naturally a logic, as we saw in a previous chapter.

Co-ordination level matching

One of the oldest matching functions in IR is co-ordination level matching. Basically it counts the number of index terms shared between a query and a document. It is enlightening to translate this matching function into the new notation. So let

$$\underline{q} = (q_1, \ldots, q_n),$$
$$\underline{x} = (x_1, \ldots, x_n),$$

and in the first instance let them be binary vectors. Geometrically, a vector $\underline{q}$ matches a vector $\underline{x}$ in the ith position when $\langle \underline{e}_i \mid \underline{q} \rangle$ and $\langle \underline{e}_i \mid \underline{x} \rangle$ are both non-zero.

More generally, to calculate the number of index terms that any two vectors $\underline{x}$ and $\underline{y}$ share we express

$$\underline{x} = x_1 \underline{e}_1 + \cdots + x_n \underline{e}_n,$$
$$\underline{y} = y_1 \underline{e}_1 + \cdots + y_n \underline{e}_n.$$

If $x_i = 1$ or 0 and $y_i = 1$ or 0, then

$$\begin{aligned} \langle \underline{x} \mid \underline{y} \rangle &= \sum_{i,j} x_i y_j \langle \underline{e}_i \mid \underline{e}_j \rangle, \text{ but } \langle \underline{e}_i \mid \underline{e}_j \rangle = \delta_{ij} \\ &= \sum_{i,j} x_i y_j \delta_{ij} \\ &= \sum_i x_i y_i, \end{aligned}$$

which counts the number of times that x_i and y_i are both 1. The formulation also shows how cosine correlation is a simple generalisation of co-ordination level matching. If $\underline{x}$ and $\underline{y}$ are two vectors as before but now every x_i and y_i is either greater than or equal to zero, then

$$\begin{aligned} \langle \underline{x} \mid \underline{y} \rangle &= \sum_i x_i y_i \langle \underline{e}_i \mid \underline{e}_i \rangle \\ &= \|\underline{x}\| \|\underline{y}\| \cos \varphi \\ \cos \varphi &= \frac{\langle \underline{x} \mid \underline{y} \rangle}{\|\underline{x}\| \|\underline{y}\|}, \\ \text{and if } \|\underline{x}\| &= \|\underline{y}\| = 1 \text{ then} \\ \cos \varphi &= \langle \underline{x} \mid \underline{y} \rangle. \end{aligned}$$

The reader will have observed that the basis vectors $\underline{e}_i$ have been retained throughout the computation. For the standard basis $\langle \underline{e}_i \mid \underline{e}_j \rangle = \delta_{ij}$, but if one were to refer $\underline{x}$ and $\underline{y}$ to a non-standard basis, that is, assuming that $\{\underline{e}_1, \ldots, \underline{e}_n\}$

were an arbitrary set of linearly independent vectors spanning the space, then that computation of the inner product referred to such a basis would become

$$\langle \underline{x} \mid \underline{y} \rangle = \sum_{i,j} x_i g_{ij} y_j, \text{ where } \langle \underline{e}_i \mid \underline{e}_j \rangle = g_{ij}.$$

The matrix $\mathbf{G} = (g_{ij})$ is called the metric matrix (Sadun, 2001). In matrix terms,

$$\langle \underline{x} \mid \underline{y} \rangle = (x_1, \ldots, x_n)\mathbf{G} \begin{pmatrix} y_1 \\ \cdot \\ \cdot \\ \cdot \\ y_n \end{pmatrix}.$$

For example, in the space R^2, let $\{(1, 0),(1, 1)\}$ be the basis, then

$$\begin{aligned} \langle \underline{e}_1 \mid \underline{e}_1 \rangle &= 1, \\ \langle \underline{e}_1 \mid \underline{e}_2 \rangle &= 1, \\ \langle \underline{e}_2 \mid \underline{e}_1 \rangle &= 1, \\ \langle \underline{e}_2 \mid \underline{e}_2 \rangle &= 2, \\ \Rightarrow \mathbf{G} &= \begin{pmatrix} 1 & 1 \\ 1 & 2 \end{pmatrix}. \end{aligned}$$

And so

$$\begin{aligned} &\text{if } \underline{b}_1 = (1, 0) \text{ and } \underline{b}_2 = (1, 1), \text{ then} \\ &\quad \underline{x} = a_1 \underline{b}_1 + a_2 \underline{b}_2, \\ &\quad \underline{y} = c_1 \underline{b}_1 + c_2 \underline{b}_2 \\ &\qquad \text{and } \langle \underline{x} \mid \underline{y} \rangle = (a_1 \quad a_2) \begin{pmatrix} 1 & 1 \\ 1 & 2 \end{pmatrix} \begin{pmatrix} c_1 \\ c_2 \end{pmatrix}. \end{aligned}$$

This is the inner product calculated with reference to the new basis $\{\underline{b}_1, \underline{b}_2\}$.

In several IR applications, for example, latent semantic indexing, a new basis is constructed, usually consisting of a small set of linearly independent vectors. If we refer our documents and queries to these new basis vectors, then the matrix **G**, the metric matrix above, allows us to calculate an inner product in a simple way.

Pseudo-relevance feedback

In relevance feedback the user is asked to judge which are the top k relevant documents in a similarity ranking presented to him or her. In pseudo-relevance feedback it is assumed that the top k documents in a ranking are relevant. From that one can then derive information to modify the query to reflect more accurately the information need of the user. One can illustrate the process geometrically in three dimensions as follows, with a basis $\{\underline{e}_1, \underline{e}_2, \underline{e}_3\}$.

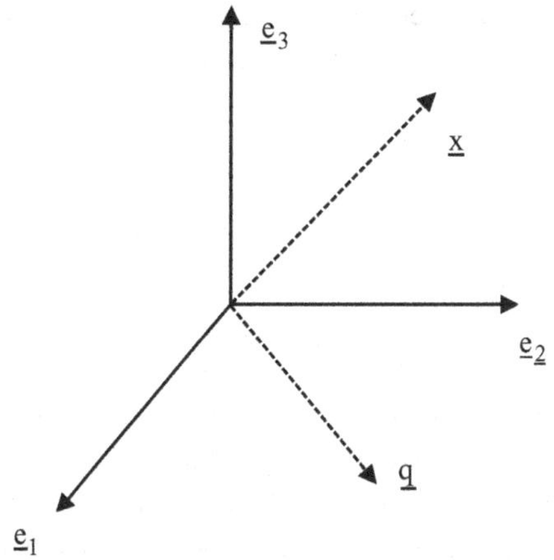

Let us say that in this 3-dimensional vector space the query $\underline{q}$ lies in the 2-dimensional plane given by $[\underline{e}_1, \underline{e}_2]$. Let $\underline{x}$ be a typical document, then the probabilistic similarity is given by

$$\mathrm{tr}(|\underline{q}\rangle\langle\underline{q} \mid \underline{x}\rangle\langle\underline{x}|) = |\langle\underline{q} \mid \underline{x}\rangle|^2 = \cos^2\theta, \qquad \text{where } \|\underline{x}\| = \|\underline{q}\| = 1.$$

The matching value $\cos^2\theta$ can be computed for each document $\underline{x}$, and a ranking of k documents is given by ranking the documents in inverse order of $\cos^2\theta$. There are essentially two ways of modifying the query in the light of the ranking.

(1) Rotate $\underline{q}$ in the plane $[\underline{e}_1, \underline{e}_2]$.
(2) Expand $\underline{q}$ so that it becomes a vector in $[\underline{e}_1, \underline{e}_2, \underline{e}_3]$.

There are many ways of implementing this (Baeza-Yates and Ribeiro-Neto, 1999). For example, if there are a number of documents, one might project each document $\underline{x}_i$ onto the plane $[\underline{e}_1, \underline{e}_2]$. This is easily expressed in our new notation. The projector $\mathbf{P}$ onto $[\underline{e}_1, \underline{e}_2]$ is denoted by $\mathbf{P} = |\underline{e}_1\rangle\langle\underline{e}_1| + |\underline{e}_2\rangle\langle\underline{e}_2|$. To project $\underline{x}_i$, which itself is $\underline{x}_i = \alpha_{i1} \mid \underline{e}_1\rangle + \alpha_{i2}|\underline{e}_2\rangle + \alpha_{i3}|\underline{e}_3\rangle$, simply compute

$$\begin{aligned}(|\underline{e}_1\rangle\langle\underline{e}_1| + |\underline{e}_2\rangle\langle\underline{e}_2|)\underline{x}_i &= \langle\underline{e}_1 \mid \underline{x}_i\rangle \mid \underline{e}_1\rangle + \langle\underline{e}_2 \mid \underline{x}_i\rangle \mid \underline{e}_2\rangle \\ &= \alpha_{i1}|\,\underline{e}_2\rangle + \alpha_{i2}|\,\underline{e}_2\rangle \\ &= \underline{z}_i.\end{aligned}$$

This calculation can be done for any $\underline{x}_i$. Now we have a bundle of vectors projected from 3-d into 2-d. A modification of $\underline{q}$ might be to transform $\underline{q}$ into a vector $\underline{q}'$ which lies somewhat closer to the set of projected document vectors. The density operator ρ representing this set would be a mixture of these vectors, so we take a convex combination of the $|\underline{z}_i\rangle\langle\underline{z}_i|$, that is

$$\rho = \sum_{i=1}^{k} \lambda_i |\underline{z}_i\rangle\langle\underline{z}_i|.$$

The trace, $\mathrm{tr}(\rho|\underline{q}\rangle\langle\underline{q}|)$, gives us the probabilistic similarity between $\underline{q}$ and the set of k projected vectors. A typical feedback operation would be to move $\underline{q}$ closer to the set of k documents. In two dimensions this can be accomplished by applying a linear transformation to $\underline{q}$. A suitable transformation in this context would be a unitary transformation,[7] which represents a rotation of the vector $\underline{q}$ through an angle ϕ into $\underline{q}'$ (see Mirsky, Chapter 8, 1990, for details). The extent of the rotation, or the size of angle ϕ, is determined by $\mathrm{tr}(\rho|\underline{q}\rangle\langle\underline{q}|)$. The relationship $\phi = f(\mathrm{tr}(\rho|\underline{q}\rangle\langle\underline{q}|))$ would need to be determined; it could be a simple mapping, f: $[0, 1] \to [0, 2\pi]$, or further heuristic information could be used to constrain or elaborate f. Here is an illustration:

$$\begin{pmatrix} q_1' \\ q_2' \end{pmatrix} = \begin{pmatrix} \cos\phi & -\sin\phi \\ \sin\phi & \cos\phi \end{pmatrix} \begin{pmatrix} q_1 \\ q_2 \end{pmatrix}.$$

The matrix represents a counter-clockwise rotation of $\underline{q}$ in the plane through ϕ, thus moving $\underline{q}$ closer to the projections of the documents $\underline{x}_i$.

This is a very simple example but it illustrates one aspect of the geometry that may have gone unnoticed. At no stage was the definition of the inner product made explicit; the choice of it was left open. So, for example, if we had chosen

$$\langle\underline{x} \mid \underline{y}\rangle = \sum_{i=1}^{n} x_i y_i.$$

the discussion would have been the same. In our example we chose a unitary matrix that represented a rotation in the plane; in higher dimensions such a nice geometric interpretation may not be available.

[7] A unitary transformation $\mathbf{A}$ is one that satisfies $\mathbf{A}^*\mathbf{A} = \mathbf{I}$; in the case where the coefficients of the representing matrix are real the transformation is called orthogonal.

Query expansion is slightly different, but using the unitary transformation above gives us the clue. To transform the query into a 3-d vector we again transform $\underline{q}$ into $\underline{q}'$, but this time the transformation moves $\underline{q}$ out of the 2-d plane into 3-d. The process is the same, but ρ is now represented as a mixture of the original (unprojected) vectors. That is,

$$\rho = \sum_i \lambda_i |\underline{x}_i\rangle\langle\underline{x}_i|, \text{ where } \sum_i \lambda_i = 1$$

and $\mathrm{tr}(\rho|\underline{q}\rangle\langle\underline{q}|)$ again gives us the matching value between the query and the set of k top ranking documents.

Relevance feedback

The situation with relevance feedback is somewhat different from that with pseudo-relevance feedback. A ranking (or set of documents) is presented to the user and he, or she, is asked to judge them choosing between relevance and non-relevance (for simplicity we will assume that unjudged ones are non-relevant). The relevance decisions are then used to construct a new query incorporating the relevance information. The two best known techniques for doing this, the one based on the probabilistic model and Rocchio's method, are both examined in Van Rijsbergen (1979a). We will describe the first of these only.

A basic formulation of the probabilistic model for relevance feedback may be summarised as follows. Given a set of retrieved documents we divide it into a set of relevant documents and a set of non-relevant ones. We now look at the frequency of occurrence of index terms in both the relevant and non-relevant sets. Thus for each index term i we can calculate p_i, the frequency with which i occurs in the relevant set, and q_i, the frequency with which i occurs in the non-relevant set. Using these p_is and q_is, there are now various formulations for implementing relevance feedback. In the decision-theoretic version described in Van Rijsbergen (1979a), a function $g(\underline{x})$ is derived:

$$g(\underline{x}) = \sum_{i=1}^{n} x_i \log\left[\frac{p_i(1-q_i)}{q_i(1-p_i)}\right] + \text{constant},$$

where $\underline{x}$ is a document on n index terms with $x_i = 1$ or 0 depending on whether the ith index term is present or absent. Then for each unseen document $\underline{x}$ the function $g(\underline{x})$ is evaluated and used either to rank documents, or as a decision function to separate the relevant from the non-relevant. We can safely ignore the constant.

If we let

$$\widetilde{\alpha}_i = \log\left[\frac{p_i(1-q_i)}{q_i(1-p_i)}\right],$$
$$g(\underline{x}) = \widetilde{\alpha}_1 x_1 + \cdots + \widetilde{\alpha}_n x_n,$$

and α_i be the rescaled version such that $\sum_{i=1}^{n} \alpha_i = 1$ and $\alpha_i \geq 0$, we have a function not too dissimilar from the one that arises in Gleason's Theorem. In $g(\underline{x})$ the variables are binary variables, so that for $x_i = 1$, $g(\underline{x})$ is incremented by α_i and for $x_i = 0$ it is ignored.

With this intuition let us express $g(\underline{.})$ as an operator to be applied to any unseen document $\underline{x}$. For this we write

$$\rho = \alpha_1 |x_1\rangle\langle x_1| + \cdots + \alpha_n |x_n\rangle\langle x_n|,$$

where $|x_i\rangle\langle x_i|$ is the orthogonal projection onto the ith basis vector[8] representing the ith index term. Now consider any unseen normalised $\underline{x}$. It can be expressed as $\underline{x} = \beta_1|x_1\rangle + \cdots + \beta_n|x_n\rangle$, where $\sum \beta_i^2 = 1$, and for $\underline{x}$ a binary vector all the β_i are equal. Now apply the operator ρ to $\underline{x}$ to get

$$\begin{aligned}\rho\underline{x} &= (\alpha_1|\mathrm{x}_1\rangle\langle x_1| + \cdots + \alpha_n|x_n\rangle\langle x_n|)(\beta_1|x_1\rangle + \cdots + \beta_n|x_n\rangle) \\ &= \alpha_1\beta_1|x_1\rangle + \cdots + \alpha_n\beta_n|x_n\rangle,\end{aligned}$$

where $\alpha_i\beta_i \geq 0$ if $\beta_i \geq 0$. If the index term is missing for $\underline{x}$ then $\beta_i = 0$ and $\alpha_i\beta_i = 0$. The expression $\rho\underline{x}$ contains the same information as $g(\underline{x})$. One further step in generalisation is needed. Instead of applying ρ to $\underline{x}$ we calculate the trace, $\mathrm{tr}(\rho\underline{x}) = \mathrm{tr}(\rho|\underline{x}\rangle\langle\underline{x}|)$. This calculation gives us the probability induced by ρ, which contains the relevance information, on the space of vectors $\underline{x}$. Clearly this process can be iterated, each time generating a different density matrix ρ.

The density matrix ρ can be thought of as a generalised query. This query is revised in the light of the relevance feedback from the user, and is applied as an operator to each document to produce a probability value via the trace calculation. These values can then be used to order the documents, after which the process can be repeated with a further algebraic application of the the operator representing the revised query. This process very nicely encapsulates the mathematics of relevance feedback in a simple manner.

There are a number of attractive things about this formulation that are worth describing.

Firstly, the particular 'index terms' chosen, that is the dimensions $|x_i\rangle$ spanning the space do not need to be the index terms in the query. This is especially important when the objects are images. The basis vectors of the space to be

8 x_i is used as a label, to label the ith basis vector.

projected onto can be determined by finding, for example, the eigenvectors of the observable representing the query.

Secondly, there is nothing to prevent the density operator ρ from being expressed as a convex combination of projectors, each of which projects on an arbitrary subspace. Thus, if there is uncertainty about the relative importance of, say, two index terms i and j, then we include a projector onto the subspace spanned by $|x_i\rangle$ and $|x_j\rangle$, or the projector $|x_i\rangle\langle x_i| + |x_j\rangle\langle x_j|$.

Thirdly, there is no intrinsic requirement that the basis vectors be orthogonal. Of course they will be so, if they are the eigenvectors of a self-adjoint linear operator.

Fourthly, the formulation readily extends to infinite dimensional spaces, which may be important when representing image objects.

Finally, the vectors do not have to be binary. $\mathrm{tr}(\rho|\underline{x}\rangle\langle\underline{x}|$ works equally well for (normalised) vectors $\underline{x}$ that are non-binary.

Dynamic clustering

In this section we give an account of the way in which the geometry of the information space presented in the earlier chapters may be applied to one class of IR problems. We have chosen clustering and in particular dynamic clustering. There are several reasons for concentrating on this area: first and foremost because the presence or need for a query is not essential. Secondly, because clustering is one of the techniques in IR (although it comes in many flavours) that attempts to exploit seriously the geometry of the information space. And thirdly, because the technique is not overly influenced by the medium of the objects. For example, text-based objects are often organised into an inverted file, or Galois connection (see Chapter 2), because of the existence of keywords, but this organisation it not the obvious one to choose for image objects. Instead some other organisation, for example clustering, may be more appropriate.

Imagine that you, the reader, as a user, are presented with a large collection of objects. Amongst those objects are some that are of interest to you and would, if you could find them, satisfy your current information need. In a fantasy world you could step into the information space, look around you, and if you did not like what you found, you could move to a different location to continue searching. If you did like what you found it would undoubtedly influence where you would look next. Notice that even in this fantasy world we use a spatial metaphor for describing how we are guided to move around it. Also, there is no question of a query, we simply examine objects, and in the light of observations we decide what to do next. To put it in terms of our paradigm, the user makes observations through interaction with objects. The results of these observations influence the way the information space is viewed from then on.

We are unable to step literally into an information space, but we can make it appear as if we do. For this we place our objects in an abstract geometric space and give the user access to this space by way of an interface through visualisation or other forms of presentation. We can keep displaying the ever-changing point of view of the user. It is never the space that changes but the perspective or point of view of the user. Pinning this down in information retrieval terms, it is the probability that an object may be found relevant that is altered, depending on what the user has found relevant thus far. This is not a completely new notion; it was alluded to many times in the earlier IR literature, for example, by Goffman, and more recently by Borland.

> . . . that the relevance of the information from one document depends upon what is already known about the subject, and in turn affects the relevance of other documents subsequently examined.
>
> *(Goffman, 1964)*

> That is the relevance or irrelevance of a given retrieved document may affect the user's current state of knowledge resulting in a change of the user's information need, which may lead to a change of the user's perception/interpretation of the subsequent retrieved documents . . .
>
> *(Borland, 2000)*

In other words, the probability of relevance is path-dependent: different paths to the same object may lead to different probabilities. Therefore a probability measure on the space varies, or equivalently it is dependent, or conditioned, on the objects that have been judged and the order in which they have been judged.

All the foregoing pre-supposes that we have some way of moving from object to object by way of a metric on the space. Such a metric is distance-like and usually has the following properties repeated here for convenience.

$$
\begin{aligned}
&d(x, y) \geq 0 \text{ for all } x, y, \\
&d(x, x) = 0 \text{ for all } x, \\
&d(x, y) = d(y, x), && \text{symmetry,} \\
&d(x, y) \leq d(x, z) + d(z, y), && \text{triangle inequality,} \\
&\{d(x, y) \leq \max\,[d(x, z), d(z, y)]\}, && \text{ultrametric inequality.}
\end{aligned}
$$

The first four conditions define a standard metric, the triangle inequality may be omitted and only the weaker fifth condition holds, thereby defining an ultrametric.

An abstract Hilbert space comes endowed with a metric structure, although the precise choice, Euclidean or non-Euclidean, is left open. So if we embed our objects in a Hilbert space we are free to choose the metric that is most meaningful from an IR point of view. There is a large literature on the choice of metrics (Harman, 1992), in which the choice is mostly resolved empirically through experimentation.

The general IR problem can now be stated. Given that the user has seen a number of objects and made decisions regarding their relevance, how can we present to the user, or direct the user to, a number of objects that are *likely* to be relevant. Notice how the word 'likely' has crept into the discussion, meaning that we expect unseen objects to vary in their estimated relevance for the user. There are in the IR literature many models that specify exactly how such an estimate may be calculated (Belew, 2000, Van Rijsbergen, 1979a, Salton and McGill, 1983, Dominich, 2001 and Sparck Jones and Willett, 1997), usually starting from a query that represents the information need. We want to leave the idea of the query out of consideration and concentrate on how a set of selected documents[9] can influence the estimation of relevance.

The original basis for this way of thinking – retrieval without query – was first detailed in Campbell and Van Rijsbergen (1996). It has been assumed that the nearness of a document to another object is evidence of likely co-relevance, an idea that has been expressed as the Cluster Hypothesis (Van Rijsbergen, 1979a) and re-expressed several times (Croft, 1978, Voorhees, 1985, Hearst and Pedersen, 1996 and Tombros, 2002). Going back to the geometry of the information space enables us to calculate a probability measure reflecting relevance in the light of already accepted objects. One possible interpretation of such a measure is that it captures aboutness, which in turn reflects relevance.

Let us illustrate this by a small abstract example. Let's say that we have accepted k objects,[10] namely, $Y = \{\underline{y}_1, \ldots, \underline{y}_k\}$ and we wish to estimate the likely relevance of all those objects not in Y. Let $\underline{z}$ be one such object, then intuitively we are interested in estimating the extent to which $\underline{z}$ is about Y. One way of capturing the extent to which $\underline{z}$ is about Y is to measure the extent to which Y implies $\underline{z}$. This is based on a view of IR as plausible inference[11] and there are many ways in which it can be formalized (Crestani *et al.*, 1998). However, the different ways have all been based on the Logical Uncertainty Principle (LUP) initially formulated in Van Rijsbergen (1986), and we will reformulate it here using the geometry of Hilbert space. We will tackle the simple case of a single object $Y = \{\underline{y}\} = \underline{y}$ plausibly implying an object $\underline{z}$.[12]

[9] We refer to documents although we could just as easily refer to the more abstract objects.

[10] The ostensive model in Campbell and Van Rijsbergen (1996) only requires an object to be pointed at for it to be accepted.

[11] For a recent treatment of plausible inference see Kyburg and Teng (2001).

[12] This way of looking at things has now been adopted by the researchers working on so-called language models, where a document 'generates' a query as opposed to implying it.

Conventionally, these objects are represented by vectors in some space and once again we assume a Hilbert space. LUP requires us to measure the uncertainty of $\underline{y} \rightarrow \underline{z}$ by measuring the amount of extra information that needs to be added to $\underline{y}$ so that $\underline{z}$ can be deduced. One way of measuring this information is to measure the size of the orthogonal projection of $\underline{y}$ onto $\underline{z}$, and use 1- (projection)^2 as that measure. In Van Rijsbergen (2000) a formal justification of this approach can be found without the use of Hilbert space theory. In the case of a real Hilbert space the projection is given by

$$\langle \underline{y} \mid \underline{x} \rangle = \|\underline{y}\| \, \|\underline{x}\| \cos\theta,$$

which has the familiar simple interpretation as the cosine of the angle between the two vectors when they are normalised, that is, when $\|\underline{y}\| = 1$ and $\|\underline{x}\| = 1$. An interpretation motivated by quantum mechanics would lead us to suggest $1 - \cos^2\theta$ as the appropriate measure,[13] because we can interpret $\cos^2\theta$ as a probability measure induced by $\underline{y}$ on the set of all subspaces of H, including of course the subspaces corresponding to the 1-dimensional vectors $\underline{z}$ (see Amati and Van Rijsbergen, 1998, p. 189–219) for a more general discussion). If the space is complex the probability measure would be given by $|\langle \underline{y} \mid \underline{z} \rangle|^2$. This example is a very special case. Let us see how to generalise it.

Although we may assert that $\underline{y}$ and $\underline{z}$ are vectors in a high-dimensional space, in practice they rarely are, as we can be sure of the values of only a small number of components in the vector, all the other components being either undefined or assumed to have some arbitrary value. Therefore, without any further knowledge, one could assume that $\underline{y}$ and $\underline{z}$ are in fact any vectors lying in the corresponding subspaces L_y and L_z. It is at this point that the power of the theory based on Gleason's Theorem comes into play. It is natural to represent a subspace by a projection operator onto it, that is, L_y is represented by $\mathbf{P}_y$ and L_z is represented by $\mathbf{P}_z$. If L_y and L_z are only 1-dimensional subspaces, that is vectors, then

$$\mathbf{P}_y = |\underline{y}\rangle\langle\underline{y}|,$$
$$\mathbf{P}_z = |\underline{z}\rangle\langle\underline{z}|$$

are the projectors onto the relevant subspaces expressed in the Dirac notation. Returning to the issue of measuring the extra information to be added to $\underline{y}$ through a probability measure on the space induced by $\mathbf{P}_y$, we can now deploy Gleason's Theorem,

$$\mu_y(L_z) = \mathrm{tr}(\mathbf{P}_y\mathbf{P}_z),$$

[13] See the Prologue and Wootters (1980b).

which gives us an algorithm for computing the probability measure for any subspace L_z induced by the subspace L_y. We repeat that

$$(\mathbf{A}, \mathbf{B}) = \text{tr}(\mathbf{A}^*\mathbf{B})$$

is a natural inner product on the space of linear operators with dimension n^2 if the dimension of $\mathbf{H}$ is n. So our probability $\mu_y(L_z)$ is the inner product between $\mathbf{P}_y$ and $\mathbf{P}_z$.

A sanity check shows that if $\mathbf{P}_y = |\underline{y}\rangle\langle\underline{y}|$ and $\mathbf{P}_z = |\underline{z}\rangle\langle\underline{z}|$ then

$$\begin{aligned}\mu_y(L_z) &= \text{tr}(|\underline{y}\rangle\langle\underline{y}||\underline{z}\rangle\langle\underline{z}|)\\ &= \text{tr}(|\underline{y}\rangle\langle\underline{y} \mid \underline{z}\rangle\langle\underline{z}|)\\ &= \langle\underline{y} \mid \underline{z}\rangle\text{tr}(|\underline{y}\rangle\langle\underline{z}|)\\ &= \langle\underline{y} \mid \underline{z}\rangle\langle\underline{z} \mid \underline{y}\rangle\\ &= |\langle\underline{y} \mid \underline{z}\rangle|^2\end{aligned}$$

as before. We can say that, a measure of the extent to which $\mathbf{P}_y \rightarrow \mathbf{P}_z$ is given by $1-\text{tr}(\mathbf{P}_y\mathbf{P}_z)$. At this point we are free to abandon the information-theoretic point of view and simply use the probability measure, which in all cases is given by 1 minus the information. The probability of course is a measure of the certainty of the implication in this context.

Now in Chapter 4 we showed that $\mathbf{P}_y \rightarrow \mathbf{P}_z$ can itself be considered a projection onto a subspace, that is, $\mathbf{P}_y \rightarrow \mathbf{P}_z$ is itself a self-adjoint idempotent linear operator, and as such can by Gleason's Theorem be used to induce a (probability) measure on the space. It brings the logic on the space within the scope of algebraic manipulation. Each logical operator has an algebraic equivalent, and Gleason's Theorem ensures that we can induce a probability measure consistent with the logic.

So far we have considered the extent to which a single object plausibly implies another. Consider now the case when we have a set of objects $Y = \{\underline{y}_1, \ldots, \underline{y}_k\}$ in which each object is of variable importance as the antecedent of the inference, that is, we weight their importance with α_i such that $\sum \alpha_i = 1$. To represent canonically such a mixture[14] of objects we use the *density operator* introduced earlier, namely

$$\rho = \alpha_1\mathbf{P}_1 + \cdots + \alpha_k\mathbf{P}_k,$$

where $\mathbf{P}_i$ is the projector onto $\underline{y}_i$. Once again Gleason's Theorem tells us that

[14] In quantum mechanics a mixture is to be distinguished from a pure state. It is not clear whether the difference between a superposition and a mixture of states plays a significant role in IR.

the probability measure of any subspace L_z is given by

$$\begin{aligned}\mu(L_z) &= \mathrm{tr}(\rho \mathbf{P}_z)\\ &= \alpha_1 \mathrm{tr}(\mathbf{P}_1 \mathbf{P}_z) + \cdots + \alpha_k \mathrm{tr}(\mathbf{P}_k \mathbf{P}_z)\\ &= \alpha_1 \mu_1(L_z) + \cdots + \alpha_k \mu_{k1}(L_z)\\ &= \alpha_1 |\langle \underline{z} \mid \underline{y}_1 \rangle|^2 + \cdots + \alpha_k |\langle \underline{z} \mid \underline{y}_k \rangle|^2,\end{aligned}$$

which is the appropriate mixture of the probabilities associated with the individual objects $\underline{y}_i$. We realise that the projectors $\mathbf{P}_i$ do not need to project onto 1-dimensional subspaces, they could equally project onto finite-dimensional subspaces of dimension greater than one. The same applies to $\mathbf{P}_z$, which could be replaced by a subspace of greater dimension. When this happens, it is expressing the fact that there is a certain amount of ignorance about the objects involved. The probability calculation carries through as before.

As already noted, ρ, the density operator, is a linear operator in the space of linear operators and

$$\mathrm{tr}(\rho \mathbf{P}_z) = \langle \rho \mid \mathbf{P}_z \rangle,$$

where the inner product is now on the space of linear operators.[15] What has emerged is that our analysis is done very simply in the dual space of linear operators with a natural geometric interpretation in the base space of objects. This very abstract way of proceeding is useful when trying to prove mathematical results about the constructs, but in practical information retrieval one is more likely to work in the base space of objects.

Ostensive retrieval

In an earlier paper (Campbell and Van Rijsbergen, 1996) a model of retrieval based on *ostension* (Quine, 1969) was proposed. Simply, this model assumes that a user browsing in information space will point at objects which are relevant. As the search enlarges, the user will have pointed at an ever increasing number of objects. The probability of relevance of an 'unseen' object is a function of the characteristics of the objects seen thus far. To make the process work a function is needed that will incorporate new relevance assessments, and at each stage calculate the probability of the objects to be considered next. This is somewhat like the pseudo-relevance feedback discussed earlier. For a detailed account see Campbell and Van Rijsbergen (1996). We are only interested in the formalisation of the function that estimates the probability of relevance.

[15] For a discussion of this inner product, the Hilbert–Schmidt inner product, see Nielsen and Chuang (2000).

If $Y = \{\underline{y}_1, \ldots, \underline{y}_k\}$ are the objects encountered so far in the order 1 to k, then the impact of the set Y on the probability calculation can be summarised by a density operator:

$$\rho = \alpha_1 |\underline{y}_1\rangle\langle\underline{y}_1| + \cdots + \alpha_k |\underline{y}_k\rangle\langle\underline{y}_k|,$$
$$\text{where } \sum \alpha_i = 1$$

and the values α_i are scaled to increase proportionately. For example, $\alpha_i = \left(\frac{1}{2}\right)^{k-i+1}$ would double the relative weight each time i was incremented by 1 up to k. However, these weights do not sum to one, the sum is $\left(\frac{1}{2}\right)^k$ short of one. So if we corrected each α_i to $\alpha_i + \frac{1}{k}\left(\frac{1}{2}\right)^k$ they would add to one.

To calculate the probability associated with an unseen object $\underline{x}$, we once again compute $\text{tr}(\rho|\underline{x}\rangle\langle\underline{x}|)$ for any $\underline{x}$.

In the original Campbell and Van Rijsbergen paper we used a slightly different calculation for the probabilities involved:

$$\begin{aligned} p_i &= P(x_i = 1 \mid \text{Rel}) \\ &= \sum_{j=1}^{k} x_{ij} \left(\frac{P_{y_j}(\text{Rel})}{\sum_{u=1}^{k} P_{y_u}(\text{Rel})} \right) \\ &= \sum_{j=1}^{k} \alpha_j x_{ij}. \end{aligned}$$

Here the set of seen documents totalling k in number were all assumed relevant, and the α_i were assumed be a specific discounting function as explained above. Thus for each index term i occurring in document j, $x_{ij} = 1$, and the α_j made a contribution, whereas if the ith term not occur in document j no contribution accrues, that is, $x_{ij} = 0$.

The calculation based on the geometry of the space is slightly different. To estimate p_i, we use

$$\begin{aligned} p_i &\approx \text{tr}(\rho|x_i\rangle\langle x_i|) \\ &= \sum_{j=1}^{k} \alpha_j \text{tr}(|y_j\rangle\langle y_j||x_i\rangle\langle x_i|) \\ &= \sum_{j=1}^{k} \alpha_j \text{tr}(|y_j\rangle\langle y_j|x_i\rangle\langle x_i|) \\ &= \sum_{j=1}^{k} \alpha_j |\langle y_j|x_i\rangle|^2. \end{aligned}$$

Now if y_j and x_i are orthogonal then $\langle y_j \mid x_i \rangle = 0$ and no contribution accrues to p_i. When $\langle y_j \mid x_i \rangle \neq 0$ the value of $|\langle y_j \mid x_i \rangle|^2$ modified by α_j contributes to p_i. Notice again that this is different from the Campbell and Van Rijsbergen (1996) calculation. Whereas in the original paper $x_{ij} = 0$ or 1, here we have $x_{ij} = |\langle y_j \mid x_i \rangle|^2$ which is a value in the interval [0, 1]. Thus it is a generalisation of the original model and it would not be difficult to modify the generalised formula for x_{ij} so that it replicated the original one.

Further reading and future research

The foregoing chapter has been well referenced at the appropriate places. The centre piece of it is undoubtedly Gleason's Theorem and its application to problems in IR. Apart from Gleason's original 1957 paper, there is the elementary proof by Cooke *et al.* (1985), and the constructive proof by Richman and Bridges (1999). Several books develop the requisite mathematics before explaining Gleason's Theorem; good examples are Cohen (1989), Jauch (1968), Parthasarathy (1992) and Varadarajan (1985). There is an important special case of the theorem where the measure is a probability measure, and it is defined in terms of a density operator. Density measures are extensively used in quantum mechanics but infrequently explained properly. For example, d'Espagnat (1976) gives a 'density matrix formalism' for QM but unfortunately devotes very little space to explaining the nature of density operators. Luckily, a thorough and standard account may be found in the widely used textbook for QM by Cohen-Tannoudji *et al.* (1977).

One of the motivations for writing this book is to lay the foundations for further research in IR using some of the tools presented here. There are several areas for immediate development; we will just mention three: *language modelling* (Croft and Lafferty, 2003), *probability of conditionals* and *information theory*. These three are not unrelated. In Lavrenko and Croft (2003) the point is specifically made: 'The simple language modelling approach is very similar to the logical implication and inference network models, . . .'. Language models, on the one hand, deal with producing generative models for $P(Q \mid D)$, where Q is the query and D a document. On the other hand, logical models are concerned with evaluating $P(D \rightarrow Q)$, where '$\rightarrow$' may be a non-standard implication such as was fully described in Chapter 5. There seems to be an intimate, largely unknown, connection between $P(Q \mid D)$ and $P(D \rightarrow Q)$, and one of the missing ingredients is an appropriate measure of information, which is required for the evaluation of the conditional by the Logical Uncertainty Principle (Van Rijsbergen, 1992).

In quantum mechanics conditional probability is defined with the help of Gleason's Theorem as

$$P^{\mathrm{W}}(P \mid P') = \frac{\mathrm{tr}(P'\mathbf{W}P'P)}{\mathrm{tr}(\mathbf{W}P')}$$

for events P and P', both projections or their corresponding subspaces. The way to read this equation in IR is as follows. W is a density matrix which may represent a mixture of states, think of it as defining a context, P' represents an observable that is measured, and thus brings about a transformation in $\mathbf{W}$:

$$\mathbf{W} \to \frac{P'\mathbf{W}P'}{\mathrm{tr}(\mathbf{W}P')},$$

which by Gleason's Theorem gives us the formula for $P^{\mathrm{W}}(P \mid P')$ shown above. Compare this with the unconditional probability $P^{\mathrm{W}}(P)$ in the context of $\mathbf{W}$,

$$P^{\mathrm{W}}(P) = \mathrm{tr}(\mathbf{W}P).$$

So here we have an algorithmic (or algebraic) representation of the conditional probability for events in Hilbert space. This general form of conditioning is called Lüders' rule (Lüders, 1951), and it has a number of special cases, one of which is Von Neumann's projection postulate (see Bub, 1997, 1982, for details). Also, when $\mathbf{W}$ indeed represents a mixture the rule is similar to Jeffrey Conditionalisation (Jeffrey, 1983, Van Fraassen, 1991, Van Rijsbergen, 1992). In general $\mathbf{W}$ represents a context where it might be a number of relevant documents, and $P^{\mathrm{W}}(P \mid P')$ would then represent the probability of P given P' in that context.

Ostensive retrieval could be viewed in terms of conditionalisation, that is, $\mathbf{W}$ could represent a weighted combination of the documents touched so far, and $P^{\mathrm{W}}(P \mid P')$ would be the probability of an unseen document $P = |\underline{\mathrm{x}}\rangle\langle\underline{\mathrm{x}}|$, given that we have observed the last one, $P' = |\underline{\mathrm{y}}\rangle\langle\underline{\mathrm{y}}|$.

Language modelling can be analysed in a similar way, but now $P = |\underline{\mathrm{q}}\rangle\langle\underline{\mathrm{q}}|$ represents the query, and $P = |\underline{\mathrm{d}}\rangle\langle\underline{\mathrm{d}}|$ is a document, whereas $\mathbf{W}$ would be some relevant documents. Again a conditional probability is calculated within a context.

For more details on the Projection Postulate the reader should consult the now extensive literature: Gibbins (1987), Herbut (1969, 1994), Martinez (1991) and Teller (1983).

It is an interesting research question to investigate to what extent $P(D \to Q)$, when $D \to Q$ is the Stalnaker conditional from Chapter 5, will function as a language model, that is, an alternative to $P(Q \mid D)$. The accessibility relation that underlies the evaluation of $D \to Q$ is defined in terms of a metric derived from the inner product on the Hilbert space (see also Herbut, 1969). Such a metric may be defined in information-theoretic terms (Amari and Nagaoka, 2000 and

Wootters, 1980a). An exploration of this largely unexplored area may well lead to a reasonable measure for the missing information in the Logical Uncertainty Principle (Van Rijsbergen, 2000).

The technique of imaging that was used to calculate $P(D \rightarrow Q)$ in earlier papers could also be reformulated algebraically making use of Gleason's Theorem and the fact that $D \rightarrow Q$ is a projection operator and corresponds to a subspace of the Hilbert space. Some guidance for this may be found in Bigelow (1976, 1977).

Appendix I

Linear algebra

> In any particular theory there is only as much real science as there is mathematics
>
> *Immanuel Kant*

Much of the mathematics in the main part of this book is concerned with Hilbert space. In general a Hilbert space is an infinite-dimensional space, but for most practical purposes we are content to work with finite-dimensional vector spaces, which indeed can be generalised to infinite-dimensional ones. In some IR applications, such as content-based image retrieval, infinite spaces may well arise, so there is good reason not to exclude them.

Here we concentrate on finite-dimensional vector spaces and collect together for reference some of the elementary mathematical results relevant to them. For this our intuitions deriving from 3-dimensional Euclidean space will stand us in good stead. The best starting point for an understanding of a vector space is to state its axioms.[1]

Vector space

Definition A vector space is a set V of objects called *vectors* satisfying the following axioms.

[1] What follows is mostly taken from Halmos (1958) with small changes, but equivalent formulations can be found in many texts on linear algebra, for example, Finkbeiner (1960), Mirsky (1990), Roman (1992), Schwarz *et al.* (1973), Birkhoff and MacLane (1957) and Sadun (2001), to name but a few. A good introduction that is slanted towards physics and quantum mechanics is Isham (1989). A readable and popular introduction is Chapter 4 of Casti (2000). Extensions to Hilbert space can be found in Debnath and Mikusinski (1999), Simmons (1963), Jordan (1969) and Bub (1997, Appendix). The Appendix to Redhead (1999) may also prove useful.

(A) To every pair, $\underline{x}$ and $\underline{y}$, of vectors in V there corresponds a vector $\underline{x} + \underline{y}$, called the sum of $\underline{x}$ and $\underline{y}$, in such a way that
  (1) addition is commutative, $\underline{x} + \underline{y} = \underline{y} + \underline{x}$,
  (2) addition is associative, $\underline{x} + (\underline{y} + \underline{z}) = (\underline{x} + \underline{y}) + \underline{z}$,
  (3) there exists in V a unique vector Φ (called the origin) such that $\underline{x} + \Phi = \underline{x}$ for every vector $\underline{x}$ in V,
  (4) to every vector $\underline{x}$ in V there corresponds a unique vector $-\underline{x}$ such that $\underline{x} + (-\underline{x}) = \Phi$.

(B) To every pair α and $\underline{x}$, where α is a scalar and $\underline{x}$ is a vector in V, there corresponds a vector $\alpha\underline{x}$, called the product of α and $\underline{x}$, in such a way that
  (1) multiplication by scalars is associative, $\alpha(\beta\underline{x}) = (\alpha\beta)\underline{x}$,
  (2) $1\underline{x} = \underline{x}$ for every $\underline{x}$,
  (3) multiplication by *scalars* is distributive with respect to vector addition, $\alpha(\underline{x} + \underline{y}) = \alpha\underline{x} + \alpha\underline{y}$,
  (4) multiplication by *vectors* is distributive with respect to scalar addition $(\alpha + \beta)\underline{x} = \alpha\underline{x} + \beta\underline{x}$.

In the main body of the text (Chapter 3) we introduce n-dimensional vectors and illustrate arithmetic operations with them. It is an easy exercise to verify that the set of n-dimensional vectors realised by n-tuples of complex numbers satisfy all the axioms of a vector space. Thus if we define for $\underline{x} = (x_1, \ldots, x_n)^{\mathrm{T}}$ and $\underline{y} = (y_1, \ldots, y_n)^{\mathrm{T}}$,

$$\underline{x} + \underline{y} = (x_1 + y_1, \ldots, x_n + y_n)^{\mathrm{T}},$$
$$\alpha\underline{x} = (\alpha x_1, \ldots, x_n)^{\mathrm{T}},$$
$$\Phi = (0, \ldots, 0)^{\mathrm{T}},$$

the axioms A and B above are satisfied for the set of n-tuples and hence C^n is a vector space. In many ways this n-dimensional space is the most important vector space since invariably it is the one used to illustrate and motivate the intuitions about abstract vector spaces.

Another simple example of a vector space is the space of nth order polynomials, including the polynomial identically zero. For example, if $n = 2$, then

$$P_1(x) = a_0 + a_1 x + a_2 x^2,$$
$$P_2(x) = b_0 + b_1 x + b_2 x^2,$$
$$P_1(x) + P_2(x) = (a_0 + b_0) + (a_1 + b_1)x + (a_2 + b_2)x^2 = P_{12},$$

and P_{12} is another second-order polynomial.

Hilbert space

A Hilbert space is a simple extension of a vector space. It requires the definition of an *inner product* on the vector space (see Chapter 3) which enables it to be called an inner product space. An example of an inner product on a finite vector space between $\underline{x}$ and $\underline{y}$ is

$$(\underline{x}, \underline{y}) = \sum_{i=1}^{n} \bar{x}_i y_i, \qquad \text{where } \bar{x}_i \text{ is the complex conjugate of } x_i.$$

If we now impose the *completeness condition* on an infinite inner product space V: that is, for every sequence of vectors $(\underline{v}_n)$, if $\|\underline{v}_m - \underline{v}_m\| \to 0$ as $n, m \to 0$ then there exists a vector $\underline{v}$ such that $\| \underline{v}_n - \underline{v} \| \to 0$.

The most straightforward example of a Hilbert space is the set of infinite sequences $(x_1, \ldots, x_k, \ldots)$ of complex numbers such that $\sqrt{\Sigma_{i=1}^{\infty}|x_i|^2}$ is finite, or equivalently, such $\Sigma_{i=1}^{\infty}|x_i|^2$ converges. Addition of sequences is defined component-wise, that is, for $\underline{x} = (x_1, \ldots, x_k, \ldots)$ and $\underline{y} = (y_1, \ldots, y_k, \ldots)$ we have $\underline{x} + \underline{y} = (x_1 + y_1, \ldots, x_k + y_k, \ldots)$; similarly for θ and $\alpha\underline{x}$. The importance of this Hilbert space of square-summable sequences, called l_2, derives from the fact that any abstract Hilbert space is isomorphic to it (Schmeidler, 1965). Hence if one imagines a Hilbert space in this concrete form one cannot go far wrong. An inner product on it is a simple extension of the one on the finite space given earlier:

$$(\underline{x}, \underline{y}) = \sum_{i=1}^{\infty} \bar{x}_i y_i.$$

Operators

A linear operator $\mathbf{T}$ on a vector space V is a correspondence that assigns to every vector $\underline{z}$ in V a vector $\mathbf{T}\underline{z}$ in V, in such a way that

$$\mathbf{T}(\alpha\underline{x} + \beta\underline{y}) = \alpha\mathbf{T}\underline{x} + \beta\mathbf{T}\underline{y}$$

for any vectors $\underline{x}$ and $\underline{y}$ and scalars α and β. The most important class of linear operators for us are the *self-adjoint* operators. An adjoint $\mathbf{T}^*$ of a linear operator $\mathbf{T}$ is defined by

$$(\mathbf{T}^*\underline{x}, \underline{y}) = (\underline{x}, \mathbf{T}\underline{y});$$

and it is self-adjoint when $\mathrm{T}^* = \mathbf{T}$. Often the name *Hermitian* is used synonymously for self-adjoint. The Hermitian operators have a number of suitable properties, such as that all their eigenvalues are real, which makes them suitable candidates as mathematical objects to represent observables in quantum mechanics and information space.

Linear functionals

There is one final abstract result that is often implicitly assumed, that is rarely explicitly stated, and it concerns linear functionals on a vector space. A *linear functional* on a vector V is a map $f\colon V \to \Gamma$, from V into the field of scalars Γ, with the properties

$$f(\alpha \underline{x} + \beta \underline{y}) = \alpha f(\underline{x}) + \beta f(\underline{y}), \text{ for all } \alpha, \beta \in \Gamma, \text{ and } \underline{x}, \underline{y} \in V.$$

The set of linear functionals on a vector space is itself a vector space known as a *dual* space to V, usually written V^* (Redhead, 1999, Appendix). If $\underline{x} \in V$ and $f \in V^*$, a 1:1 correspondence φ between V and V^* is defined by writing

$$f(\underline{y}) = (\underline{x}, \underline{y}), \quad \underline{y} \in V, \text{ and then setting } \underline{x} = \varphi(f).$$

The result is a theorem that for any f there exists an $\underline{x}$ and the $\underline{x}$ is unique. There is more about duality in Sadun (2001).

At this point we can take a quick dip into the world of IR to illustrate the use of duality. Say we have defined the usual cosine correlation on the space of documents to represent the inner product between documents. We can have a linear functional that associates with each document a scalar, and then the theorem tells us that for the particular inner product there is a vector $\underline{x}$ with respect to which the inner product with each document $\underline{y}$ will result in the same scalar value. The reverse is true too: the inner product between each $\underline{y}$ and a given $\underline{x}$ will generate a linear functional on the space V. One way to interpret $\underline{x}$ is that it can represent the query as a vector on the document space.

Dirac notation

We are now in a position to introduce the succinct Dirac notation that is used at various places in the book, especially in Chapter 6. Paul Dirac (1958) was responsible for introducing the 'bra' and 'ket' notation. A vector $\underline{y}$ in a Hilbert space **H** is represented by $|\underline{y}\rangle$, a ket. The linear functional f associated with $\underline{x}$ is denoted by $\langle\underline{x}|$, the bra, thus forming the 'bra(c)ket' $\langle\underline{x} \mid \underline{y}\rangle$ the inner product. The bra (the linear functional) has the linearity property shown as follows in the Dirac notation:

$$\langle\underline{x}|(\alpha \mid \underline{y}\rangle + \beta \mid \underline{z}\rangle) = \alpha\langle\underline{x} \mid \underline{y}\rangle + \beta\langle\underline{x} \mid \underline{z}\rangle.$$

The set of linear functionals is a vector space itself, as we observed above, and so they can be added and multiplied by complex numbers in the usual way:

$$[\alpha\langle\underline{u}| + \beta\langle\underline{v}|](|\underline{z}\rangle) = \alpha\langle\underline{u}\,|\,\underline{z}\rangle + \beta\langle\underline{v}\,|\,\underline{z}\rangle.$$

The 1:1 mapping between V and V^*, φ above, is often denoted by a star *, the same symbol used for indicating the adjoint of an operator. In the Dirac notation this rarely causes confusion, and if it does, it can be resolved by the judicious use of brackets.

We have the two relations

$$\langle\underline{x}| = (|\underline{x}\rangle)^* \text{ and } |\underline{x}\rangle = (\langle\underline{x}|)^*.$$

The star operation is antilinear, reflecting the fact that the inner product is antilinear in its left argument,

$$(\alpha|\underline{y}\rangle + \beta|\underline{z}\rangle)^* = \alpha^*\langle\underline{y}| + \beta^*\langle\underline{z}|,$$
$$(\gamma\langle\underline{u}| + \delta\langle\underline{v}|)^* = \gamma^*|\underline{u}\rangle + \delta^*|\underline{v}\rangle.$$

One final piece of the Dirac notation is concerned with linear operators. The inner product of a vector $|\underline{x}\rangle$ in $\mathbf{H}$ with the ket $\mathbf{T}|\underline{y}\rangle$ can be written as

$$(|\underline{x}\rangle)^*\mathbf{T}|\underline{y}\rangle = \langle\underline{x}|\mathbf{T}|\underline{y}\rangle.$$

$\langle\underline{x}|\mathbf{T}|\underline{y}\rangle$ is the famous 'sandwich' notation, which if it seems uninformative during a manipulation can always be replaced by the more elaborate left-hand side of its definition.

Dyads

A special class of operators, known as *dyads*, is particularly useful when it comes to deriving results using the Dirac notation. A dyad is the outer product of a ket with a bra, and can be defined by

$$|\underline{x}\rangle\langle\underline{y}\,|\,(|\underline{z}\rangle) = |\underline{x}\rangle\langle\underline{y}\,|\,\underline{z}\rangle = \langle\underline{y}|\underline{z}\rangle|\underline{x}\rangle.$$

Here the operator $|\underline{x}\rangle\langle\underline{y}|$ is applied to a vector $|\underline{z}\rangle$ to produce the vector $|\underline{x}\rangle$ multiplied by a scalar $\langle\underline{y}\ \}\ \underline{z}\rangle$.

Especially important dyads are the projectors, which are of the form $|\underline{u}\rangle\langle\underline{u}|$, where $\underline{u}$ is the vector onto which the projection is made. For example,

$$|\underline{u}\rangle\langle\underline{u}|(|\underline{z}\rangle) = |\underline{u}\rangle\langle\underline{u}\,|\,\underline{z}\rangle = \langle\underline{u}\,|\,\underline{z}\rangle|\underline{u}\rangle,$$

where the application of the projector to vector $|\underline{z}\rangle$ results in $|\underline{u}\rangle$ multiplied by a scalar. A projector of this kind is therefore a linear transformation that takes any vector and maps it onto another vector.

Multiplying dyads is especially easy:

$$|\underline{u}\rangle\langle\underline{v}||\underline{x}\rangle\langle z| = \langle\underline{v}\mid\underline{x}\rangle|\underline{u}\rangle\langle\underline{z}|,$$

resulting in another dyad multiplied by the scalar $\langle\underline{v}\mid\underline{x}\rangle$. The multiplication quickly demonstrates that operators in general do not *commute*, for

$$|\underline{x}\rangle\langle\underline{z}||\underline{u}\rangle\langle\underline{v}| = \langle\underline{z}\mid\underline{u}\rangle|\underline{x}\rangle\langle\underline{v}|,$$

and in general these two resulting dyads are not equal,

$$\langle\underline{v}\mid\underline{x}\rangle|\underline{u}\rangle\langle\underline{z}| \neq \langle\underline{z}\mid\underline{u}\rangle|\underline{x}\rangle\langle\underline{v}|.$$

Useful identities in Dirac notation

We now collect together a number of identities, using Dirac notation, that may prove useful. Let $\{\varphi_1, \ldots, \varphi_n\}$ be an orthonormal basis for an n-dimensional Hilbert space, that is $\sqrt{\langle\varphi_k|\varphi_k\rangle} = 1$ and $\langle\varphi_i\mid\varphi_j\rangle = \delta_{ij}$. Although we produce these five identities for a finite space, they also hold for an infinite-dimensional space.

The set of dyads $\{|\varphi_1\rangle\langle\varphi_1|, \ldots, |\varphi_n\rangle\langle\varphi_n|\}$ is a set of projectors, one for each basis vector, and projecting onto that vector. They satisfy a completeness property, or resolution of identity, namely

$$\sum_{k=1}^{n} |\varphi_k\rangle\langle\varphi_k| = \mathbf{I},$$

where **I** is the identity operator. They are also mutually orthogonal, that is

$$|\varphi_i\rangle\langle\varphi_i||\varphi_j\rangle\langle\varphi_j| = |\varphi_i\rangle\langle\varphi_i\mid\varphi_j\rangle\langle\varphi_j| = \delta_{ij}|\varphi_i\rangle\langle\varphi_i|.$$

The matrix representation of an operator **T** with respect to an orthonormal basis such as $\{\varphi_1, \ldots, \varphi_n\}$ is given by $\langle\varphi_j|\mathbf{T}|\varphi_k\rangle$, that is, it represents the jkth element of the matrix.

$$|\psi\rangle = \left(\sum_{k=1}^{n} |\varphi_k\rangle\langle\varphi_k|\right)|\psi\rangle = \sum_{k=1}^{n} \langle\varphi_k\mid\psi\rangle|\varphi_k\rangle$$

shows how to resolve a vector into its components.

$$\langle\chi\mid\psi\rangle = \langle\chi|\sum_{k=1}^{n} |\varphi_k\rangle\langle\varphi_k\mid\psi\rangle = \sum_{k=1}^{n} \langle\chi\mid\varphi_k\rangle\langle\varphi_k\mid\psi\rangle$$

shows the inner product as a sum of pair-wise products of components.

$$\langle\varphi_j|\mathbf{T}|\psi\rangle = \langle\varphi_j|\mathbf{T}\sum_{k=1}^{n}|\varphi_k\rangle\langle\varphi_k|\psi\rangle = \sum_{k=1}^{n}\langle\varphi_j|\mathbf{T}|\varphi_k\rangle\langle\varphi_k \mid \psi\rangle$$

calculates the effect of **T** on a vector $|\psi\rangle$ in terms of matrix multiplication.

$$\mathbf{T}|\varphi_j\rangle = \sum_{k=1}^{n}|\varphi_k\rangle\langle\varphi_k|\mathrm{T}|\varphi_j\rangle = \sum_{k=1}^{n}\langle\varphi_k|\mathbf{T}|\varphi_j\rangle|\varphi_k\rangle$$

expresses the effect of **T** on the *j*th basis vector as a linear combination of the basis vectors with matrix elements as weights.

$$\langle\varphi_j|\mathbf{TS}|\varphi_k\rangle = \langle\varphi_j|\mathbf{T}\sum_{i=1}^{n}|\varphi_i\rangle\langle\varphi_i|\mathbf{S}|\varphi_k\rangle = \sum_{i=1}^{n}\langle\varphi_j|\mathbf{T}|\varphi_i\rangle\langle\varphi_i|\mathbf{S}|\varphi_k\rangle$$

illustrates the product of **T** and **S** in terms of the product of the corresponding matrix representations.

It is a good exercise in the use of Dirac notation to show that the five identities hold. For further details the reader should consult Jordan (1969). An explanation of how the Dirac notation relates to standard mathematical notation for vector spaces is quite hard to find, but one of the most recent can be found in Sadun (2001). Dirac (1958) himself of course explained and motivated the notation in his groundbreaking book, where it was developed along with an introduction to quantum mechanics. The recent book by Griffiths (2002) has a clear explanation, but again it is intertwined with details of quantum mechanics. Developing an understanding of the Dirac notation is well worthwhile as it opens up many of the books and papers in quantum mechanics, especially the classics. One of the greatest is Von Neumann's (1983), which uses the notation to great effect to discuss the foundations of quantum mechanics. The power of the notation comes from the fact that it accomplishes some very complicated manipulations whilst at the same time taking care of the 'bookkeeping', thus making sure, almost by sleight of hand, that mathematical correctness is preserved.

A good example of the power of the Dirac notation shows in the derivation of the Cauchy–Schwartz inequality, which will be used in the next appendix.

Cauchy–Schwartz inequality

The Cauchy–Schwartz inequality states that for two vectors $|\varphi\rangle$ and $|\Psi\rangle$ we have $|\langle\varphi \mid \psi\rangle|^2 \leq \langle\varphi \mid \varphi\rangle\langle\psi \mid \psi\rangle$. To derive this result, construct a orthonormal basis $\{\varphi_1, \ldots, \varphi_n\}$ for the Hilbert space. Let $|\varphi_1\rangle = |\psi\rangle/\sqrt{\langle\psi \mid \psi\rangle}$, then

$$\begin{aligned}
\langle\varphi \mid \varphi\rangle\langle\psi \mid \psi\rangle &= \langle\varphi| \sum_i |\varphi_i\rangle\langle\varphi_i||\varphi\rangle\langle\psi \mid \psi\rangle \\
&= \sum_i \langle\varphi \mid \varphi_i\rangle\langle\varphi_i \mid \varphi\rangle\langle\psi \mid \psi\rangle \\
&\geq \frac{\langle\varphi \mid \psi\rangle\langle\psi \mid \varphi\rangle}{\langle\psi \mid \psi\rangle}\langle\psi \mid \psi\rangle \\
&= \langle\varphi \mid \psi\rangle\langle\psi \mid \varphi\rangle = |\langle\varphi \mid \psi\rangle|^2,
\end{aligned}$$

where we have used the resolution of the identity **I**, and ignored all the (non-negative) terms in the sum bar the first.

Appendix II
Quantum mechanics

> One should keep the need for a sound mathematical basis dominating one's search for a new theory. Any physical or philosophical ideas that one has must be adjusted to fit the mathematics. Not the other way around.
>
> *Dirac, 1978.*

This appendix will give a brief, highly simplified introduction to a number of the principles underlying quantum theory. It is convenient to collect them here independent of information retrieval. We will use the Dirac notation introduced in the previous appendix to express the necessary mathematics.[1] Before examining the few principles underlying quantum mechanics let us make two comments. The first is that there is no general agreement about whether probabilistic quantum statements apply to individual isolated systems or only to ensembles of such systems identically prepared. The second comment is that there is no distinct preference whether to develop quantum theory fully in terms of vectors in a Hilbert space, or in terms of the density operators applied to that space. We will not take a strong position on either

[1] There are, it is hardly necessary to say, many more complete and deeper introductions. Usually they are wrapped up with philosophical considerations, or physical phenomena. For example, Hughes (1989), Van Fraassen (1991) and Bub (1997) give excellent philosophical accounts, whereas Peres (1998), Omnès (1994) and Schwinger (2001) are good introductions linked with physical phenomena. One of the best pure mathematical accounts, in sympathy with the approach taken in this book, is Varadarajan (1985). Of course, the original books by Dirac (1958), Von Neumann (1983) and Feynman *et al.* (1965) are good sources of inspiration and understanding. Outstanding bibliographies can be found in Suppes (1976) and Auletta (2000); the website www.arXiv.org gives access to many recent papers in quantum mechanics. One of the best all-round introductions, combining the mathematical, philosophical and physical is Griffiths (2002).

There are remarkably few principles underlying modern quantum mechanics. Different versions can be found in d'Espagnat (1976), Auyang (1995) and Wootters (1980), where they are spelt out explicitly.

division. For convenience we will assume that statements are applicable to single systems, and that when it suits, either vectors or density operators can be used.

To begin with we will consider only pure states of single systems and observables with discrete non-degenerate spectra.[2] This will keep the mathematics simple.

There are four significant fundamental concepts to consider: physical states, observables, measurements and dynamics; and of course the interplay between these.

Physical states

A quantum state is the complete and maximal summary of the characteristics of the quantum system at a moment in time. Schrödinger, see Wheeler and Zurek (1983), already held this view: 'It (ψ-function) is now the means for predicting probability of measurement results. In it is embodied momentarily-attained sum of theoretically based future expectation, somewhat as laid down in a catalogue.' The state of a system is represented mathematically by a unit vector $|\varphi\rangle$ in a complex Hilbert space. That is, the states are such that

$$\|\varphi\|^2 = \langle\varphi \mid \varphi\rangle = 1.$$

The ensemble interpretation would say that the ensemble of identically prepared systems is represented by $|\varphi\rangle$. The same physical state as $|\varphi\rangle$ is represented by $e^{i\theta}|\varphi\rangle$, its norm remains unity, and θ is called the phase factor.

Observables

These are represented by self-adjoint operators on the Hilbert space. It is assumed that every physical property that is to be measured is representable by such an operator, and that the spectrum of the operator comprises all possible values that can be found if the observable is measured. Thus, certain values called eigenvalues of the self-adjoint operator, which are all real, are all the outcomes of a measurement that are possible. The eigenvectors corresponding to the eigenvalues, are called the eigenstates of the system. A famous postulate[3] of

[2] This is standard terminology to express that the eigenvalues of the operators representing observable are unique: a single eigenvector per eigenvalue.

[3] The postulate is generally referred to as Von Neumann's Projection Postulate. There are other related ones, for example one due to Lüders (1951).

Von Neumann required that immediately after a measurement a system could be deemed to be in the eigenstate corresponding to the observed eigenvalue. This would ensure that a measurement of the same observable immediately after its first measurement would produce the same eigenvalue with probability 1.

Measurements

Let us assume that we have a physical system whose quantum state is described by the ket $|\varphi\rangle$, and suppose that we measure the observable **T** which is represented by the self-adjoint operator **T**. In classical physics such a measurement would produce a definite result. However, in quantum theory the outcome of a measurement can only be predicted with a certain probability, making the claim that measurement is intrinsically probabilistic, and that the probability of outcome of a measurement depends on the state of the system, that is, it depends on $|\varphi\rangle$. This fundamental relationship is codified in the following manner for n-dimensional operators with a non-degenerate spectrum

$$P_\varphi(\mathbf{T}, \lambda_i) = \left\langle \varphi \,\middle|\, \mathbf{E}_i^{\mathrm{T}} \varphi \right\rangle = \langle \varphi \mid \psi_i \rangle \langle \psi_i \mid \varphi \rangle = |\langle \varphi \mid \psi_i \rangle|^2, \text{ where}$$

φ is the normalised vector in Hilbert space representing the system,[4]
T is the self-adjoint operator representing the observable **T**,[5]
$\mathbf{E}_i^{\mathrm{T}}$ is the projector $|\psi_i\rangle\langle\psi_i|$ onto the 1-dimensional subspace spanned by ψ_i,
ψ_i is one of the n eigenvectors associated with **T**, and
λ_i is the ith eigenvalue associated with the ith eigenvector ψ_i.

P_φ (**T**, λ_i) is the probability that a measurement of **T** conducted on a system in state φ will yield a result λ_i with a probability given by $|\langle\varphi \mid \psi_i\rangle|^2$. In an n-dimensional Hilbert space any vector φ can be expressed as a linear combination of the basis vectors. The eigenvectors $\{\psi_1, \ldots, \psi_n\}$ form an orthonormal basis and hence $\varphi = c_1\psi_1 + c_2\psi_2 + \cdots + c_n\psi_n$, where the c_i are complex numbers such that $\Sigma_{i=1}^n |c_i|^2 = 1$, and hence $|\langle\varphi \mid \psi_i\rangle|^2 = |c_i^* c_i| = |c_i|^2$. Observe that the probabilities sum to unity, as they must.

From this algorithm for calculating the probability $P_\varphi(.\,,.)$ it is immediately possible to derive the statistical quantities, *expected value* and *variance* of an observable, which we will need below to derive the famous Heisenberg

[4] φ and $|\varphi\rangle$ are in 1:1 correspondence and will be treated as names for the same object.
[5] It is conventional in quantum mechanics to use the same symbol for an observable and the self-adjoint operator representing it.

Uncertainty Principle. The expected value $\langle \mathbf{T} \rangle$ of an obervable $\mathbf{T}$ is calculated as follows:

$$\begin{aligned}\langle \mathbf{T} \rangle &= \sum_{i=1}^{n} |\langle \varphi \mid \psi_i \rangle|^2 \lambda_i = \sum_{i=1}^{n} \langle \varphi | \mathbf{E}_i^{\mathrm{T}} | \varphi \rangle \lambda_i \\ &= \langle \varphi | \sum_{i=1}^{n} \lambda_i \mathbf{E}_i^{\mathrm{T}} | \varphi \rangle \\ &= \langle \varphi | \mathbf{T} | \varphi \rangle.\end{aligned}$$

The last step in the derivation above is given by the Spectral Decomposition Theorem (see Chapter 4).

The variance of a quantity is usually a measure of the extent to which it deviates from the expected value. In quantum mechanics the variance $(\Delta\mathbf{T})^2$ of an observable $\mathbf{T}$ in state φ is defined as

$$(\Delta\mathbf{T})^2 = \langle \mathbf{T}\varphi - \langle \mathbf{T} \rangle \varphi \mid \mathbf{T}\varphi - \langle \mathbf{T} \rangle \varphi \rangle = \|\mathbf{T}\varphi - \langle \mathbf{T} \rangle \varphi\|^2.$$

Let us demonstrate the expected value and variance with some examples. If the system is in one of its eigenstates, say $|\psi_i\rangle$, then for a measurement of the observable $\mathbf{T}$ you expect $\langle \mathbf{T} \rangle$to be λ_i with zero variance, that is with complete certainty. Let us check this:

$$\begin{aligned}&\langle \mathbf{T} \rangle = \langle \psi_i | \mathbf{T} | \psi_i \rangle = \langle \psi_i \mid \lambda_i \psi_i \rangle = \lambda_i \langle \psi_i \mid \psi_i \rangle = \lambda_i \text{ because } \langle \psi_i \mid \psi_i \rangle = 1; \\ &(\Delta\mathbf{T}) = \|\mathbf{T}\psi_i - \langle \mathbf{T} \rangle \psi_i\| = \|\mathbf{T}\psi_i - \lambda_i \psi_i\| = \|\mathbf{T}\psi_i - \mathbf{T}\psi_i\| = 0.\end{aligned}$$

Another interesting case is to look at the expectation of a projector onto an eigenvector $|\psi_i\rangle$when the system is in state $|\varphi\rangle$. Let $\mathbf{T}_i = |\psi_i\rangle\langle\psi_i|$; then

$$\langle |\psi_i\rangle\langle\psi_i| \rangle = \langle \varphi \mid \psi_i \rangle \langle \psi_i \mid \varphi \rangle = |\langle \varphi \mid \psi_i \rangle|^2,$$

which is the probability that a measurement of $\mathbf{T}_i$ conducted on a system in state φ will yield a result λ_i.[6] Projection operators can be interpreted as simple questions that have a 'yes' or 'no' answer, because they have two eigenvalues, namely 1 and 0.

$$\begin{aligned}&\mathbf{T}_i|\psi_i\rangle = |\psi_i\rangle\langle\psi_i \mid \psi_i\rangle = 1|\psi_i\rangle; \\ &\mathbf{T}_i|\psi_j\rangle = |\psi_i\rangle\langle\psi_i \mid \psi_j\rangle = 0|\psi_i\rangle \text{ because } \langle \psi_i \mid \psi_j \rangle = \delta_{ij}.\end{aligned}$$

Given one such question $\mathbf{T}_i$, $\langle \mathbf{T}_i \rangle$ is the expected relative frequency with which the observable $\mathbf{T}_i$ when measured will return an answer 'yes'. Because any self-adjoint operator can be decomposed into a linear combination of projectors, it implies that any observable can be reduced to a set of 'yes'/'no'

[6] Remember that λ_i is the eigenvalue associated with the eigenvector ψ_i.

questions. Mackey(1963) developed this '*question-oriented*' approach to quantum mechanics in some detail, constructing what he called question-valued measures.

Heisenberg Uncertainty Principle[7]

Surprisingly, this famous principle in quantum mechanics can be derived from Hilbert space theory for non-commuting self-adjoint operators without any reference to physics. It uses some simple facts about complex numbers and the Cauchy–Schwartz inequality (see Chapter 3). Its statement for two observables **T** and **S** is that when **T** and **S** are measured for a system whose quantum state is given by $|\psi\rangle$, then the product of the variances of **T** and **S** are bounded from below as follows:

$$\Delta\mathbf{T}\Delta\mathbf{S} \geq \tfrac{1}{2}|\langle\psi|\mathbf{TS} - \mathbf{ST}|\psi\rangle|.$$

To derive it we need first to introduce some notation and some elementary mathematical results. For any two observables **A** and **B** we can define the *commutator* $[\mathbf{A}, \mathbf{B}]$ and *anti-commutator* $\{\mathbf{A}, \mathbf{B}\}$

$$[\mathbf{A}, \mathbf{B}] \equiv \mathbf{AB} - \mathbf{BA},$$
$$\{\mathbf{A}, \mathbf{B}\} \equiv \mathbf{AB} + \mathbf{BA}.$$

Let x and y be real variables and $x + \mathrm{i}y$ a complex number.

$$\begin{aligned} \langle\psi|\mathbf{AB}|\psi\rangle &= x + \mathrm{i}y \\ \langle\psi|[\mathbf{A}, \mathbf{B}]|\psi\rangle &= \langle\psi|\mathbf{AB}|\psi\rangle - \langle\psi|\mathbf{BA}|\psi\rangle = x + \mathrm{i}y - x + \mathrm{i}y = 2\mathrm{i}y, \\ \langle\psi|\{\mathbf{A}, \mathbf{B}\}|\psi\rangle &= \langle\psi|\mathbf{AB}|\psi\rangle + \langle\psi|\mathbf{BA}|\psi\rangle = x + \mathrm{i}y + x - \mathrm{i}y = 2x. \end{aligned}$$

Doing the complex number arithmetic, we can derive

$$|\langle\psi|[\mathbf{A}, \mathbf{B}]|\psi\rangle|^2 + |\langle\psi|\{\mathbf{A}, \mathbf{B}\}|\psi\rangle|^2 = 4|\langle\psi|\mathbf{AB}|\psi\rangle|^2.$$

By the Cauchy–Schwartz inequality, we get

$$|\langle\psi|\mathbf{AB}|\psi\rangle|^2 \leq \langle\psi|\mathbf{A}^2|\psi\rangle\langle\psi|\mathbf{B}^2|\psi\rangle.$$

Combining this with the previous equation and dropping the term involving $\{\mathbf{A}, \mathbf{B}\}$, we get

$$|\langle\psi|[\mathbf{A}, \mathbf{B}]|\psi\rangle|^2 \leq 4\langle\psi|\mathbf{A}^2|\psi\rangle\langle\psi|\mathbf{B}^2|\psi\rangle.$$

[7] See Heisenberg (1949) for an account by the master, and Popper (1982) for an enthusiastic critique.

Now, to derive the principle we substitute $\mathbf{A} = \mathbf{T} - \langle\mathbf{T}\rangle\mathbf{I}$ and $\mathbf{B} = \mathbf{S} - \langle\mathbf{S}\rangle\mathbf{I}$, where $\mathbf{T}$ and $\mathbf{S}$ are observables and $\mathbf{I}$ is the identity operator, and we get

$$\begin{aligned}(\Delta\mathbf{T})^2 &= \langle\psi|\mathbf{A}^2|\psi\rangle,\\ (\Delta\mathbf{S})^2 &= \langle\psi|\mathbf{B}^2|\psi\rangle,\\ \langle\psi|[\mathbf{A},\mathbf{B}]|\psi\rangle &= \langle\psi|(\mathbf{T} - \langle\mathbf{T}\rangle\mathbf{I})(\mathbf{S} - \langle\mathbf{S}\rangle\mathbf{I})|\psi\rangle = \langle\psi|[\mathbf{T},\mathbf{S}]|\psi\rangle.\end{aligned}$$

Substituting into the inequality above gives the Heisenberg Uncertainty Principle:

$$\Delta\mathbf{T}\Delta\mathbf{S} \geq \frac{|\langle\psi|[\mathbf{T},\mathbf{S}]|\psi\rangle|}{2}.$$

There are some interesting things to observe about this inequality and its derivation. Time did not play a role in the derivation, so the result is independent of time. More importantly, one must be clear about its interpretation. The inequality does not quantify how the measurement of one observable inteferes with the accuracy of another. The correct way to interpret it is as follows: when a large number of quantum systems are prepared in an identical state represented by $|\psi\rangle$, then peforming a measurement of $\mathbf{T}$ on some of these systems, and $\mathbf{S}$ on others, the variances $(\Delta\mathbf{T})^2$ and $(\Delta\mathbf{S})^2$ will satisfy the Heisenberg inequality. It is important to emphasise once again that no physics was used in the derivation, and the only extra mathematical results used, apart from standard Hilbert space geometry, were the Cauchy–Schwartz inequality and the fact that in general operators do not commute, that is, $\mathbf{AB} - \mathbf{BA} \neq 0$. In the case where the operators do commute, the commutator $[\mathbf{A}, \mathbf{B}]$ reduces to zero and the lower bound on the product of the variances is zero, and hence no bound at all. It is surprising that such a famous principle in physics is implied by the choice of mathematical representation for state and observable in Hilbert space.

In this appendix the time evolution of the quantum state has been ignored, because in this book, time evolution is not considered. Nevertheless, it is important to remember that the evolution in time of a state vector $|\psi\rangle$ is governed by the famous Schrödinger equation. An excellent exposition of this equation may be found in Griffiths (2002).

Further reading

The following is a list of references for further elementary, and in some cases more philosophical, introductions to quantum mechanics. The reader might like to consult the bibliography for the annotations with respect to each reference. They are Aerts (1999), Baggott (1997), Barrett (1999), Greenstein and

Zajonc (1997), Healey (1990), Heisenberg (1949), Isham (1995), Lockwood (1991), London and Bauer (1982), Murdoch (1987), Packel (1974), Pais (1991), Reichenbach (1944) and Van der Waerden (1968).

Although this book is not about quantum computation, much of the literature referenced below contains excellent introductions to the mathematics for quantum mechanics in which the application to physics is minimized and instead the relationship with computing science is emphasized. Good examples are Bouwmeester *et al.* (2001), Deutsch (1997), Grover (1997), Gruska (1999), Hirvensalo (2001), Lo *et al.* (1998), Nielsen and Chuang (2000) and Pittenger (2000). Grover (1997) is not a book but a seminal paper on the application of quantum computation to searching.

A book that deserves special mention is the one by Lomonaco (2002); although it is primarily an introduction to quantum computation, the first chapter contains one of the best introductions to quantum mechanics this author has encountered.

Appendix III
Probability

Therefore the true logic for this world is the calculus of Probabilities which is, or ought to be, in a reasonable man's mind.

James Clerk Maxwell

Classical probability

The usual starting point for classical probability theory is with Kolmogorov's axioms, first stated in his book published in 1933 and translated into English in 1950. Ever since then these axioms have been used and repeated in many publications, and may be considered as orthodoxy.[1] The Kolmogorov axioms define a probability measure on a field $\Im$ of sets, which is a collection of subsets of the set Ω, the universe of basic events. This universe Ω can be a set of anything; it is the subsets which are members of Ω that are important. $\Im$ is a *field* because it is closed with respect to the operations of complementation, countable union and intersection. Furthermore, it contains the empty set Φ, and hence by complementation the entire set Ω.

We can now define a probability measure on $\Im$. It is a positive-valued function $\mu: \Im \to \Re^+$, a mapping from the field of subsets into the set of positive real numbers[2] with the following properties:

$$\mu(\Phi) = 0; \quad \mu(\Omega) = 1.$$

[1] A recent version is given in Jaynes (2003), where we also find very detailed and annotated references to the earlier literature on probability, for example Jeffreys (1961), Keynes (1929), Feller (1957)), Good (1950), Cox (1961), de Finetti (1974) and Williams (2001). For introductions to probability theory motivated by the needs of quantum mechanics one should look at Jauch (1968), Sneed (1970) and Sutherland (2000).

[2] The positive shall include zero.

For any pairwise disjoint sequence S_n, that is $S_i \cap S_j = \Phi$ for $i \neq j$, we have

$$\mu\left(\bigcup S_n\right) = \bigcup_n \mu(S_n) \quad (\sigma\text{-additivity})$$

and a requirement for continuity at zero, that if a sequence $S_1 \supseteq S_2 \supseteq S_3 \supseteq \cdots$ tends to the empty set, then $\mu(S_n) \to 0$. All this abstract theory can be summarised by saying that a numerical probability is a measure μ on a Boolean σ-algebra $\Im$ of subsets of a set Ω, such that $\mu(\Omega) = 1$ (Halmos, 1950).

We rarely work with probability functions in this form, and we usually see them defined slightly differently $P(.)$ is a positive real-valued function on an event space, where E_0 is the empty event, E_1 the universal event, and then

$$P(E_0) = 0 \text{ and } P(E_1) = 1,$$
$$P(E_i \cup E_j) = P(E_i) + P(E_j) \text{ provided that } E_i \cap E_j = E_0.$$

A conditional probability is then defined by

$$P(E \mid F) = \frac{P(E \cap F)}{P(F)} \text{ provided that } P(F) \neq 0.$$

One can then transform this latter equation into Bayes' Theorem, which is

$$P(E \mid F) = \frac{P(F \mid E)P(E)}{P(F)}.$$

Because of a famous corollary to the Stone Representation Theorem: every Boolean algebra is isomorphic to a field of sets (Halmos, 1963), it is possible to substitute propositional variables for events. Thus we can define probability as a real-valued function P on an algebra of propositions satisfying the following axioms:

$$P(p) \geq 0 \text{ for all } p \text{ belonging to the algebra},$$
$$P(T) = 1, \text{ where } T = p \vee \bar{p} \text{ is a tautology},$$
$$P(p \vee q) = P(p) + P(q), \text{ whenever } \overline{p \vee q}.$$

Conditional probability and Bayes' Theorem can then be re-expressed in terms of propositions instead of subsets.

Quantum probability

When it comes to defining a probability function for quantum mechanics the situation is somewhat different. There is an excellent paper by Jauch (1976) in Suppes (1976) that shows how to define probability and random variables for quantum mechanics, with definitions motivated by the classical definitions.

In essence the powerset of subsets of a set of outcomes (the sample space) which forms a Boolean lattice is replaced by a non-Boolean lattice on which a probability measure is defined thus.

Let L be the lattice of elementary events. Then a probability measure on L, a function $\mu: L \to [0, 1]$, is defined on L with values in [0, 1] satisfying the following conditions:

$$\sum \mu(a_i) = \mu(\cup a_i), \quad \text{for } a_i \in L, \quad i = 1, 2, \ldots, \quad a_i \perp a_j, \text{ when } i \neq j;$$

$\mu(\Phi) = 0, \quad \mu(\mathrm{I}) = 1,$ where Φ is the smallest and I is the largest element in L;

if $\mu(a) = \mu(b) = 1$ then $\mu(a \cap b) = 1$.

This definition is made more concrete if the lattice elements are interpreted as the subspaces of a Hilbert space **H**. It is a well known result that this $\wp(\mathbf{H})$, the lattice of closed subspaces of a complex Hilbert space, is a non-Boolean lattice of a special kind (see, for example, Birkhoff and Von Neumann, 1936, or Beltrametti and Cassinelli, 1981).

A less abstract definition of the probability measure can now be given in terms of the closed subspaces of **H**. Let φ be any normalised vector in the Hilbert space **H**, then a probability measure μ on the set of subspaces $L = \wp(\mathbf{H})$ is defined as follows:

$$\mu_\varphi(\Phi) = 0,$$
$$\mu_\varphi(\mathbf{H}) = 1.$$

For subspaces L_i and L_j, $\mu_\varphi(L_i \oplus L_j) = \mu_\phi(L_i) + \mu_\varphi(L_j)$ provided $L_i \cap L_j = \Phi$. Observe that the measure μ is defined with respect to a particular vector φ, a different measure for different vectors. The symbol $\oplus$ is used to indicate the linear span of two subspaces, which in the classical axioms would have been the union of two sets. For a more general form of the probability axioms, interested readers should consult Parthasarathy (1992).

A concrete realisation of such a probability measure can be given. To do this we need to define briefly *trace* and *density operator* (see Chapter 6).

$$\mathrm{tr}(\mathbf{A}) = \sum_i \langle \varphi_i | \mathbf{A} | \varphi_i \rangle, \text{ where } \langle \varphi | \mathbf{A} | \varphi \rangle > 0 \ \forall \varphi \in \mathbf{H},$$
$$\text{and } \{\varphi_i\} \text{ is a orthonormal basis for } \mathbf{H}.$$

The trace tr(.) has the following properties if the traces are finite and α a scalar:

$$\mathrm{tr}(\alpha \mathbf{A}) = \alpha \mathrm{tr}(\mathbf{A}),$$
$$\mathrm{tr}(\mathbf{A} + \mathbf{B}) = \mathrm{tr}(\mathbf{A}) + \mathrm{tr}(\mathbf{B}).$$

Now a *density operator* $\mathbf{D}$ is such that $\langle\varphi|\mathbf{D}|\varphi\rangle > 0 \ \forall \ \varphi \in \mathbf{H}$ and $\mathrm{tr}(\mathbf{D}) = 1$. So, for example, every projection operator onto a 1-dimensional subspace is a density operator, and its trace is unity. Moreover, any linear combination $\sum_i \alpha\mathbf{P}_i$ of such projectors $\mathbf{P}_i$, where $\sum_i \alpha = 1$, is a density operator. If we now define for any projector $\mathbf{P}_L$ onto subspace L the quantity $\mathrm{tr}(\mathbf{DP}_L)$ for a density operator $\mathbf{D}$, we find that it is a probability measure on the subspaces L: $\mu(L) = \mathrm{tr}(\mathbf{DP}_L)$, conforming to the axioms defined above. Significantly, the reverse is true as well, that is that given a probability measure on the closed subspaces of a Hilbert space $\mathbf{H}$, then there exists a density operator that 'computes' the probability for each subspace (Gleason, 1957).

Let us do a simple example. Let $\mathbf{D} = |\varphi\rangle\langle\varphi|$ and $\mathrm{P}_\psi = |\psi\rangle\langle\psi|$. Then

$$\begin{aligned}\mathrm{tr}(\mathbf{DP}_\psi) &= \mathrm{tr}(|\varphi\rangle\langle\varphi||\psi\rangle\langle\psi|) = \mathrm{tr}(|\varphi\rangle\langle\varphi \mid \psi\rangle\langle\psi|)\\ &= \langle\varphi \mid \psi\rangle\mathrm{tr}(|\varphi\rangle\langle\psi|) = \langle\varphi \mid \psi\rangle\langle\psi \mid \varphi\rangle = |\langle\varphi \mid \psi\rangle|^2,\end{aligned}$$

which by now is a familiar result showing that the probability of getting a yes answer to the question $\mathbf{P}_\psi$ when the system is in state $\mathbf{D}$ is $|\langle\varphi \mid \psi\rangle|^2$ (refer to Appendix II for more details).

Further reading

Williams (2001), apart from being an excellent book on probability theory, contains a comprehensive chapter on quantum probability. For the real enthusiast we recommend Pitowsky (1989), which describes and explains many results in quantum probability in great detail and makes appropriate connections with quantum logic.

Bibliography

Accardi, L. and A. Fedullo (1982). 'On the statistical meaning of complex numbers in quantum mechanics.' *Lettere al nuovo cimento* **34**(7): 161–172. Gives a technical acount of the necessity for using complex rather than real Hilbert spaces in quantum mechanics. There is no equivalent argument for IR (yet).

Aerts, D. (1999). 'Foundations of quantum physics: a general realistic and operational approach.' *International Journal of Theoretical Physics* **38**(1): 289–358. This is a careful statement of the basic concepts of quantum mechanics. Most of it is done from first principles and the paper is almost self-contained. The foundations are presented from an operational point of view.

Aerts, D., T. Durt, A. A. Grib, B. van Bogaert and R. R. Zupatrin (1993). 'Quantum structures in macroscopic reality.' *International Journal of Theoretical Physics* **32**(3): 489–498. They construct an artificial, macroscopic device that has quantum properties. The corresponding lattic is non-Boolean. This example may help in grasping non-Boolean lattices in the abstract.

Albert, D. Z. (1994). *Quantum Mechanics and Experience*, Harvard University Press. This is one of the best elementary introductions to quantum mechanics, written with precision and very clear. The examples are very good and presented with considerable flair. It uses the Dirac notation and thus provides a good entry point for that too, although the mathematical basis for it is never explained.

Albert, D. and B. Loewer (1988). 'Interpreting the many worlds interpretation.' *Synthese* **77**: 195–213. The many worlds interpretation is worth considering as a possible model for interpreting the geometry of information retrieval. Albert and Loewer give a clear and concise introduction to the many world approach as pioneered by Everett (DeWitt and Graham, 1973).

Amari, S.-i. and H. Nagaoka (2000). *Methods of Information Geometry*, Oxford University Press. This one is not for the faint hearted. It covers the connection between geometric structures and probability distribution, but in a very abstract way. Chapter 7 gives an account of 'information geometry' for quantum systems. It defines a divergence measure for quantum systems equivalent to the Kullback divergence. For those interested in quantum information this may prove of interest.

Amati, G. and C. J. van Rijsbergen (1998). 'Semantic information retrieval.' In *Information Retrieval: Uncertainty and Logics*, F. Crestani, M. Lalmas and

C. J. van Rijsbergen (eds.). Kluwer, pp. 189–219. Contains a useful discussion on various formal notions of information content.

Arveson, W. (2000). *A short course on spectral theory*. Springer Verlag. Alternative to Halmos (1951). A fairly dense treatment.

Auletta, G. (2000). *Foundations and Interpretation of Quantum Mechanics; in the Light of a Critical-Historical Analysis of the Problem and of a Synthesis of the Results*. World Scientific. This book is encyclopedic in scope. It is huge – 981 pages long and contains a large bibliography with a rough guide as to where each entry is relevant, and the book is well indexed. One can find a discussion of almost any aspect of the interpretation of QM. The mathematics is generally given in its full glory. An excellent source reference. The classics are well cited.

Auyang, S. Y. (1995). *How is Quantum Field Theory Possible?* Oxford University Press. Here one will find a simple and clear introduction to the basics of quantum mechanics. The mathematics is kept to a minimum.

Bacciagaluppi, G. (1993). 'Critique of Putnam's quantum logic.' *International Journal of Theoretical Physics* **32**(10): 1835–1846. Relevant to Putnam (1975).

Baeza-Yates, R. and B. Ribeiro-Neto (1999). *Modern Information Retrieval*, Addison Wesley. A solid introduction to information retrieval emphasising the computational aspects. Contains an interesting and substantial chapter on modelling. Contains a bibliography of 852 references, also has a useful glossary.

Baggott, J. (1997). *The Meaning of Quantum Theory*, Oxford University Press. Fairly leisurely introduction to quantum mechanics. Uses physical intuition to motivate the Hilbert space mathematics. Nice examples from physics, and a good section on the Bohr–Einstein debate in terms of their thought experiment 'the photon box experiment'. It nicely avoids mathematical complications.

Barrett, J. A. (1999). *The Quantum Mechanics of Minds and Worlds*, Oxford University Press. This book is for the philosophically minded. It concentrates on an elaboration of the many-worlds interpretation invented by Everett, and first presented in his doctoral dissertation in 1957.

Barwise, J. and J. Seligman (1997). *Information Flow: The Logic of Distributed Systems*, Cambridge University Press. Barwise has been responsible for a number of interesting developments in logic. In particular, starting with the early work of Dretske, he developed together with Perry an approach to situation theory based on notions of information, channels and information flow. What is interesting about this book is that in the last chapter of the book, it relates their work to quantum logic. For this it used the theory of manuals developed for quantum logic, which is itself explained in detail in Cohen (1989).

Belew, R. (2000). *Finding Out About: a Cognitive Perspective on Search Engine Technology and the WWW*. Cambridge University Press. Currently one of the best textbooks on IR in print. It does not shy away from using mathematics. It contains a good section introducing the vector space model pioneered by Salton (1968) which is useful material as background to the Hilbert space approach adopted in GIR. The chapter on mathematical foundations will also come in handy and is a useful reference for many of the mathematical techniques used in IR. There is a CD insert on which one will find, among other useful things, a complete electronic version of Van Rijsbergen (1979a).

Bell, J. S. (1993). *Speakable and Unspeakable in Quantum Mechanics*, Cambridge University Press. A collection of previously published papers by the famous Bell, responsible for the Bell inequalities. Several papers deal with hidden variable theories. Of course it was Bell who spotted a mistake in Von Neumann's original proof that there was no hidden-variable theory for quantum mechanics. It contains a critique of Everett's many-worlds interpretation of quantum mechanics. It also contains 'Beables for quantum field theory'.

Beltrametti, E. G. and G. Cassinelli (1977). 'On state transformation induced by yes–no experiments, in the context of quantum logic.' *Journal of Philosophical Logic* **6**: 369–379. The nature of the conditional in logic as presented by Stalnaker and Hardegree can be shown to play a special role in quantum logic. Here we have a discussion of how YES–NO experiments can be useful in giving meaning to such a conditional.

— (1981). *The Logic of Quantum Mechanics*. Addison-Wesley Publishing Company. This is a seminal book, a source book for many authors writing on logic and probability theory in quantum mechanics. Most of the mathematical results are derived from first principles. Chapter 9 is a good summary of the Hilbert space formulation which serves as an introduction to Part II: one of the best introductions to the mathematical structures for quantum logics. It is well written. Chapter 20 is a very good brief introduction to quantum logic.

Beltrametti, E. G. and B. C. van Fraassen, eds. (1981). *Current Issues in Quantum Logic*. Plenum Press. This volume collects together a number of papers by influential thinkers on quantum logic. Many of the papers are written as if from first principles. It constitutes an excellent companion volume to Beltrametti and Cassinelli (1981) and Van Fraassen (1991). Many of the authors cited in this bibliography have a paper in this volume, for example, Aerts, Bub, Hardegree, Hughes and Mittelstaedt. A good place to start one's reading on quantum logic.

Bigelow, J. C. (1976). 'Possible worlds foundations for probability.' *Journal of Philosophical Logic* **5**: 299–320. Based on the notion of similarity heavily used by David Lewis to define a semantics for counterfactuals; Bigelow uses it to define probability. This is good background reading for Van Rijsbergen (1986).

— (1977). 'Semantics of probability.' *Synthese* **36**: 459–472. A useful follow-on paper to Bigelow (1976).

Birkhoff, G. and S. MacLane (1957). *A Survey of Modern Algebra*. The Macmillan Company. One of the classic textbooks on algebra by two famous and first rate mathematicians. This is the Birkhoff that collaborated with John von Neumann on the logic of quantum mechanics and in 1936 published one of the first papers ever on the subject. Most elementary results in linear algebra can be found in the text. There is a nice chapter on the algebra of classes which also introduces partial orderings and lattices.

Birkhoff, G. and J. von Neumann (1936). 'The logic of quantum mechanics.' *Annals of Mathematics* **37**: 823–843. Reprinted in Hooker (1975), this is where it all started! 'The object of the present paper is to discover what logical structure one may hope to find in physical theories which, like quantum mechanics, do not conform to classical logic. Our main conclusion, based on admittedly heuristic arguments, is that one can reasonable expect to find a calculus of propositions which is formally indistinguishable from the calculus of linear subspaces with respect to set products, linear sums, and orthogonal complements – and resembles the usual calculus of propositions with respect to and, or, and not.' Ever since this seminal work there has been a steady output of papers and ideas on how to make sense of it.

Blair, D. C. (1990). *Language and Representation in Information Retrieval.* Elsevier. A thoughtful book on the philosophical foundations of IR, it contains elegant descriptions of some of the early formal models for IR. Enjoyable to read.

Blum, K. (1981). 'Density matrix theory and applications.' In *Physics of Atoms and Molecules*, P. G. Burke (ed.) Plenum Press, pp. 1–62. It is difficult to find an elementary introduction to density matrices. This is one, although it is mixed up with applications to atomic physics. Nevertheless Chapter 2, which is on general density matrix theory, is a good self-contained introduction which uses the Dirac notation throughout.

Borland, P. (2000). *Evaluation of Interactive Information Retrieval Systems.* Abo Akademi University. Here one will find a methodology for the evaluation of IR systems that goes beyond the now standard 'Cranfield paradigm'. There is a good discussion of the concept of relevance and the book concentrates on retrieval as an interactive process. The framework presented in GIR should be able to present and formalise such a process.

Bouwmeester, D., A. Ekert and A. Zeiliager, eds. (2001). *The Physics of Quantum Information*, Springer-Verlag. Although not about quantum computation per se, there are some interesting connections to be made. This collection of papers covers quantum cryptography, teleportation and computation. The editors are experts in their field and have gone to some trouble to make the material accessible to the non-expert.

Bruza, P. D. (1993). *Stratified Information Disclosure: a Synthesis between Hypermedia and Information Retrieval.* Katholieke University Nijmegen. A good example of the use of non-standard logic in information retrieval.

Bub, J. (1977). 'Von Neumann's projection postulate as a probability conditionalization rule in quantum mechanics.' *Journal of Philosophical Logic* **6**: 381–390. The title says it all. The Von Neumann projection postulate has been a matter of debate ever since he formulated it; it was generalised by Lüders in 1951. Bub gives a nice introduction to it in this paper. The interpretation as a conditionalisation rule is important since it may be a useful way of interpreting the postulate in IR. Van Fraassen (1991, p. 175) relates it to *Jeffrey* conditionalisation (Jeffrey,1983).

— (1982). 'Quantum logic, conditional probability, and interference.' *Philosophy of Science* **49**: 402–421. Good commentary on Friedman and Putnam (1978).

— (1997). *Interpreting the Quantum World*, Cambridge University Press. Bub has been publishing on the interpretation of quantum mechanics for many years. One of his major interests has been the projection postulates, and their interpretation as a collapse of the wave function. The first two chapters of the book are well worth reading, introducing many of the main concepts in QM. The mathematical appendix is an excellent introduction to Hilbert space machinery.

Busch, P., M. Grabowski and P. J. Lanti (1997). *Operational Quantum Physics*, Springer-Verlag. There is a way of presenting quantum theory from the point of view of positive operator valued measures, which is precisely what this book does in great detail.

Butterfield, J. and J. Melia (1993). 'A Galois connection approach to superposition and inaccessibility.' *International Journal of Theoretical Physics* **32**(12): 2305–2321. In Chapter 2 on inverted files and natural kinds, we make use of a Galois connection. In this paper quantum logic is discussed in terms of a Galois connection. A fairly technical paper, most proofs are omitted.

Campbell, I. and C. J. van Rijsbergen (1996). *The Ostensive Model of Developing Information Needs.* CoLIS 2, Second International Conference on Conceptions of Library and Information Science: Integration in Perspective, Copenhagen, The Royal School of Librarianship. A description of an IR model to which the theory presented in GIR will be applied. It is the companion paper to Van Rijsbergen (1996).

Carnap, R. (1977). *Two Essays on Entropy*, University of California Press. For many years these essays remained unpublished. An introduction by Abner Shimony explains why. Carnap's view on the nature of information diverged significantly from that of Von Neumann's. John Von Neumann maintained that there was one single physical concept of information, whereas Carnap, in line with his view of probability, thought this was not adequate. Perhaps these essays should be read in conjunction with Cox (1961) and Jaynes (2003).

Cartwright, N. (1999). *How the Laws of Physics Lie*, Clarendon Press. Essay 9 of this book contains a good introduction to what has become known in QM as 'The Measurement Problem': the paradox of the time evolution of the wave function versus the collapse of the wave function. A clear and elementary account.

Casti, J. L. (2000). *Five More Golden Rules: Knots, Codes, Chaos, and Other Great Theories of Twentieth Century Mathematics.* Wiley. Contains a semi-popular introduction to functional analysis. The section on quantum mechanics is especially worth reading.

Cohen, D. W. (1989). *An Introduction to Hilbert Space and Quantum Logic*, Springer-Verlag. Good introduction to quantum logics, explaining the necessary Hilbert space as needed. It gives a useful proof of Gleason's Theorem, well actually almost, as it leaves it to be proved as a number of guided projects. Here the reader will also find a good introduction to 'manuals' with nice illustrative examples. Note in particular the 'firefly in a box' example.

Cohen-Tannoudji, C., B. Diu and F. Laloë (1977). *Quantum Mechanics.* Wiley. A standard and popular textbook on QM. It is one of the few that has a comprehensive section on density operators.

Collatz, L. (1966). *Functional Analysis and Numerical Mathematics*, Academic Press. Contrary to what the title may lead one to believe, almost half of this book is devoted to a very clear, self-contained, introduction to functional analysis. For example, it is has a thorough introduction to operators in Hilbert space.

Colodny, R. G., ed. (1972). *Paradigms and Paradoxes. The Philosophical Challenge of the Quantum Domain*, University of Pittsburgh Press. The lion's share of this book is devoted to a lengthy paper by C. A. Hooker on quantum reality. However, the papers by Arthur Fine and David Finkelstein on conceptual issues to do with probability and logic in QM are well worth reading.

Cooke, R., M. Keane and W. Moran (1985). 'An Elementary Proof of Gleason's Theorem.' *Mathematical Proceedings of the Cambridge Philosophical Society* **98**: 117–128. Gleason's Theorem is central to the mathematical approach in GIR.

Gleason published his important result in 1957. The proof was quite difficult and eventually an elementary proof was given by Cooke *et al.* in 1985. Hughes (1989) has annotated the proof in an Appendix to his book. Richman and Bridges (1999) give a constructive prooof. The theorem is of great importance in QM and hence is derived in a number of standard texts on quantum theory, for example Varadarajan (1985), Parthasarathy (1992) and Jordan (1969).

Cox, R. T. (1961). *The Algebra of Probable Inference.* The Johns Hopkins Press. This is a much cited and quoted book on the foundations of probability. For example, in his recent book on Probability Theory, Jaynes (2003) quotes results from Cox. The book has sections on probability, entropy and expectation. It was much influenced by Keynes' *A Treatise on Probability* (1929), another good read.

Crestani, F., M. Lalmas and C. J. van Rijsbergen, eds. (1998). *Information Retrieval: Uncertainty and Logics: Advanced Models for the Representation and Retrieval of Information.* Kluwer. After the publication of Van Rijsbergen (1986), which is reprinted here, a number of researchers took up the challenge to define and develop appropriate logics for information retrieval. Here we have a number of research papers showing the progress that was made in this field, that is now often called the 'Logical model for IR'. The papers trace developments from around 1986 to roughly 1998. The use of the Stalnaker conditional (Stalnaker, 1970) for IR was first proposed in the 1986 paper discussed in some detail in Chapter 5 in GIR.

Crestani, F. and C. J. van Rijsbergen (1995). 'Information retrieval by logical imaging.' *Journal of Documentation* **51**: 1–15. A detailed account of how to use imaging (Lewis, 1976) in IR.

Croft, W. B. (1978). *Organizing and Searching Large Files of Document Descriptions. Cambridge, Computer Laboratory*, Cambridge University. A detailed evaluation of document clustering based on the single link hierarchical classification method.

Croft, W. B. and J. Lafferty, eds. (2003). *Language Modeling for Information Retrieval.* Kluwer. The first book on language modelling. It contains excellent introductory papers by Lafferty and Xhia, as well as by Lavrenk and Croft.

Dalla Chiara, M. L. (1986). 'Quantum logic.' In *Handbook of Philosophical Logic*, D. Gabbay and F. Guenthner (eds.). Reidel Publishing Company III, pp. 427–469. A useful summary of quantum logic given by a logician.

— (1993). 'Empirical Logics.' *International Journal of Theoretical Physics* **32**(10): 1735–1746. A logician looks at quantum logics. The result is a fairly sceptical view not too dissimilar from Gibbins (1987).

Davey, B. A. and H. A. Priestley (1990). *Introduction to Lattices and Order*, Cambridge University Press. Here you will find all you will ever need to know about lattices. The final chapter on formal concept analysis introduces the Galois Connection.

De Broglie, L. (1960). *Non-Linear Wave Mechanics. A Causal Interpretation*, Elsevier Publishing Company. A classic book. Mainly of historical interest now. De Broglie is credited with being the first to work out the implications of $l = h/mv$ (page 6), the now famous connection between wavelength and momentum, h is Planck's constant.

De Finetti, B. (1974). *Theory of Probability.* Wiley. A masterpiece by the master of the subjectivist school of probability. Even though it has been written from the point of view of a subjectivist, it is a rigorous complete account of the basics of probability theory. He discusses fundamental notions like independence in great depth. The book has considerable philosophical depth; De Finetti does not shy away from defending his point of view at length, but since it is done from a deep knowledge of the subject, following the argument is always rewarding.

Debnath, L. and P. Mikusinski (1999). *Introduction to Hilbert spaces with Applications*, Academic Press. A standard textbook on Hilbert spaces. Many of the important results are presented and proved here. It treats QM as one of a number of applications.

Deerwester, S., S. T. Dumais, G. F. W. Furnas, T. K. Landauer and R. Harsman (1990). 'Indexing by Latent Semantic Analysis.' *Journal of the American Society for Information Science* **4**: 391–407. This is one of the earliest papers on latent semantic indexing. Despite many papers on the subject since the publication of this one, it is still worth reading. It presents the basics ideas in a simple and clear way. It is still frequently cited.

D'Espagnat, B. (1976). *Conceptual Foundations of Quantum Mechanics*, W. A. Benjamin, Inc. Advanced Book Program. This must be one of the very first books on the conceptual foundations of QM. It takes the approach that a state vector represents an ensemble of identically prepared quantum systems. It gives a very complete account of the density matrix formalism in Chapter 6, but beware of some trivial typos. It is outstanding for its ability to express and explain in words all the important fundamental concepts in QM. It also gives accurate mathematical explanations. This book is worth studying in detail.

— (1990). *Reality and the Physicist. Knowledge, Duration and the Quantum World*, Cambridge University Press. This is a more philosophical and leisurely treatment of some of the material covered in d'Estaganat (1976).

Deutsch, D. (1997). *The Fabric of Reality*, Allen Lane. The Penguin Press. This is a very personal account of the importance of quantum theory for philosophy and computation. David Deutsch was one of the early scientists to lay the foundations for quantum computation. His early papers sparked much research and debate about the nature of computation. This book is written entirely without recourse to rigorous mathematical argument. It contains copious references to Turing's ideas on computability.

Deutsch, F. (2001). *Best Approximation in Inner Product Spaces*, Springer. Inner products play an important role in the development of quantum theory. Here one will find inner products discussed in all their generality. Many other algebraic results with a geometric flavour are presented here.

DeWitt, B. S. and N. Graham, eds. (1973). *The Many-Worlds Interpretation of Quantum Mechanics*. Princeton Series in Physics, Princeton University Press. Here are collected together a number of papers about the many-worlds interpretation, including a copy of Everett's original dissertation on the subject, entitled, 'The Theory of the Universal Wave Function'. This latter paper is relatively easy to read. It makes frequent use of statistical information theory in a way not unknown to information retrievalists.

Dirac, P. A. M. (1958). *The Principles of Quantum Mechanics*, Oxford University Press. One of the great books of quantum mechanics. The first one hundred pages are still worth reading as an introduction to QM. Dirac motivates the introduction of the mathematics. In particular he defends the use of the Dirac notation. He takes as one of his guiding principles the superposition of states, and takes some time to defend his reason. This book is still full of insights, well worth spending time on.

— (1978). 'The mathematical foundations of quantum theory.' In *The Mathematical Foundations of Quantum Theory*. A. R. Marlow (ed.). Academic Press: 1–8. This paper is by way of a preface to the edited volume by Marlow. It contains a late statement of the master's personal philosophy concerning foundational research. The quote: 'Any physical or philosophical ideas that one has must be adjusted to fit the mathematics.' is taken from this paper.

Dominich, S. (2001). *Mathematical Foundations of Information Retrieval*, Kluwer Academic Publishers. A very mathematical approach to information retrieval.

Dowty, D., R. Wall and S. Peters (1981). *Introduction to Montague Semantics*. Reidel. Still one of the best introductions to Montague Semantics. Is is extremely well written. If one wishes to read Montague's original writings this is a good place to start.

Einstein, A., B. Podolsky and N. Rosen (1935). Can quantum mechanical descriptions of physical reality be considered complete? *Physical Review* **47**: 777–780

Engesser, K. and D. M. Gabbay (2002). 'Quantum Logic, Hilbert Space, Revision Theory.' *Artificial Intelligence* **136**: 61–100. This is a look at quantum logic by logicians with a background in computer science. It has a little to say about probability measures on the subspaces of a Hilbert space.

Fairthorne, R. A. (1958). 'Automatic Retrieval of Recorded Information.' *The Computer Journal* **1**: 36–41. Fairthorne's paper, reprinted in Fairthorne (1961), is now mainly of historical interest. The opening section of the paper throws some light on the history of IR; Vannevar Bush is usually cited as the source of many of the early ideas in IR, but Fairthorne gives details about much earlier original work.

— (1961). *Towards Information Retrieval*, Butterworths. One of the very first books on information retrieval, it is of particular interest because Fairthorne was an early proponent of the use of Brouwerian logics in IR. A useful summary of this approach is given in Salton (1968).

Fano, G. (1971). *Mathematical Methods of Quantum Mechanics*, McGraw-Hill Book Company. A fine introduction to the requisite mathematics for QM. It is clearly geared to QM although the illustrations are mostly independent of QM. It contains a useful explanation of the Dirac notation (section 2.5). Its section (5.8) on the spectral decomposition of a self-adjoint operator is important and worth reading in detail.

Feller, W. (1957). *An Introduction to Probability Theory and Its Applications*. One of the classic mathematical introductions to probability theory.

Feynman, R. P. (1987). 'Negative probability.' In *Quantum Implications*, B. J. Hiley and F. D. Peat (eds.) Routledge & Kegan Paul, pp. 235–248. This paper is of interest because it represents an example of using a 'non-standard' model for probability theory, to be compared with using complex numbers instead of real numbers. It illustrates how intermediate steps in analysis may fail to have simple naïve interpretations.

Feynman, R. P., R. B. Leiguton and M. Sands (1965). *The Feynman Lectures on physics*, vol. III, Addison-Wesley.

Finch, P. D. (1975). 'On the structure of quantum logic.' In *The Logico-Algebraic Approach to Quantum Mechanics*, Vol I., C. A. Hooker (ed.) pp. 415–425. An account of quantum logic without using the usual physical motivation.

Fine, A. (1996). *The Shaky Game. Einstein Realism and the Quantum Theory*, The University of Chicago Press. Einstein never believed in the completeness of quantum mechanics. He did not accept that probability had an irreducible role in fundamental physics. He famously coined the sentence 'God does not play dice'. Here we have an elaboration of Einstein's position. This book should be seen as a contribution to the philosophy and history of QM.

Finkbeiner, D. T. (1960). *Matrices and Linear Transformations*, W. H. Freeman and Company. A standard textbook on linear algebra. It is comparable to Halmos (1958), and it covers similar material. It uses a postfix notation for operator application which can be awkward. Nevertheless it is clearly written, even though with less flair than Halmos. It contains numerous good examples and exercises.

Fisher, R. A. (1922). *On the Dominance Ratio.* Royal Society of Edinburgh. This paper is referred to by Wootters (1980a). The claim is that it is one of the first papers to describe a link between probability and geometry for vector spaces. It is not easy to establish that. The reference is included for the sake of completeness.

Frakes, W. B. and R. Baeza-Yates, eds. (1992). *Information Retrieval – Data Structures & Algorithms*, Prentice Hall. A good collection of IR papers covering topics such as file structures, NLP algorithms, ranking and clustering algorithms. Good source for technical details of well-known algorithms.

Friedman, A. (1982). *Foundations of Modern Analysis*, Dover Publications, Inc. The first chapter contains a good introduction to measure theory.

Friedman, M. and H. Putnam (1978). 'Quantum logic, conditional probability, and interference.' *Dialectica* **32**(3–4): 305–315. The authors wrote this now influential paper, claiming 'The quantum logical interpretation of quantum mechanics gives an explanation of interference that the Copenhagen interpretation cannot supply.' It all began with Putnam's original 1968 'Is logic empirical?', subsequently updated and published as Putnam (1975). It has been a good source for debate ever since, for example, Gibbins (1981) Putnam (1981) and Bacciagaluppi (1993), to name but a few papers.

Ganter, B. and R. Wille (1999). *Formal Concept Analysis – Mathematical Foundations*, Springer-Verlag. This is a useful reference for the material in Chapter 2 of this book.

Garden, R. W. (1984). *Modern Logic and Quantum Mechanics*, Adam Hilger Ltd., Bristol. One could do a lot worse than start with this as a first attempt at understanding the role of logic in classical and quantum mechanics. Logic is first used in classical mechanics, which motivates its use in quantum mechanics. The pace is very gentle. The book finishes with Von Neumann's quantum logic as first outlined in the paper by Birkhoff and Von Neumann (1936).

Gibbins, P. (1981). 'Putnam on the Two-Slit Experiment.' *Erkenntnis* **16**: 235–241. A critique of Putnam's 1969 paper (Putnam, 1975).

— (1987). *Particles and Paradoxes: the Limits of Quantum Logic*, Cambridge University Press. An outstanding informal introduction to the philosophy and interpretations of QM. It has a unusual Chapter 9, which gives a natural deduction formulation of quantum logic. Gibbins is quite critical of the work on quantum logic and in the final chapter he summarises some of his criticisms.

Gillespie, D. T. (1976). *A Quantum Mechanics Primer. An Elementary Introduction to the Formal Theory of Non-relativistic Quantum Mechanics*, International Textbook Co. Ltd. A modest introduction to QM. Avoids the use of Dirac notation. It was an Open University Set Book and is clearly written.

Gleason, A. M. (1957). 'Measures on the closed subspaces of a Hilbert space.' *Journal of Mathematics and Mechanics* **6**: 885–893. This is the original Gleason paper containing the theorem frequently referred to in GIR. Simpler versions are to found in Cooke *et al.* (1985), and Hughes (1989).

— (1975). 'Measures of the closed subspaces of a Hilbert space.' In *The Logico-Algebraic Approach to Quantum Mechanics*, C. A. Hooker (ed.) pp. 123–133. This is a reprint of Gleason's original paper published in 1957.

Goffman, W. (1964). 'On relevance as a measure.' *Infomation Storage and Retrieval* **2**: 201–203. Goffman was one of the early dissenters from the standard view of the concept of relevance.

Goldblatt, R. (1993). *Mathematics of Modality*, CSLI Publications. The material on orthologic and orthomodular structures is relevant. The treatment is dense and really aimed at logicians.

Golub, G. H. and C. F. van Loan (1996). *Matrix Computations*, The Johns Hopkins University Press. A standard textbook on matrix computation.

Good, I. J. (1950). *Probability and the weighing of evidence*. Charles Griffin & Company Limited. Mainly of historical interest now, but contains a short classification of theories of probability.

Greechie, R. J. and S. P. Gudder (1973). 'Quantum logics.' In *Contemporary Research in the Foundations and Philosophy of Quantum Theory*, C. A. Hooker (ed.), D. Reidel Publishing Company, pp. 143–173. A wonderfully clear account of the mathematical tools neeeded for the study of axiomatic quantum mechanics.

Greenstein, G. and A. G. Zajonc (1997). *The Quantum Challenge. Modern Research on the Foundations of Quantum Mechanics*, Jones and Bartlett. A relatively short and thorough introduction to QM. The emphasis is on conceptual issues, mathematics is kept to a minimum. Examples are taken from physics.

Gribbin, J. (2002). *Q is for Quantum: Particle Physics from A to Z*. Phoenix Press. A popular glossary for particle physics, but contains a large number of entries for QM.

Griffiths, R. B. (2002). *Consistent Quantum Theory*, Cambridge University Press. A superb modern introduction to quantum theory. The important mathematics is introduced very clearly. Toy examples are used to avoid complexities. It contains a thorough treatment of histories in QM, which although not used in this book, could easily be adapted for IR purposes. Tensor products are explained. Some the paradoxical issues in logic for QM are addressed. This is possibly one of the best modern introductions to QM for those interested in applying it outside physics.

Grover, L. K. (1997). 'Quantum mechanics helps in searching for a needle in a haystack.' *Physical Review Letters* **79**(2): 325–328. The famous paper on 'finding a needle in a haystack' by using quantum computation and thereby speeding up the search compared with what is achievable on a computer with a Von Neumann architecture.

Gruska, J. (1999). *Quantum Computing*, McGraw Hill. For the sake of completeness a number of books on quantum computation are included. This is one of them. It contains a brief introduction to the fundamentals of Hilbert space; useful for someone in a hurry to grasp the gist of it.

Halmos, P. R. (1950). *Measure Theory*. Van Nostrand Reinhold Company. A classic introduction to the subject. It is written with the usual Halmos upbeat style. It has an excellent chapter on probability from the point of view of measure theory.

— (1951). *Introduction to Hilbert Space and the Theory of Spectral Multiplicity*, Chelsea Publishing Company. This is a very lively introduction to Hilbert space and explains the details behind spectral measures. This book should be read and consulted in conjunction with Halmos (1958). Even though it is very high powered it is written in an easy style, and it should be compared with Arveson (2002) and Retherford (1993); both these are more recent introductions to spectral theory.

— (1958). *Finite-Dimensional Vector Spaces*, D. van Nostrand Company, Inc. This is one of the best books on finite-dimensional vector spaces, even though it was published so many years ago. It is written in a deceptively simple and colloquial style. It is nicely divided into 'bite size' chunks and probably you will learn more than you ever would want to know about vector spaces. It is also a good introduction to Halmos's much more sophisticated and harder book on Hilbert spaces.

— (1963). *Lectures on Boolean Algebra*. D. Van Nostrand Company. All you might ever want to know about Boolean Algebra can be found here. Contains a proof of the Stone Representation Theorem.

Halpin, J. F. (1991). 'What is the logical form of probability assignment in quantum mechanics?' *Philosophy of Science* **58**: 36–60. Looks at a number of proposals taking into account the work of Stalnaker and Lewis on counterfactuals.

Hardegree, G. M. (1975). 'Stalnaker conditionals and quantum logic.' *Journal of Philosophical Logic* **4**: 399–421. The papers by Hardegree are useful reading as background to Chapter 5.

— (1976). 'The conditional in quantum logic.' In *Logic and Probability in Quantum Mechanics*, P. Suppes (ed.), D. Reidel Publishing Company, pp. 55–72. The material in this paper is drawn on significantly for Chapter 5 on conditonal logic for IR.

— (1979). 'The conditional in abstract and concrete quantum logic.' In *Logico-Algebraic Approach to Quantum Mechanics*. II. C. A. Hooker (ed.), D. Reidel Publishing Company, pp. 49–108. This is a much more extensive paper than Hardegree (1976). It deals with a taxonomy of quantum logics. The emphasis is still on the conditional.

— (1982). 'An approach to the logic of natural kinds.' *Pacific Philosophical Quarterly* **63**: 122–132. This paper is relevant to Chapter 2, and would make good background reading.

Harman, D. (1992). Ranking algorithms. In *Information Retrieval – Data Structures, and Algorithms*, Frakes, W. B. and R. Baeza-Yates (eds.), Prentice Hall, pp. 363–392.

Harper, W. L., R. Stalnaker and G. Peare eds. (1981). *Ifs*. Reidel. This contains reprints of a number of influential papers on counterfactual reasoning and conditionals. In particular it contains important classic papers by Stalnaker and Lewis.

Hartle, J. B. (1968). 'Quantum mechanics of individual systems.' *American Journal of Physics* **36**(8): 704–712. A paper on an old debate: does it make sense to make probabilistic assertions about individual systems, or should we stick to only making assertions about ensembles?

Healey, R. (1990). *The Philosophy of Quantum Mechanics. An Interactive Interpretation*, Cambridge University Press. Despite its title this is quite a technical book. The idea of interaction is put centre stage and is to be compared with the approach by Kochen and Specker (1965a).

Hearst, M. A. and J. O. Pedersen (1996). 'Re-examining the cluster hypothesis: scatter/gather on retrieval results.' *Proceedings of the 19th Annual ACM SIGIR Conference*. pp. 76–84. Another test of the cluster hypothesis.

Heelan, P. (1970a). 'Quantum and classical logic: their respective roles.' *Synthese* **21**: 2–23. An attempt to clear up some of the confused thinking about quantum logics.

Heelan, P. (1970b). 'Complementarity, context dependence, and quantum logic.' *Foundations of Physics* **1**(2): 95–110. Mainly interesting because of the role that context plays in descriptions of quantum-mechanical events.

Heisenberg, W. (1949). *The Physical Principles of the Quantum Theory*, Dover Publications, Inc. By one of the pioneers of QM. It is mainly of historical interest now.

Hellman, G. (1981). 'Quantum logic and the projection postulate.' *Philosophy of Science* **48**: 469–486. Another forensic examination of the 'Projection Postulate'.

Herbut, F. (1969). 'Derivation of the change of state in measurement from the concept of minimal measurement.' *Annals of Physics* **55**: 271–300. A detailed account of how to define a simple and basic concept of physical measurement for an arbitrary observable. Draws on the research surrounding the Lüders–Von Neumann debate on the projection postulate. The paper is well written and uses sensible notation.

— (1994). 'On state-dependent implication in quantum mechanics.' *J. Phys. A: Math. Gen.* **27**: 7503–7518. This paper should be read after Chapter 5 in GIR.

Hiley, B. J. and F. D. Peat (1987). *Quantum Implications. Essays in honour of David Bohm*. Routlege & Kegan Paul. The work of David Bohm, although much respected, was controversial. He continued to work on hidden variable theories despite the so-called impossibility proofs. The contributors to this volume include famous quantum physicists, such as Bell and Feynman, and well known popularisers, such as Kilmister and Penrose. A book worth dipping into. It contains the article by Feynman on negative probability.

Hirvensalo, M. (2001). *Quantum Computing*, Springer-Verlag. A clearly written book with good appendices to quantum physics and its mathematical background.

Holland, S. P. (1970). 'The current interest in orthomodular lattices.' *Trends in Lattice Theory*, J. C. Abbott (ed.). Van Nostrand Reinhold. There are many introductions to lattice theory. What distinguishes this one is that it relates the material to subspace structures of Hilbert space and to quantum logic. The explanations are relatively complete and easy to follow.

Hooker, C. A., ed. (1975). *The Logico-Algebraic Approach to Quantum Mechanics*. Vol. 1: *Historical Evolution*. The University of Western Ontario Series in Philosophy of Science. D. Reidel Publishing Company. This is Volume 1 of a two-volume set containing a number of classic papers, for example, reprints of Birkhoff and Von Neumann (1936), Gleason (1957), Kochen and Specker (1965b) and Holland (1970).

Hooker, C. A., ed. (1979). *The Logico-Algebraic Approach to Quantum Mechanics*. Vol. 2: *Contemporary Consolidation*. The University of Western Ontario Series in Philosophy of Science. D. Reidel Publishing Company. Following the historical papers in Volume 1, this second volume contains more recent material. A useful paper is Hardegree (1979) as a companion to Hardegree (1976).

Horn, R. A. and C. R. Johnson (1999). *Matrix Analysis*, Cambridge University Press. One of several well-known, standard references on matrix theory, excellent companion for Golub and Van Loan (1996).

Hughes, R. I. G. (1982). 'The logic of experimental questions.' *Philosophy of Science* **1**: 243–256. A simple introduction to how a quantum logic arises out of giving a mathematical structure to the process of asking experimental questions of a quantum system. Chapter 5 of Jauch (1968) gives a more detailed account of this mode of description, and presents the necessary preliminary mathematics in the earlier chapters. This particular way of viewing the logic of quantum mechanics was also explained synoptically by Mackey (1963).

— (1989). *The Structure and Interpretation of Quantum Mechanics.* Harvard University Press. A lucid and well-written book. It introduces the relevant mathematics at the point where it is needed. It contains an excellent discussion of Gleason's Theorem. It has a good chapter on quantum logic. It also introduces density operators in a simple manner. Much attention is paid to the philosophical problem of 'properties'. An appendix contains an annotated version of the proof of Gleason's Theorem by Cooke *et al.* (1985).

Huibers, T. (1996). *An Axiomatic Theory for Information Retrieval.* Katholieke University Nijmegen. Presents a formal set of inference rules that are intended to capture retrieval. A proof system is specified for the rules, and used to prove theorems about 'aboutness'.

Ingwersen, P. (1992). *Information Retrieval Interaction.* Taylor Graham. This is a formulation of IR from a cognitive standpoint. In many ways it is in sympathy with the approach taken in GIR, especially in that it puts interaction with the user at the centre of the discipline. Its approach is non-mathematical.

Isham, C. J. (1989). *Lectures on Groups and Vector Spaces for Physicists.* World Scientific. A well-paced introduction to vector spaces amongst other things. It starts from first principles and introduces groups before it discusses vector spaces. Gives examples from physics and quantum mechanics. It is a good companion volume to Isham (1995).

Isham, C. J. (1995). *Lectures on Quantum Theory: Mathematical and Structural Foundations.* Imperial College Press. The two books by Isham (1989,1995) go together. This book is a fairly complete lecture course on QM. The 1989 book contains a thorough introduction to vector spaces which is needed for the book on QM. Although a technical introduction, it also contains considerable philosophical comment and is very readable. In introducing quantum theory it begins with a statement of four simple rules that define a general mathematical framework within which all quantum-mechanical systems can be described. Technical developments come after a discussion of the rules.

Jauch, J. M. (1968). *Foundations of Quantum Mechanics*, Addison-Wesley Publishing Company. Another classic monograph on QM. Jauch is a proponent of the mode of description of physical systems in terms of so-called 'yes-no experiments'. Section 3-4 on projections is extremely interesting, it shows how the operation of union and intersection of subspaces are expressed algebraically in terms of the corresponding projections. An excellent introduction, one of the best, to the foundations of QM.

— (1972). 'On bras and kets.' In *Aspects of Quantum Theory*, A. Salam and E. P. Wigner (eds.). Cambridge University Press, pp. 137–167. Exactly that!

— (1973). *Are Quanta Real? A Galilean Dialogue*. Indiana University Press. A three-way discussion written by a fine quantum physicist. Perhaps this could be read after the prologue in GIR which has been done in the same spirit. It contains a physical illustration, in terms of polarising filters, of the intrinsic probability associated with measuring a property of a single photon.

— (1976). 'The quantum probability calculus.' In *Logic and Probability in Quantum Mechanics, Suppes, P.* (ed.). D. Reidel Publishing Company, pp. 123–146. Starting with the classical probability calculus, it gives an account, from first principles, of the probability calculus in quantum mechanics.

Jaynes, E. T. (2003). *Probability Theory: The Logic of Science*. Cambridge University Press. Jaynes' *magnum opus*. He is has worked for many years on probability theory and maximum entropy. This book is the result of over sixty years of thinking about the nature of probability: it is a *tour de force*. It is one of the best modern reference works on probability. It contains a good annotated bibliography.

Jeffrey, R. C. (1983). *The Logic of Decision*. University of Chicago Press. This is the best source for a discussion of Jeffrey Conditionalisation and the role that the 'passage of experience' plays in that. The Von Neumann projection postulate can be related to this form of conditonalisation (see Van Fraassen, 1991, p. 175).

Jeffreys, H. (1961). *Theory of Probability*. Oxford University Press. One of the classic introductions to probability theory. Jeffreys is sometimes associated with the subjectivist school of probability – which is somewhat surprising since he was he was a distinguished mathematical physicist. He was an early proponent of Bayesian inference and the use of priors. The first chapter on fundamental notions is still one of the best elementary introductions to probable inference ever written.

Jordan, T. F. (1969). *Linear Operators for Quantum Mechanics*, John Wiley & Sons, Inc. There are a number of books frequently referred to in the quantum mechanics literature for the relevant background mathematics. Here we have identified three: Jordan (1969), Fano (1971) and Reed and Simon (1980). All three cover similar material, perhaps Reed and Simon is the most pure-mathematical in approach, whereas Jordan makes explicit connections with quantum mechanics.

Kägi-Romano, U. (1977). 'Quantum logic and generalized probability theory.' *Journal of Philosophical Logic* **6**: 455–462. A brief attempt to modify the classical Kolmogorov (1933) theory so that it becomes applicable to quantum mechanics.

Keynes, M. (1929). *A Treatise on Probability*. Macmillan. Keynes' approach to probability theory represents a logical approach; probability is seen as a logical relation between propositions. After Frank Ramsey's devastating critique of it, it lost favour. However, it may be that there is more to be said about Keynes' theory, especially in the light of the way quantum probability is defined. The first one hundred pages of Keynes' treatise is still a wonderful historical account of the evolution of the theory of probability – full of insights that challenge the foundations of the subject.

Kochen, S. and E. P. Specker (1965a). 'Logical structures arising in quantum theory.' In *Symposium on the Theory of Models*, eds. J. Addison, J. L. Henkin and A. Tarski. North Holland, pp. 177–189. An early account of how logical structures arise in quantum theory by two eminent theoreticians.

— (1965b). 'The calculus of partial propositional functions.' In *Logic, Methodology, and Philosophy of Science*. Y. Bar-Hillel (ed.). North-Holland, pp. 45–57. A follow-on paper to their earlier 1965 paper; in fact here they deny a conjecture made in the first paper.

Kolmogorov, A. N. (1950). *Foundations of the theory of probability*. Chelsea Publishing Co. Translation of Kolmogorov's original 1933 monograph. An approach to probability theory phrased in the language of set theory and measure theory. Kolmogorov's axiomatisation is now the basis of most current work on probability theory. For important dissenters consult Jaynes (2003).

Korfhage, R. R. (1997). *Information Storage and Retrieval*. Wiley Computer Publishing. A simple and elementary introduction to information retrieval, presented in a traditional way.

Kowalski, G. J. and M. T. Maybury (2000). *Information Retrieval Systems: Theory and Implementation*. Kluwer. 'This work provides a theoretical and practical explanation of the advancements in information retrieval and their application to existing systems. It takes a system approach, discussing all aspects of an Information Retrieval System. The major difference between this book and the first edition is the addition to this text of descriptions of the automated indexing of multimedia documents, as items in information retrieval are now considered to be a combination of text along with graphics, audio, image and video data types.' – publisher's note.

Kyburg, H. E., Jr. and C. M. Teng (2001). *Uncertain Inference*. Cambridge University Press. A comprehensive, up-to-date survey and explanation of various theories of uncertainty. Has a good discussion on the range of interpretations of probability. Also, does justice to Dempster–Shafer belief revision. Covers the work of Carnap and Popper in some detail.

Lafferty, J. and C. X. Zhia (2003). 'Probabilistic relevance models based on document and query generation.' In *Language Modeling for Information Retrieval*. W. B. Croft and J. Lafferty (eds.). Kluwer, pp. 1–10. A very clear introduction to language modeling in IR.

Lakoff, G. (1987). *Women, Fire, and Dangerous Things. What Categories Reveal about the Mind*. The University of Chicago Press. A wonderfully provocative book about the nature of classification. It also discusses the concept of natural kinds in a number of places. A real page turner.

Lavrenko, V. and W. B. Croft (2003). 'Relevance models in information retrieval.' In *Language Modeling for Information Retrieval*. W. B. Croft and J. Lafferty (eds.). Kluwer. Describes how relevance can be brought into language models. Also, draws parallels between language models and other forms of plausible inference in IR.

Lewis, D. (1973). *Counterfactuals*. Basil Blackwell. Classic reference on the possible world semantics for counterfactuals.

— (1976). 'Probabilities of conditionals and conditional probabilities.' *Philosophy of Science* **85**: 297–315. Lewis shows here how the Stalnaker Hypothesis is subject to a number of triviality results. He also defines a process known as *imaging* that was used in Crestani and Van Rijsbergen (1995a) to evaluate the probability of conditonals in IR.

Lo, H.-K., S. Popescu and T. Spiller, eds. (1998). *Introduction to Quantum Computation and Information.* World Scientific Publishing. A collection of semi-popular papers on quantum computation. Mathematics is kept to a minimum.

Lock, P. F. and G. M. Hardegree (1984). 'Connections among quantum logics. Part 1. Quantum propositional logics.' *International Journal of Theoretical Physics* **24**(1): 43–61. The work of Hardegree is extensively used in Chapter 5 of GIR.

Lockwood, M. (1991). *Mind, Brain and the Quantum. The Compound 'I'.* Blackwell Publishers. This book is concerned with QM and consciousness. It is almost entirely philosophical and uses almost no mathematics. It should probably be read at the same time as Penrose (1989, 1994).

Lomonaco, S. J., Jr., ed. (2002). *Quantum Computation: A Grand Mathematical Challenge for the Twenty-First Century and the Millennium.* Proceedings of Symposia in Applied Mathematics. Providence, Rhode Island, American Mathematical Society. The first lecture by Lomonaco, 'A Rosetta stone for quantum mechanics with an introduction to quantum computation', is one of the best introductions this author has seen. It accomplishes in a mere 65 pages what most authors would need an entire book for. The material is presented with tremendous authority. A good collection of references.

London, F. and E. Bauer (1982). 'The theory of observation in quantum mechanics.' In *Quantum Theory and Measurement.* J. A. Wheeler and W. H. Zurek (eds.) Princeton University Press, pp. 217–259. The authors claim this to be a 'treatment both concise and simple' as an introduction to the problem of measurement in quantum mechanics. They have taken their cue from Von Neumann's original 1932 foundations and tried to make his deep discussions more accessible. They have succeeded. The original version was first published in 1939 in French.

Lüders, G. (1951). 'Über die Zustandsänderung durch den Messprozess.' *Annalen der Physik* **8**: 323–328. The original paper by Lüders that sparked the debate about the Projection Postulate.

Mackay, D. (1950). 'Quantal aspects of scientific information', *Philosophical Magazine*, **41**, 289–311.

— (1969). *Information, Mechanism and Meaning*, MIT Press.

Mackey, G. W. (1963). *Mathematical Foundations of Quantum Mechanics.* Benjamin. One of the early well known mathematical introductions, it is much cited. He introduced the suggestive terminology 'question-valued measure'.

Marciszewski, W., ed. (1981). *Dictionary of Logic – as Applied in the Study of Language.* Nijhoff International Philosophy Series, Martinus Nijhoff Publishers. This dictionary contains everything that you have always wanted to know about logic (but were ashamed to ask). It contains entries for the most trivial up to the most sophisticated. Everything is well explained and references are given for further reading.

Maron, M. E. (1965). 'Mechanized documentation: The logic behind a probabilistic interpretation.' In *Statistical Association Methods for Mechanized Documentation.* M. E. Stevens *et al.*, (eds.) National Bureau of Standards Report **269**: 9–13. 'The purpose of this paper is to look at the problem of document identification and retrieval from a logical point of view and to show why the problem must be interpreted by means of probability concepts.' This quote from Maron could easily be taken as a part summary of the approach adopted in GIR. Maron was one of the very first to start thinking along these lines, less surprising if one considers that Maron's Ph.D. dissertation, 'The meaning of the probability concept', was supervised by Hans Reichenbach, one of early contributors to the foundations of QM.

Martinez, S. (1991). 'Lüders's rule as a description of individual state transformations.' *Philosophy of Science* **58**: 359–376. Lüders paper on the projection postulate generalising Von Neumann's rule has played a critical role in quantum theory. A number of papers have examined it in detail. Here is one such paper.

Mirsky, L. (1990). *An Introduction to Linear Algebra.* Dover Publications, Inc. A traditional introduction emphasising matrix representation for linear operators. It contains a nice chapter on orthogonal and unitary matrices, an important class of matrices in QM. This material is used in Chapter 6 to explain relevance feedback.

Mittelstaedt, P. (1972). 'On the interpretation of the lattice of subspaces of the Hilbert space as a propositional calculus.' *Zeitschrift für Naturforschung* **27a**: 1358–1362. Here is a very nice and concise set of lattice-theoretic results derived from the original paper by Birkhoff and Von Neumann (1936). In particular it shows how a quasi-implication, defined in the paper, is a generalisation of classical implication.

— (1998). *The Interpretation of Quantum Mechanics and the Measurement Process.* Cambridge University Press. A recent examination of the measurement problem in QM.

Mizzaro, S. (1997). 'Relevance: the whole history.' *Journal of the American Society for Information Science* **48**: 810–832. Mizzaro brings the debate on 'relevance' up to date. It is worth reading Saracevic (1975) first.

Murdoch, D. (1987). *Niels Bohr's Philosophy of Physics* Cambridge University Press. This is of historical interest. Amongst other things it traces the development of Bohr's ideas on complementarity. Worth reading at the same time as Pais' (1991) biography of Bohr.

Nie, J.-Y., M. Brisebois and F. Lepage (1995). 'Information retrieval as counterfactual.' *The Computer Journal* **38**(8): 643–657. Looks at IR as counterfactual reasoning, drawing heavily on Lewis (1973).

Nie, J.-Y. and F. Lepage (1998). 'Toward a broader logical model for information retrieval.' In *Information Retrieval: Uncertainty and Logics: Advanced Models for the Representation and Retrieval of Information.* F. Crestani, M. Lalmas and C. J. van Rijsbergen (eds.). Kluwer: 17–38. In this paper the logical approach to IR is revisited and the authors propose that situational factors be included to enlarge the scope of logical modelling.

Nielsen, M. A. and I. L. Chuang (2000). *Quantum Computation and Quantum Information* Cambridge University Press. Without doubt this is currently one of the best of its kind. The first one hundred pages serves extremely well as an introduction to quantum mechanics and its relevant mathematics. It has a good bibliography with references to www.arXiv.org whenever a paper is available for downloading. It is also well indexed.

Ochs, W. (1981). 'Some comments on the concept of state in quantum mechanics.' *Erkenntnis* **16**: 339–356. The notion of state is fundamental both in classical and quantum mechanics. The difference between a pure and mixed state in QM is of some importance, and the mathematics is designed to reflect this difference. There is an interpretation of mixed states as the 'ignorance interpretation of states'. Here is a discussion of that interpretation.

Omnès, R. (1992). 'Consistent interpretations of quantum mechanics.' *Reviews of Modern Physics* **64**(2): 339–382. Excellent supplementary reading to Griffiths (2002).

— R. (1994). *The Interpretation of Quantum Mechanics* Princeton University Press. A complete treatment of the interpretation of QM. It is hard going but all the necessary machinery is introduced. There is a good chapter on a logical framework for QM. Gleason's Theorem is presented. His other book, Omnès (1999), is a much more leisurely treatment of some of the same material.

— (1999). *Understanding Quantum Mechanics* Princeton University Press. See Omnes (1994).

Packel, E. W. (1974). 'Hilbert space operators and quantum mechanics.' *American Mathematical Monthly* **81**: 863–873. Convenient self-contained discussion of Hilbert space operators and QM. Written with mathematical rigour.

Pais, A. (1991). *Niels Bohr's Times, in Physics, Philosophy, and Polity*, Oxford University Press. A wonderful book on the life and times of Niels Bohr. Requisite reading before seeing the play *Copenhagen* by Michael Frayn.

Park, J. L. (1967). 'Nature of quantum states.' American Journal of Physics **36**: 211–226. Yet another paper on states in QM. This one explains in detail the difference between pure and mixed states.

Parthasarathy, K. R. (1970). 'Probability theory on the closed subspaces of a Hilbert space.' *Les Probabilites sur Structures Algebriques*, CNRS. **186**: 265–292. An early version of a proof of Gleason's Theorem, it is relatively self-contained. The version in the author's 1992 book may be easier to follow since the advanced mathematics is first introduced.

— (1992). *An Introduction to Quantum Stochastic Calculus*, Birkhäuser Verlag. The first chapter on events, observable and states is an extraordinarily clear and condensed exposition of the underlying mathematics for handling probability in Hilbert space. Central to the chapter is yet another proof of Gleason's Theorem. The mathematical concepts outer product and trace are very clearly defined.

Pavicic, M. (1992). 'Bibliography on quantum logics and related structures.' *International Journal of Theoretical Physics* **31**(3): 373–461. A useful bibliography emphasising papers on quantum logic.

Penrose, R. (1989). *The Emperor's New Mind: Concerning Computers, Minds, and the Laws of Physics*, Oxford University Press. A popular book containing a section on quantum magic and mystery, writtten with considerable zest.

— (1994). *Shadows of the Mind. A Search for the Missing Science of Consciousness*, Oxford University Press. A popular book containing a substantial section on the quantum world.

Peres, A. (1998). *Quantum Theory: Concepts and Methods*, Kluwer Academic Publishers. This book is much liked by researchers in quantum computation for providing the necessary background in quantum mechanics. Contains good discussion of Bell's inequalities, Gleason's Theorem and the Kochen–Specker Theorem.

Petz, D. and J. Zemánek (1988). Characterizations of the Trace. *Linear Algebra and Its Applications*, Elsevier Science Publishing. **111**: 43–52. Useful if you want to know more about the properties of the trace function.

Pippard, A. B., N. Kemmer, M. B. Hesse, M. Pryce, D. Bohn and N. R. Hanson (1962). *Quanta and Reality*, The Anchor Press Ltd. Popular book.

Piron, C. (1977). 'On the logic of quantum logic.' *Journal of Philosophical Logic* **6**: 481–484. A clarification of the connection between classical logic and quantum logic. Very short and simply written.

Pitowsky, I. (1989). *Quantum Probability – Quantum Logic* Springer-Verlag. A thorough and detailed analysis of the two ideas. Many of the arguments are illustrated with simple concrete examples. Recommended reading after first consulting Appendix III in GIR.

Pittenger, A. O. (2000). *An Introduction to Quantum Computing Algorithms*, Birkhäuser. A slim volume giving a coherent account of quantum computation.

Plotnitsky, A. (1994). *Complementarity. Anti-Epistemology after Bohr and Derrida*, Duke University Press. Incomprehensible but fun.

Polkinghorne, J. C. (1986). *The Quantum World*. Pelican. Elementary, short and simple. It also contains a nice glossary; for example, *non-locality* – the property of permitting a cause at one place to produce immediate effects at a distant place.

— (2002). *Quantum Theory: a Very Short Introduction*. Oxford University Press. The title says it all. Nice mathematical appendix.

Popper, K. R. (1982). *Quantum Theory and the Schism in Physics* Routledge. An exhilarating read. Popper is never uncontroversial! Contains a thought-provoking analysis of the Heisenberg Uncertainty Principle.

Priest, G. (2001). *An Introduction to Non-classical Logic*. Cambridge University Press. An easy-going introduction to non-classical logics. It begins with classical logic, emphasising the material conditional, and then moves on to to the less standard logics. The chapter devoted to conditional logics is excellent and worth reading as background to the logical discussion in Chapter 5 in GIR.

Putnam, H. (1975). 'The logic of quantum mechanics.' In *Mathematics, Matter and Method: Philosophical Papers*, vol. I (ed.). H. Putnam. Cambridge University Press. pp. 174–197. The revised version of the 1968 paper that sparked a continuing debate about the nature of logic, arguing that 'logic is, in a certain sense, a natural science'.

— (1981). 'Quantum mechanics and the observer.' *Erkenntnis* **16**: 193–219. A revision of some of Putnam's views as expressed in Putnam (1975).

Quine, W. v. O. (1969). *Ontological Relativity and Other Essays*. Columbia University Press. Contains a Chapter on natural kinds that is relevant to Chapter 2 of GIR.

Rae, A. (1986). *Quantum Physics: Illusion or Reality?* Cambridge University Press. A fine short popular introduction to quantum mechanics.

Rédei, M. (1998). *Quantum Logic in Algebraic Approach* Kluwer Academic Publishers. A very elaborate book on quantum logic and probability. It builds on the early work of Von Neumann. It mainly contains pure mathematical results and as such is a useful reference work. To be avoided unless one is interested in pursuing quantum logic (and probability) on various kinds of lattices in great depth.

Rédei, M. and M. Stöltzner, eds. (2001). *John von Neumann and the Foundations of Quantum Physics*. Vienna Circle Institute Yearbook, Kluwer Academic Publishers. A collection of papers dealing with the contributions that John von Neumann made to QM. It also contains some previously unpublished material by John von Neumann. One of the unpublished lectures, 'Unsolved Problems in Mathematics', is extensively quoted from in Chapter 1.

Redhead, M. (1999). *Incompleteness Non-locality and Realism. A Prolegomenon to the Philosophy of Quantum Mechanics*, Clarendon Press. Although philosophical in thrust and intent, it is quite mathematical. It gives a competent introduction to QM. The Einstein–Podolsky–Rosen incompleteness argument is discussed, followed by non-locality and the Bell inequality as well the Kochen–Specker Paradox. It has a good mathematical appendix.

Reed, M. and B. Simon (1980). *Methods of Modern Mathematical Physics*, Vol. I *Functional Analysis* Academic Press. Compare this book with Fano (1971) and Jordan (1969).

Reichenbach, H. (1944). *Philosophic Foundations of Quantum Mechanics*, University of California Press. Still a valuable and well-written account. His views on multi-valued and three-valued logic for QM are now discounted.

Retherford, J. R. (1993). *Hilbert Space: Compact Operators and the Trace Theorem*, Cambridge University Press. Slim volume, worth consulting on elementary spectral theory.

Richman, F. and D. Bridges (1999). 'A constructive proof of Gleason's Theorem.' *Journal of Functional Analysis* **162**: 287–312. Another version of the proof of Gleason's Theorem.

Riesz, F. and B. Sz.-Nagy (1990). *Functional Analysis*, Dover Publications, Inc. A classic reference on functional analysis. It contains a good section on self-adjoint transformations.

Robertson, S. E. (1977). 'The probability ranking principle in IR.' *Journal of Documentation* **33**: 294–304. A seminal paper. It is the first detailed formulation of why ranking documents by the probability of relevance can be optimal. Contains an interesting discussion of the principle in relation to the Cluster Hypothesis, and makes reference to Goffman's early work. It is reprinted in Sparck Jones and Willett (1997).

Román, L. (1994). 'Quantum logic and linear logic.' *International Journal of Theoretical Physics* **33**(6): 1163–1172. Linear logic is an important development in computer science; here is a paper that clarifies its relation to quantum logic.

Roman, S. (1992). *Advanced Linear Algebra*, Springer-Verlag. A fairly recent textbook on linear algebra. Excellent chapter on eigenvectors and eigenvalues.

Sadun, L. (2001). *Applied Linear Algebra. The Decoupling Principle* Prentice Hall. It is hard to find any textbooks on linear algebra that deal with bras, kets and duality. This is such a rare find. It also discusses the Heisenberg Uncertainty Principle for bandwidth and Fourier transforms, that is, independent of QM. Apart from that, it is a clear and well presented introduction to linear algebra.

Salton, G. (1968). *Automatic Information Organization and Retrieval* McGraw-Hill Book Company. A classic IR reference. This is a compendium of early results in IR based on the Smart system that was originally designed at Harvard between 1962 and 1965. It continues to operate at Cornell to this day. Even though this book is dated it still contains important ideas that are not readily accessible elsewhere.

Salton, G. and M. J. McGill (1983). *Introduction to Modern Information Retrieval*, McGraw-Hill Book Company. An early textbook on IR, still much used and cited.

Saracevic, T. (1975). 'Relevance: A review of and a framework for the thinking on the notion in information science.' *Journal of the American Society for Information Science* **26**: 321–343. Although somewhat dated, this is still one of the best surveys of the concept of relevance. It takes the reader through the different ways of conceptualising relevance. One gets a more up-to-date view of this topic by reading Mizzaro (1997), and the appropriate sections in Belew (2000).

Schmeidler, W. (1965). *Linear Operators in Hilbert Space* Academic Press. A gentle introduction to linear operators in Hilbert space, it begins with a simple introduction to Hilbert spaces.

Schrödinger, E. (1935). 'Die gegenwartige Situation in der Quantenmechanik.' *Naturwissenschaften* **22**: 807–812, 823–828, 844–849. The original of the translated version in Wheeler and Zurek (1983, pp. 152–167). In our Prologue there is a quote from the translation. Schrödinger was at odds with the quantum mechanics orthodoxy for most of his life. He invented the Schrödinger's Cat Paradox to illustrate the absurdity of some of its tenets.

Schwarz, H. R., H. Rutishauser and E. Stiefel (1973). *Numerical Analysis of Symmetric Matrices*. Prentice-Hall, Inc. Despite its title this is an excellent introduction to vector spaces and linear algebra. The numerical examples are quite effective in aiding the understanding of the basic theory. It uses a very clear notation.

Schwinger, J. (1959). 'The algebra of microscopic measurement.' *Proceedings of the National Academy of Science* **45**: 1542–1553. Full version of the paper reprinted in Schwinger (1991).

— (1960). 'Unitary operator bases.' *Proceedings of the National Academy of Science* **46**: 570–579. Reprinted in Schwinger (1991).

— (1960). 'The geometry of quantum states.' *Proceedings of the National Academy of Science* **46**: 257–265. Reprinted in Schwinger (1991).

— (1991). *Quantum Kinematics and Dynamics*, Perseus Publishing. A preliminary and less formal version of material in Schwinger (2001). This is a good book to start with if one wishes to read Schwinger in detail.

— (2001). *Quantum Mechanics: Symbolism of Atomic Measurements*, Springer-Verlag. Schwinger received the Nobel prize for physics at the same time as Feynman in 1965. His approach to QM was very intuitive, motivated by the process of measurement. The first chapter introduces QM through the notion of measurement algebra. It is an idiosyncratic approach but some may find it a more accessible way than through Hilbert space theory.

Sibson, R. (1972). 'Order invariant methods for data analysis.' *The Journal of the Royal Statistical Society, Series B(Methodology)* **34**(3): 311–349. A lucid discussion on classification methods without recourse to details of specifc algorithms.

Simmons, G. F. (1963). *Introduction to Topology and Modern Analysis*, McGraw-Hill. Contains an excellent introduction to Hilbert spaces.

Sneath, P. H. A. and R. R. Sokal (1973). *Numerical Taxonomy*, W. H. Freeman and Company. An excellent compendium on classification methods. Although now over thirty years old, it is still one of the best books on automatic classification. It contains an very thorough and extensive bibliography.

Sneed, J. D. (1970). 'Quantum mechanics and classical probability theory.' *Synthese* **21**: 34–64. The author argues that 'there is an interpretation of the quantum mechanical formalism which is both physically acceptable and consistent with classical probability theory (Kolmogorov's)'.

Sober, E. (1985). 'Constructive empiricism and the problem of aboutness.' *British Journal of the Philosophy of Science* 1985: 11–18. The concept of 'aboutness' is a source of potential difficulty in IR. Here is a philosophical discussion of the notion.

Sparck Jones, K. and P. Willett, eds. (1997). *Readings in Information Retrieval*. The Morgan Kaufmann Series in Multimedia Information and Systems, Morgan Kaufmann Publishers, Inc. A major source book for important IR papers published in the last fifty years. It contains, for example, the famous paper by Maron and Kuhns. It also has a chapter on models describing the most important ones. Not covered are latent semantic indexing and language models in IR.

Stairs, A. (1982). 'Discussion: quantum logic and the Lüders rule.' *Philosophy of Science* **49**: 422–436. Contribution to the debate sparked by Putnam (1975). A response to the Friedman and Putnam (1978) paper.

Stalnaker, R. (1970). 'Probability and conditionals.' *Philosophy of Science* **37**: 64–80. It is here that Stalnaker stated the Stalnaker Hypothesis that the probability of a conditional goes as the conditional probability. David Lewis subsequently produce a set of triviality results. All this is well documented in Harper *et al.* (1981).

Suppes, P., ed. (1976). *Logic and Probability in Quantum Mechanics*. Synthese Library. D. Reidel Publishing Company. This still remains one of the best collections of papers on logic and probability in quantum mechanics despite its age. It contains an excellent classified bibliography of almost one thousand references. The headings of the classification are very helpful, for example, 'quantum logic' is a heading under which one will find numerous references to items published before 1976. It is well indexed: the author index gives separate access to the bibliography.

Sutherland, R. I. (2000). 'A suggestive way of deriving the quantum probability rule.' *Foundations of Physics Letters* **13**(4): 379–386. An elementary and simple derivation of the rule that probability in QM goes as the 'modulus squared'.

Teller, P. (1983). 'The projection postulate as a fortuitous approximation.' *Philosophy of Science* **50**: 413–431. Another contribution to the debate sparked by Friedman and Putnam (1978). It also contains an excellent section on the Projection Postulate.

Thomason, R. H., ed. (1974). *Formal Philosophy: Selected papers of Richard Montague*. Yale University Press. Once one has read the introduction by Dowty *et al.* (1981) on Montague Semantics one may wish to consult the master. Thomason has collected together probably the most important papers published by Montague. Montague's papers are never easy going but always rewarding.

Tombros, A. (2002). *The Effectiveness of Query-based Hierarchic Clustering of Documents for Information Retrieval. Computing Science Department*, Glasgow University. A thorough examination of document clustering. Contains a very good up-to-date literature survey. There is an excellent discussion on how to measure the effectiveness of document clustering.

Van der Waerden, B. L., ed. (1968). *Sources of Quantum Mechanics*, Dover Publications, Inc. Contains original papers by Bohr, Born, Dirac, Einstein, Ehrenfest, Jordan, Heisenberg and Pauli, but sadly omits any by Schrödinger.

Van Fraassen, B. C. (1976). 'Probabilities of conditionals.' In *Foundations of Probability Theory, Statistical Inference, and Statistical Theories of Science*. W. L. Harper and C. A. Hooker (eds.). Reidel, pp. 261–300. This is a beautifully written paper, it examines the Stalnaker Thesis afresh and examines under what conditions it can be sustained.

— (1991). *Quantum Mechanics. An Empiricist View* Clarendon Press. This is a superb introduction to modern quantum mechanics. Its notation is slightly awkward, and it avoids the use of Dirac notation. It aims to present and discuss a number of interpretations of quantum mechanics. For example, there is an extensive consideration of modal interpretations. Hilbert space theory is kept to a minimum. The mathematics is intended to be understood by philosophers with little or no background.

Van Rijsbergen, C. J. (1970). 'Algorithm 47. A clustering algorithm.' *The Computer Journal* **13**: 113–115. Contains a programme for the L^* algorithm mentioned in Chapter 2.

— (1979a). *Information Retrieval*. Butterworths. A popular textbook on IR, still much used. It has been made available on number of web sites, for example, a search with Google on the author's name will list www.dcs.gla.ac.uk/Keith/Preface.html. An electronic version on CD is also contained in Belew (2000).

— (1979b). 'Retrieval effectiveness.' In *Progress in Communication Sciences*. M. J. Voigt and G. J. Hanneman, (eds.). ABLEX Publishing Corporation. Vol. I, pp. 91–118. A foundational paper on the measurement of retrieval effectiveness, paying particular attention to averaging techniques. Expresses some of the standard parameters of effectiveness, such as precision and recall, in terms of general measures.

— (1979c). 'Foundation of evaluation.' *Journal of Documentation* **30**: 365–373. Contains a complete derivation of the E and F measure for measuring retrieval effectiveness based on the theory of measurement.

— (1986). 'A non-classical logic for information retrieval.' *The Computer Journal* **29**: 481–485. The paper that launched a number of papers dealing with the logical model for information retrieval. Reprinted in Sparck Jones and Willett (1997).

— (1992) 'Probabilistic retrieval revisited.' *The Computer Journal* **35**: 291–298.

— (1996). *Information, Logic, and Uncertainty in Information Science*. CoLIS 2, Second International Conference on Conceptions of Library and Information Science: Integration in Perspective, Copenhagen, The Royal School of Librarianship. Here is the first detailed published account of the conceptualisation underlying the approach in GIR. An argument is made for an interaction logic taking its inspiration from quantum logic.

— (2000). 'Another look at the logical uncertainty principle.' *Information Retrieval* **2**: 15–24. Useful background reading for Chapter 2.

Varadarajan, V. S. (1985). *Geometry of Quantum Theory* Springer-Verlag. A one volume edition of an earlier, 1968, two-volume set. It contains a very detailed and thorough treatment of logics for quantum mechanics followed by logics associated with Hilbert spaces. The material is beautifully presented, a real labour of love.

— (1993). 'Quantum theory and geometry: sixty years after Von Neumann.' *International Journal of Theoretical Physics* **32**(10): 1815–1834. Mainly of historical interest, but written by one of the foremost scholars of quantum theory. It reviews some of the developments in mathematical foundations of QM since the publication of Von Neumann (1932). Written with considerable informality.

Von Neumann, J. (1932). *Mathematische Grundlagen der Quantenmechanik*. Springer. The original edition of his now famous book on QM.

— (1961). *Collected Works*. Vol. I: *Logic, Theory of Sets and Quantum Mechanics*, Pergamon Press. This volume contains most of John von Neumann's published papers on quantum mechanics (in German).

— (1983). *Mathematical Foundations of Quantum Mechanics*, Princeton University Press. This is the 1955 translation by Robert T. Beyer of John von Neumann (1932), originally published by Princeton University Press. It is the starting point for most work in the last 70 years on the philosophy and interpretation of quantum mechanics. It contains a so-called proof of the 'no hidden variables' result, a result that was famously challenged in detail by Bell (1993), and much earlier by Reichenbach (1944, p.14). Nevertheless, this book was and remains one of the great contributions to the foundations of QM. Its explanations, once the notation has been mastered, are outstanding for their clarity and insight.

Von Weizsäcker, C. F. (1973). 'Probability and quantum mechanics.' *British Journal of Philosophical Science* **24**: 321–337. An extremely informal but perceptive account of probability in QM.

Voorhees, E. M. (1985). *The Effectiveness and Efficiency of Agglomerative Hierarchic Clustering in Document Retrieval. Computing Science Department*, Cornell University. One of the first thorough evaluations of the Cluster Hypothesis.

Wheeler, J. A. (1980). 'Pregeometry: motivation and prospects.' In *Quantum Theory and Gravitation.* A. R. Marlow (ed.). Academic Press, pp. 1–11. Provocative article about the importance and role of geometry in quantum mechanics. The quote: 'No elementary phenomenon is a phenomenon until it is an observed (registered) phenomenon' is taken from this essay.

Wheeler, J. A. and W. H. Zurek, eds. (1983). *Quantum Theory and Measurement.* Princeton University Press. Here is a collection of papers that represents a good snapshot of the state of debate about the 'measurement problem'. Many of the classic papers on the problem are reprinted here, for example, Schrödinger (1935), London and Bauer (1982) and Einstein, Podolsky and Rosen (1935).

Whitaker, A. (1996). *Einstein, Bohr and the Quantum Dilemma*, Cambridge University Press. Should the reader get interested in the debate between Bohr and Einstein that took place between 1920 and 1930, this is a good place to start.

Wick, D. (1995). *The Infamous Boundary: Seven Decades of Heresy in Quantum Physics.* Copernicus. This is a wonderfully lucid book about the well-known paradoxes in quantum mechanics. It is written in an informal style and pays particular attention to the history of the subject. It contains a substantial appendix on probability in quantum mechanics prepared by William G. Farris.

Wilkinson, J. H. (1965). *The Algebraic Eigenvalue Problem.* Clarendon Press. This is perhaps the 'Bible' of mathematics for dealing with the numerical solutions of the eigenvalue problem. It is written with great care.

Williams, D. (2001). *Weighing the Odds: a Course in Probability and Statistics.* Cambridge University Press. A modern introduction. It would make a good companion to Jaynes (2003) simply because it presents the subject in a neutral and mathematical way, without the philosophical bias of Jaynes. It contains a useful chapter on quantum probability and quantum computation: a rare thing for books on probability theory.

Witten, I. H., A. Moffat and T. C. Bell (1994). *Managing Gigabytes – Compressing and Indexing Documents and Images* Van Nostrand Reinhold. A useful book about the nuts and bolts of IR. There is now a second edition published in 1999.

Wootters, W. K. (1980a). *The Acquisition of Information from Quantum Measurements.* Center for Theoretical Physics, Austin, The University of Texas at Austin. Wootters summarises his results in this thesis by '. . . the observer's ability to distinguish one state from another seems to be reflected in the structure of quantum mechanics itself'. He gives an information-theoretic argument for a particular form of a probabilistic law which is used in the Prologue of this book.

— (1980b). 'Information is maximised in photon polarization measurements.' In *Quantum Theory and Gravitation.* A. R. Marlow (ed.). Academic Press, pp. 13–26. A self-contained account of a central idea described in the thesis by Wootters (1980a). His idea is used in the Prologue of GIR.

Zeller, Eduard (1888). *Plato and the Older Academy*, translated by Sarah Alleyne and Alfred Goodwin, Longmens, Green and Co., pp. 21–22, note 41.

Zhang, F. (1999). *Matrix Theory: Basic Results and Techniques* Springer. A standard modern reference on matrices; contains a good chapter on Hermitian matrices.

Author index

Index